Functional Python Programming

Create succinct and expressive implementations
with functional programming in Python

Steven Lott

BIRMINGHAM - MUMBAI

Functional Python Programming

First published: January 2015

Production reference: 1270115

Published by Packt Publishing Ltd.
Livery Place
35 Livery Street
Birmingham B3 2PB, UK.

ISBN 978-1-78439-699-2

www.packtpub.com

Credits

Author
Steven Lott

Reviewers
Oleg Broytman
Rui Carmo
Ian Cordasco
Julien Danjou
Amoatey Harrison
Shivin Kapur
Gong Yi

Commissioning Editor
Ed Gordon

Acquisition Editor
Owen Roberts

Content Development Editor
Sumeet Sawant

Technical Editor
Abhishek R. Kotian

Copy Editors
Roshni Banerjee
Pranjali Chury
Deepa Nambiar
Karuna Narayanan
Nithya P

Project Coordinator
Danuta Jones

Proofreaders
Stephen Copestake
Maria Gould
Bernadette Watkins

Indexer
Hemangini Bari

Graphics
Abhinash Sahu

Production Coordinator
Melwyn D'sa

Cover Work
Melwyn D'sa

About the Author

Steven Lott has been programming since the 1970s, when computers were large, expensive, and rare. As a contract software developer and architect, he has worked on hundreds of projects, from very small to very large. He's been using Python to solve business problems for over 10 years. He's particularly adept struggling with gnarly data representation problems. His other titles include *Mastering Object-Oriented Python* and *Python for Secret Agents*, both by Packt Publishing. After spending years as a technomad — living in various places on the east coast of the US — he has dropped the hook in the Chesapeake Bay. He blogs at `http://slott-softwarearchitect.blogspot.com`.

About the Reviewers

Oleg Broytman is a software developer currently working with web technologies on Unix/Linux using the Python programming language on the server side and Javascript on the client side. Oleg started to work with computers even before the IBM PC era. He worked with DOS for some time and then switched to Unix, mostly Linux and FreeBSD. For about 25 years, he has been working in the medicine field in Moscow, Russia.

You can contact him at phd@phdru.name.

> I'd like to thank my wife Olga! She supports everything I do any way I do it (well, mostly!). Her love and support make me happy and allow me to achieve as much as I do.

Rui Carmo is a systems architect with 20 years' experience in telecoms and Internet, having worked in software development, product management, mobile network planning, systems engineering, virtualization, cloud services, and a lot of what the industry is currently trying to roll into the "DevOps" moniker. He has been coding in Python for over a decade (starting with Python 2.3) and has gravitated towards Clojure, Erlang, and Hy (an LISP that leverages the Python AST) in the past few years due to the intrinsic advantages of functional programming.

He currently lives in the wonderful city of Lisbon, Portugal, with his wife and two children, and he blogs at http://taoofmac.com. You can find him on GitHub, Twitter, and Hacker News as @rcarmo.

Julien Danjou is an open source hacker working at Red Hat. He started his career as a Debian developer and contributed to a lot of free software (GNU Emacs, Freedesktop, and so on), writing some software on his own, such as the awesome window manager.

Nowadays, Julien contributes to OpenStack, an open source cloud platform entirely written in Python. He has been a Python developer since then, worked on Hy (an LISP dialect in Python), and written a self-published book titled *The Hacker's Guide to Python* in 2014.

Amoatey Harrison is a Python programmer with a passion for building software systems to solve problems. When he is not programming, he is playing video games, swimming, or simply hanging out with friends.

After graduating from the Kwame Nkrumah University of Science and Technology with a degree in computer engineering, he is doing his national service at the GCB Bank Head Office in Accra, Ghana.

He would like to think of himself as a cool nerd.

Shivin Kapur is an aspiring computer science student who is passionate about learning new things.

Gong Yi is a software developer working in Shanghai, China. He maintains an open source project at https://github.com/topikachu/python-ev3, which can control LEGO® MINDSTORMS® EV3 by Python language.

> I thank my wife Zhu Xiaoling for her patience and love, and I thank my son Yang Yang for being the best thing ever.

www.PacktPub.com

Support files, eBooks, discount offers, and more

For support files and downloads related to your book, please visit www.PacktPub.com.

Did you know that Packt offers eBook versions of every book published, with PDF and ePub files available? You can upgrade to the eBook version at www.PacktPub.com and as a print book customer, you are entitled to a discount on the eBook copy. Get in touch with us at service@packtpub.com for more details.

At www.PacktPub.com, you can also read a collection of free technical articles, sign up for a range of free newsletters and receive exclusive discounts and offers on Packt books and eBooks.

https://www2.packtpub.com/books/subscription/packtlib

Do you need instant solutions to your IT questions? PacktLib is Packt's online digital book library. Here, you can search, access, and read Packt's entire library of books.

Why subscribe?

- Fully searchable across every book published by Packt
- Copy and paste, print, and bookmark content
- On demand and accessible via a web browser

Free access for Packt account holders

If you have an account with Packt at www.PacktPub.com, you can use this to access PacktLib today and view 9 entirely free books. Simply use your login credentials for immediate access.

Table of Contents

Preface

Programming languages sometimes fit neatly into tidy categories like imperative and functional. Imperative languages might further subdivide into those that are procedural and those that include features for object-oriented programming. The Python language, however, contains aspects of all of these three language categories. Though Python is not a purely functional programming language, we can do a great deal of functional programming in Python.

Most importantly, we can leverage many design patterns and techniques from other functional languages and apply them to Python programming. These borrowed concepts can lead us to create succinct and elegant programs. Python's generator expressions, in particular, avoid the need to create large in-memory data structures, leading to programs which may execute more quickly because they use fewer resources.

We can't easily create purely functional programs in Python. Python lacks a number of features that would be required for this. For example, we don't have unlimited recursion, lazy evaluation of all expressions, and an optimizing compiler.

Generally, Python emphasizes strict evaluation rules. This means that statements are executed in order and expressions are evaluated from left to right. While this deviates from functional purity, it allows us to perform manual optimizations when writing in Python. We'll take a hybrid approach to functional programming using Python's functional features when they can add clarity or simplify the code and use ordinary imperative features for optimization.

There are several key features of functional programming languages that are available in Python. One of the most important is the idea that functions are first-class objects. In some languages, functions exist only as a source code construct: they don't exist as proper data structures at runtime. In Python, functions can use functions as arguments and return functions as results.

Python offers a number of higher-order functions. Functions like `map()`, `filter()`, and `functools.reduce()` are widely used in this role. Less obvious functions like `sorted()`, `min()`, and `max()` are also higher-order functions; they have a default function and, consequently, different syntax from the more common examples.

Functional programs often exploit immutable data structures. The emphasis on stateless objects permits flexible optimization. Python offers tuples and namedtuples as complex but immutable objects. We can leverage these structures to adapt some design practices from other functional programming languages.

Many functional languages emphasize recursion but exploit Tail-Call Optimization (TCO). Python tends to limit recursion to a relatively small number of stack frames. In many cases, we can think of a recursion as a generator function. We can then simply rewrite it to use a `yield from` statement, doing the tail-call optimization ourselves.

We'll look at the core features of functional programming from a Python point of view. Our objective is to borrow good ideas from functional programming languages, and use these ideas to create expressive and succinct applications in Python.

What this book covers

Chapter 1, Introducing Functional Programming, introduces some of the techniques that characterize functional programming. We'll identify some of the ways to map these features to Python, and finally, we'll also address some ways that the benefits of functional programming accrue when we use these design patterns to build Python applications.

Chapter 2, Introducing Some Functional Features, will delve into six central features of the functional programming paradigm. We'll look at each in some detail to see how they're implemented in Python. We'll also point out some features of functional languages that don't apply well to Python. In particular, many functional languages have complex type-matching rules required to support compilation and optimization.

Chapter 3, Functions, Iterators, and Generators, will show how to leverage immutable Python objects and generator expressions, and adapt functional programming concepts to the Python language. We'll look at some of the built-in Python collection and how we can leverage them without departing too far from functional programming concepts.

Chapter 4, Working with Collections, shows how we can use a number of built-in Python functions to operate on collections of data. This section will focus on a number of relatively simple functions such as `any()` and `all()`, which will reduce a collection of values to a single result.

Chapter 5, Higher-order Functions, examines the commonly used higher order functions such as `map()` and `filter()`. The chapter also includes a number of other functions that are also higher-order functions, as well as how we can create our own higher-order functions.

Chapter 6, Recursions and Reductions, shows how we can design an algorithm using recursion and then optimize it into a high performance `for` loop. We'll also look at some other reductions that are widely used, including the `collections.Counter()` function.

Chapter 7, Additional Tuple Techniques, shows a number of ways in which we can use immutable tuples and namedtuples instead of stateful objects. Immutable objects have a much simpler interface: we never have to worry about abusing an attribute and setting an object into some inconsistent or invalid state.

Chapter 8, The Itertools Module, examines a number of functions in the standard library module. This collection of functions simplifies writing programs that deal with collections or generator functions.

Chapter 9, More Itertools Techniques, covers the combinatoric functions in the itertools module. These functions are somewhat less useful. This chapter includes some examples that illustrate ill-considered uses of these functions and the consequences of combinatoric explosion.

Chapter 10, The Functools Module, will show how to use some of the functions in this module for functional programming. A few of the functions in this module are more appropriate for building decorators, and are left for the next chapter. The other functions, however, provide several more ways to design and implement function programs.

Chapter 11, Decorator Design Techniques, shows how we can look at a decorator as a way to build a composite function. While there is considerable flexibility here, there are also some conceptual limitations: we'll look at ways in which overly complex decorators can become confusing rather than helpful.

Chapter 12, The Multiprocessing and Threading Modules, points out an important consequence of good functional design: we can distribute the processing workload. Using immutable objects means that we can't corrupt an object because of poorly synchronized write operations.

Chapter 13, Conditional Expressions and the Operator Module, will show some ways in which we can break out of Python's strict order of evaluation. There are limitations to what we can achieve here. We'll also look at the operator module and how the operator module can lead to some slight clarification of some simple kinds of processing.

Chapter 14, The PyMonad Library, examines some of the features of the PyMonad library. This provides some additional functional programming features. This also provides a way to learn more about monads. In some functional languages, monads are an important way to force a particular order for operations that might get optimized into an undesirable order. Since Python already has strict ordering of expressions and statements, the monad feature is more instructive than practical.

Chapter 15, A Functional Approach to Web Services, shows how we can think of web services as a nested collection of functions that transform a request into a reply. We'll see ways in which we can leverage functional programming concepts for building responsive, dynamic web content.

Chapter 16, Optimizations and Improvements, includes some additional tips on performance and optimization. We'll emphasize techniques like memoization because they're easy to implement and can—in the right context—yield dramatic performance improvements.

What you need for this book

This book presumes some familiarity with Python 3 and general concepts of application development. We won't look deeply at subtle or complex features of Python; we'll avoid much consideration of the internals of the language.

We'll presume some familiarity with functional programming. Since Python is not a functional programming language, we can't dig deeply into functional concepts. We'll pick and choose the aspects of functional programming that fit well with Python and leverage just those that seem useful.

Some of the examples use Exploratory Data Analysis (EDA) as a problem domain to show the value of functional programming. Some familiarity with basic probability and statistics will help with this. There are only a few examples that move into more serious data science.

You'll need to have Python 3.3 or 3.4 installed and running. For more information on Python, visit `http://www.python.org/`.

In *Chapter 14, The PyMonad Library*, we'll look at installing this additional library. If you have Python 3.4 ,which includes pip and Easy Install, this will be very easy. If you have Python 3.3, you might have already installed pip or Easy Install or both. Once you have an installer, you can add PyMonad. Visit `https://pypi.python.org/pypi/PyMonad/` for more details.

Who this book is for

This book is for programmers who want to create succinct, expressive Python programs by borrowing techniques and design patterns from functional programming languages. Some algorithms can be expressed elegantly in a functional style; we can—and should—adapt this to make Python programs more readable and maintainable.

In some cases, a functional approach to a problem will also lead to extremely high performance algorithms. Python makes it too easy to create large intermediate data structures, tying up memory and processor time. With functional programming design patterns, we can often replace large lists with generator expressions that are equally expressive, but take up much less memory and run much more quickly.

Conventions

In this book, you will find a number of styles of text that distinguish between different kinds of information. Here are some examples of these styles, and an explanation of their meaning.

Code words in text are shown as follows: "We can create a `Pool` object of concurrent worker processes, assign tasks to them, and expect the tasks to be executed concurrently."

A block of code is set as follows:

```
GIMP Palette
Name: Crayola
Columns: 16
#
```

Any command-line input or output is written as follows:

```
def max(a, b):
    f = {a >= b: lambda: a, b >= a: lambda: b}[True]
    return f()
```

Warnings or important notes appear in a box like this.

Tips and tricks appear like this.

Reader feedback

Feedback from our readers is always welcome. Let us know what you think about this book—what you liked or may have disliked. Reader feedback is important for us to develop titles that you really get the most out of.

To send us general feedback, simply send an e-mail to feedback@packtpub.com, and mention the book title through the subject of your message.

If there is a topic that you have expertise in and you are interested in either writing or contributing to a book, see our author guide on www.packtpub.com/authors.

Customer support

Now that you are the proud owner of a Packt book, we have a number of things to help you to get the most from your purchase.

Downloading the example code

You can download the example code files for all Packt books you have purchased from your account at http://www.packtpub.com. If you purchased this book elsewhere, you can visit http://www.packtpub.com/support and register to have the files e-mailed directly to you.

Errata

Although we have taken every care to ensure the accuracy of our content, mistakes do happen. If you find a mistake in one of our books—maybe a mistake in the text or the code—we would be grateful if you would report this to us. By doing so, you can save other readers from frustration and help us improve subsequent versions of this book. If you find any errata, please report them by visiting http://www.packtpub.com/support, selecting your book, clicking on the **errata submission form** link, and entering the details of your errata. Once your errata are verified, your submission will be accepted and the errata will be uploaded to our website, or added to any list of existing errata, under the Errata section of that title.

Piracy

Piracy of copyright material on the Internet is an ongoing problem across all media. At Packt, we take the protection of our copyright and licenses very seriously. If you come across any illegal copies of our works, in any form, on the Internet, please provide us with the location address or website name immediately so that we can pursue a remedy.

Please contact us at copyright@packtpub.com with a link to the suspected pirated material.

We appreciate your help in protecting our authors, and our ability to bring you valuable content.

Questions

You can contact us at questions@packtpub.com if you are having a problem with any aspect of the book, and we will do our best to address it.

1
Introducing Functional Programming

Functional programming defines a computation using expressions and evaluation—often encapsulated in function definitions. It de-emphasizes or avoids the complexity of state change and mutable objects. This tends to create programs that are more succinct and expressive. In this chapter, we'll introduce some of the techniques that characterize functional programming. We'll identify some of the ways to map these features to **Python**. Finally, we'll also address some ways in which the benefits of functional programming accrue when we use these design patterns to build Python applications.

Python has numerous functional programming features. It is not a purely functional programming language. It offers enough of the right kinds of features that it confers to the benefits of functional programming. It also retains all optimization power available from an imperative programming language.

We'll also look at a problem domain that we'll use for many of the examples in this book. We'll try to stick closely to **Exploratory Data Analysis (EDA)** because its algorithms are often good examples of functional programming. Furthermore, the benefits of functional programming accrue rapidly in this problem domain.

Our goal is to establish some essential principles of functional programming. The more serious Python code will begin in *Chapter 2, Introducing Some Functional Features*.

 We'll focus on Python 3 features in this book. However, some of the examples might also work in Python 2.

Identifying a paradigm

It's difficult to be definitive on what fills the universe of programming paradigms. For our purposes, we will distinguish between just two of the many programming paradigms: **Functional programming** and **Imperative programming**. One important distinguishing feature between these two is the concept of state.

In an imperative language, like Python, the state of the computation is reflected by the values of the variables in the various namespaces. The values of the variables establish the state of a computation; each kind of statement makes a well-defined change to the state by adding or changing (or even removing) a variable. A language is imperative because each statement is a command, which changes the state in some way.

Our general focus is on the assignment statement and how it changes state. Python has other statements, such as `global` or `nonlocal`, which modify the rules for variables in a particular namespace. Statements like `def`, `class`, and `import` change the processing context. Other statements like `try`, `except`, `if`, `elif`, and `else` act as guards to modify how a collection of statements will change the computation's state. Statements like `for` and `while`, similarly, wrap a block of statements so that the statements can make repeated changes to the state of the computation. The focus of all these various statement types, however, is on changing the state of the variables.

Ideally, each statement advances the state of the computation from an initial condition toward the desired final outcome. This "advances the computation" assertion can be challenging to prove. One approach is to define the final state, identify a statement that will establish this final state, and then deduce the precondition required for this final statement to work. This design process can be iterated until an acceptable initial state is derived.

In a functional language, we replace state—the changing values of variables—with a simpler notion of evaluating functions. Each function evaluation creates a new object or objects from existing objects. Since a functional program is a composition of a function, we can design lower-level functions that are easy to understand, and we will design higher-level compositions that can also be easier to visualize than a complex sequence of statements.

Function evaluation more closely parallels mathematical formalisms. Because of this, we can often use simple algebra to design an algorithm, which clearly handles the edge cases and boundary conditions. This makes us more confident that the functions work. It also makes it easy to locate test cases for formal unit testing.

It's important to note that functional programs tend to be relatively succinct, expressive, and efficient when compared to imperative (object-oriented or procedural) programs. The benefit isn't automatic; it requires a careful design. This design effort is often easier than functionally similar procedural programming.

Subdividing the procedural paradigm

We can subdivide imperative languages into a number of discrete categories. In this section, we'll glance quickly at the procedural versus object-oriented distinction. What's important here is to see how object-oriented programming is a subset of imperative programming. The distinction between procedural and object-orientation doesn't reflect the kind of fundamental difference that functional programming represents.

We'll use code examples to illustrate the concepts. For some, this will feel like reinventing a wheel. For others, it provides a concrete expression of abstract concepts.

For some kinds of computations, we can ignore Python's object-oriented features and write simple numeric algorithms. For example, we might write something like the following to get the range of numbers:

```
s = 0
for n in range(1, 10):
    if n % 3 == 0 or n % 5 == 0:
        s += n
print(s)
```

We've made this program strictly procedural, avoiding any explicit use of Python's object features. The program's state is defined by the values of the variables s and n. The variable, n, takes on values such that $1 \leq n < 10$. As the loop involves an ordered exploration of values of n, we can prove that it will terminate when n == 10. Similar code would work in C or Java using their primitive (non-object) data types.

We can exploit **Python's Object-Oriented Programming (OOP)** features and create a similar program:

```
m = list()
for n in range(1, 10):
    if n % 3 == 0 or n % 5 == 0:
        m.append(n)
print(sum(m))
```

This program produces the same result but it accumulates a stateful collection object, m, as it proceeds. The state of the computation is defined by the values of the variables m and n.

The syntax of m.append(n) and sum(m) can be confusing. It causes some programmers to insist (wrongly) that Python is somehow not purely Object-oriented because it has a mixture of the function() and object.method() syntax. Rest assured, Python is purely Object-oriented. Some languages, like C++, allow the use of primitive data type such as int, float, and long, which are not objects. Python doesn't have these primitive types. The presence of prefix syntax doesn't change the nature of the language.

To be pedantic, we could fully embrace the object model, the subclass, the list class, and add a sum method:

```
class SummableList(list):
    def sum( self ):
        s= 0
        for v in self.__iter__():
            s += v
        return s
```

If we initialize the variable, m, with the SummableList() class instead of the list() method, we can use the m.sum() method instead of the sum(m) method. This kind of change can help to clarify the idea that Python is truly and completely object-oriented. The use of prefix function notation is purely syntactic sugar.

All three of these examples rely on variables to explicitly show the state of the program. They rely on the assignment statements to change the values of the variables and advance the computation toward completion. We can insert the assert statements throughout these examples to demonstrate that the expected state changes are implemented properly.

The point is not that imperative programming is broken in some way. The point is that functional programming leads to a change in viewpoint, which can, in many cases, be very helpful. We'll show a function view of the same algorithm. Functional programming doesn't make this example dramatically shorter or faster.

Using the functional paradigm

In a functional sense, the sum of the multiples of 3 and 5 can be defined in two parts:

- The sum of a sequence of numbers
- A sequence of values that pass a simple test condition, for example, being multiples of three and five

The sum of a sequence has a simple, recursive definition:

```
def sum(seq):
    if len(seq) == 0: return 0
    return seq[0] + sum(seq[1:])
```

We've defined the sum of a sequence in two cases: the **base case** states that the sum of a zero length sequence is 0, while the **recursive case** states that the sum of a sequence is the first value plus the sum of the rest of the sequence. Since the recursive definition depends on a shorter sequence, we can be sure that it will (eventually) devolve to the base case.

The + operator on the last line of the preceding example and the initial value of 0 in the base case characterize the equation as a sum. If we change the operator to * and the initial value to 1, it would just as easily compute a product. We'll return to this simple idea of generalization in the following chapters.

Similarly, a sequence of values can have a simple, recursive definition, as follows:

```
def until(n, filter_func, v):
    if v == n: return []
    if filter_func(v): return [v] + until( n, filter_func, v+1 )
    else: return until(n, filter_func, v+1)
```

In this function, we've compared a given value, v, against the upper bound, n. If v reaches the upper bound, the resulting list must be empty. This is the base case for the given recursion.

There are two more cases defined by the given `filter_func()` function. If the value of v is passed by the `filter_func()` function, we'll create a very small list, containing one element, and append the remaining values of the `until()` function to this list. If the value of v is rejected by the `filter_func()` function, this value is ignored and the result is simply defined by the remaining values of the `until()` function.

We can see that the value of v will increase from an initial value until it reaches n, assuring us that we'll reach the base case soon.

Here's how we can use the `until()` function to generate the multiples of 3 or 5. First, we'll define a handy `lambda` object to filter values:

```
mult_3_5= lambda x: x%3==0 or x%5==0
```

(We will use lambdas to emphasize succinct definitions of simple functions. Anything more complex than a one-line expression requires the `def` statement.)

We can see how this lambda works from the command prompt in the following example:

```
>>> mult_3_5(3)
True
>>> mult_3_5(4)
False
>>> mult_3_5(5)
True
```

This function can be used with the `until()` function to generate a sequence of values, which are multiples of 3 or 5.

The `until()` function for generating a sequence of values works as follows:

```
>>> until(10, lambda x: x%3==0 or x%5==0, 0)
[0, 3, 5, 6, 9]
```

We can use our recursive `sum()` function to compute the sum of this sequence of values. The various functions, such as `sum()`, `until()`, and `mult_3_5()` are defined as simple recursive functions. The values are computed without restoring to use intermediate variables to store state.

We'll return to the ideas behind this purely functional recursive function definition in several places. It's important to note here that many functional programming language compilers can optimize these kinds of simple recursive functions. Python can't do the same optimizations.

Using a functional hybrid

We'll continue this example with a mostly functional version of the previous example to compute the sum of the multiples of 3 and 5. Our **hybrid** functional version might look like the following:

```
print( sum(n for n in range(1, 10) if n%3==0 or n%5==0) )
```

We've used **nested generator expressions** to iterate through a collection of values and compute the sum of these values. The `range(1, 10)` method is an iterable and, consequently, a kind of generator expression; it generates a sequence of values $\{n | 1 \le n < 10\}$. The more complex expression, `n for n in range(1, 10) if n%3==0 or n%5==0`, is also an iterable expression. It produces a set of values $\{n | 1 \le n < 10 \wedge (n \bmod 3 = 0 \vee n \bmod 5 = 0)\}$. A variable, n, is bound to each value, more as a way of expressing the contents of the set than as an indicator of the state of the computation. The `sum()` function consumes the iterable expression, creating a final object, 23.

The bound variable doesn't change once a value is bound to it. The variable, n, in the loop is essentially a shorthand for the values available from the `range()` function.

The `if` clause of the expression can be extracted into a separate function, allowing us to easily repurpose this with other rules. We could also use a higher-order function named `filter()` instead of the `if` clause of the generator expression. We'll save this for *Chapter 5, Higher-order Functions*.

As we work with generator expressions, we'll see that the bound variable is at the blurry edge of defining the state of the computation. The variable, n, in this example isn't directly comparable to the variable, n, in the first two imperative examples. The `for` statement creates a proper variable in the local namespace. The generator expression does not create a variable in the same way as a `for` statement does:

```
>>> sum( n for n in range(1, 10) if n%3==0 or n%5==0 )
23
>>> n
Traceback (most recent call last):
  File "<stdin>", line 1, in <module>
NameError: name 'n' is not defined
```

Because of the way Python uses namespaces, it might be possible to write a function that can observe the n variable in a generator expression. However, we won't. Our objective is to exploit the functional features of Python, not to detect how those features have an object-oriented implementation under the hood.

Looking at object creation

In some cases, it might help to look at intermediate objects as a history of the computation. What's important is that the history of a computation is not fixed. When functions are commutative or associative, then changes to the order of evaluation might lead to different objects being created. This might have performance improvements with no changes to the correctness of the results.

Consider this expression:

```
>>> 1+2+3+4
10
```

We are looking at a variety of potential computation histories with the same result. Because the + operator is commutative and associative, there are a large number of candidate histories that lead to the same result.

Of the candidate sequences, there are two important alternatives, which are as follows:

```
>>> ((1+2)+3)+4
10
>>> 1+(2+(3+4))
10
```

In the first case, we fold in values working from left to right. This is the way Python works implicitly. Intermediate objects 3 and 6 are created as part of this evaluation.

In the second case, we fold from right-to-left. In this case, intermediate objects 7 and 9 are created. In the case of simple integer arithmetic, the two results have identical performance; there's no optimization benefit.

When we work with something like the `list` append, we might see some optimization improvements when we change the association rules.

Here's a simple example:

```
>>> import timeit
>>> timeit.timeit("((([]+[1])+[2])+[3])+[4]")
0.8846941249794327
>>> timeit.timeit("[]+([1]+([2]+([3]+[4])))")
1.0207440659869462
```

In this case, there's some benefit in working from left to right.

What's important for functional design is the idea that the + operator (or `add()` function) can be used in any order to produce the same results. The + operator has no hidden side effects that restrict the way this operator can be used.

The stack of turtles

When we use Python for functional programming, we embark down a path that will involve a hybrid that's not strictly functional. Python is not **Haskell, OCaml**, or **Erlang**. For that matter, our underlying processor hardware is not functional; it's not even strictly object-oriented—CPUs are generally procedural.

All programming languages rest on abstractions, libraries, frameworks and virtual machines. These abstractions, in turn, may rely on other abstractions, libraries, frameworks and virtual machines. The most apt metaphor is this: the world is carried on the back of a giant turtle. The turtle stands on the back of another giant turtle. And that turtle, in turn, is standing on the back of yet another turtle.

It's turtles all the way down.

– Anonymous

There's no practical end to the layers of abstractions.

More importantly, the presence of abstractions and virtual machines doesn't materially change our approach to designing software to exploit the functional programming features of Python.

Even within the functional programming community, there are more pure and less pure functional programming languages. Some languages make extensive use of monads to handle stateful things like filesystem input and output. Other languages rely on a hybridized environment that's similar to the way we use Python. We write software that's generally functional with carefully chosen procedural exceptions.

Our functional Python programs will rely on the following three stacks of abstractions:

- Our applications will be functions — all the way down — until we hit the objects
- The underlying Python runtime environment that supports our functional programming is objects — all the way down — until we hit the turtles
- The libraries that support Python are a turtle on which Python stands

The operating system and hardware form their own stack of turtles. These details aren't relevant to the problems we're going to solve.

A classic example of functional programming

As part of our introduction, we'll look at a classic example of functional programming. This is based on the classic paper *Why Functional Programming Matters* by John Hughes. The article appeared in a paper called *Research Topics in Functional Programming*, edited by D. Turner, published by Addison-Wesley in 1990.

Here's a link to the paper *Research Topics in Functional Programming*:

```
http://www.cs.kent.ac.uk/people/staff/dat/miranda/whyfp90.pdf
```

This discussion of functional programming in general is profound. There are several examples given in the paper. We'll look at just one: the Newton-Raphson algorithm for locating the roots of a function. In this case, the function is the square root.

It's important because many versions of this algorithm rely on the explicit state managed via `loops`. Indeed, the Hughes paper provides a snippet of the **Fortran** code that emphasizes stateful, imperative processing.

The backbone of this approximation is the calculation of the next approximation from the current approximation. The `next_()` function takes x, an approximation to the `sqrt(n)` method and calculates a next value that brackets the proper root. Take a look at the following example:

```
def next_(n, x):
    return (x+n/x)/2
```

This function computes a series of values $a_{i+1} = (a_i + n/a_i)/2$. The distance between the values is halved each time, so they'll quickly get to converge on the value such that $a = n/a$, which means $a = \sqrt{n}$. We don't want to call the method `next()` because this name would collide with a built-in function. We call it the `next_()` method so that we can follow the original presentation as closely as possible.

Here's how the function looks when used in the command prompt:

```
>>> n= 2
>>> f= lambda x: next_(n, x)
>>> a0= 1.0
>>> [ round(x,4) for x in (a0, f(a0), f(f(a0)), f(f(f(a0))),) ]
[1.0, 1.5, 1.4167, 1.4142]
```

We've defined the `f()` method as a `lambda` that will converge on $\sqrt{2}$. We started with 1.0 as the initial value for a_0. Then we evaluated a sequence of recursive evaluations: $a_1 = f(a_0)$, $a_2 = f(f(a_0))$ and so on. We evaluated these functions using a generator expression so that we could round off each value. This makes the output easier to read and easier to use with `doctest`. The sequence appears to converge rapidly on $\sqrt{2}$.

We can write a function, which will (in principle) generate an infinite sequence of a_i values converging on the proper square root:

```
def repeat(f, a):
    yield a
    for v in repeat(f, f(a)):
        yield v
```

This function will generate approximations using a function, `f()`, and an initial value, a. If we provide the `next_()` function defined earlier, we'll get a sequence of approximations to the square root of the n argument.

> The `repeat()` function expects the `f()` function to have a single argument, however, our `next_()` function has two arguments. We can use a `lambda` object, `lambda x: next_(n, x)`, to create a partial version of the `next_()` function with one of two variables bound.
>
> The Python generator functions can't be trivially recursive, they must explicitly iterate over the recursive results, yielding them individually. Attempting to use a simple `return repeat(f, f(a))` will end the iteration, returning a generator expression instead of yielding the sequence of values.

We have two ways to return all the values instead of returning a generator expression, which are as follows:

- We can write an explicit `for` loop as follows:

  ```
  for x in some_iter: yield x.
  ```

- We can use the `yield from` statement as follows:

  ```
  yield from some_iter.
  ```

Both techniques of yielding the values of a recursive generator function are equivalent. We'll try to emphasize `yield from`. In some cases, however, the `yield` with a complex expression will be more clear than the equivalent mapping or generator expression.

Of course, we don't want the entire infinite sequence. We will stop generating values when two values are so close to each other that we can call either one the square root we're looking for. The common symbol for the value, which is close enough, is the Greek letter **Epsilon**, ε, which can be thought of as the largest error we will tolerate.

In Python, we'll have to be a little clever about taking items from an infinite sequence one at a time. It works out well to use a simple interface function that wraps a slightly more complex recursion. Take a look at the following code snippet:

```
def within(ε, iterable):
    def head_tail(ε, a, iterable):
        b= next(iterable)
        if abs(a-b) <= ε: return b
        return head_tail(ε, b, iterable)
    return head_tail(ε, next(iterable), iterable)
```

We've defined an internal function, head_tail(), which accepts the tolerance, ε, an item from the iterable sequence, a, and the rest of the iterable sequence, iterable. The next item from the iterable bound to a name b. If $|a-b| \le \varepsilon$, then the two values that are close enough together that we've found the square root. Otherwise, we use the b value in a recursive invocation of the head_tail() function to examine the next pair of values.

Our within() function merely seeks to properly initialize the internal head_tail() function with the first value from the iterable parameter.

Some functional programming languages offer a technique that will put a value back into an iterable sequence. In Python, this might be a kind of unget() or previous() method that pushes a value back into the iterator. Python iterables don't offer this kind of rich functionality.

We can use the three functions next_(), repeat(), and within() to create a square root function, as follows:

```
def sqrt(a0, ε, n):
    return within(ε, repeat(lambda x: next_(n,x), a0))
```

We've used the repeat() function to generate a (potentially) infinite sequence of values based on the next_(n,x) function. Our within() function will stop generating values in the sequence when it locates two values with a difference less than ε.

When we use this version of the sqrt() method, we need to provide an initial seed value, a0, and an ε value. An expression like sqrt(1.0, .0001, 3) will start with an approximation of 1.0 and compute the value of $\sqrt{3}$ to within 0.0001. For most applications, the initial a0 value can be 1.0. However, the closer it is to the actual square root, the more rapidly this method converges.

The original example of this approximation algorithm was shown in the Miranda language. It's easy to see that there are few profound differences between Miranda and Python. The biggest difference is Miranda's ability to construct cons, a value back into an iterable, doing a kind of unget. This parallelism between Miranda and Python gives us confidence that many kinds of functional programming can be easily done in Python.

Exploratory Data Analysis

Later in this book, we'll use the field of EDA as a source for concrete examples of functional programming. This field is rich with algorithms and approaches to working with complex datasets; functional programming is often a very good fit between the problem domain and automated solutions.

While details vary from author to author, there are several widely accepted stages of EDA. These include the following:

- Data preparation: This might involve extraction and transformation for source applications. It might involve parsing a source data format and doing some kinds of data scrubbing to remove unusable or invalid data. This is an excellent application of functional design techniques.

- Data exploration: This is a description of the available data. This usually involves the essential statistical functions. This is another excellent place to explore functional programming. We can describe our focus as univariate and bivariate statistics but that sounds too daunting and complex. What this really means is that we'll focus on mean, median, mode, and other related descriptive statistics. Data exploration may also involve data visualization. We'll skirt this issue because it doesn't involve very much functional programming. I'll suggest that you use a toolkit like `SciPy`.

  Visit the following link to get more information how SciPY works and its usage:

  ```
  https://www.packtpub.com/big-data-and-business-intelligence/
  learning-scipy-numerical-and-scientific-computing or https://
  www.packtpub.com/big-data-and-business-intelligence/learning-
  python-data-visualization
  ```

- Data modeling and machine learning: This tends to be proscriptive as it involves extending a model to new data. We're going to skirt this because some of the models can become mathematically complex. If we spend too much time on these topics, we won't be able to focus on functional programming.

- Evaluation and comparison: When there are alternative models, each must be evaluated to determine which is a better fit for the available data. This can involve ordinary descriptive statistics of model outputs. This can benefit from functional design techniques.

The goal of EDA is often to create a model that can be deployed as a decision support application. In many cases, a model might be a simple function. A simple functional programming approach can apply the model to new data and display results for human consumption.

Summary

We've looked at programming paradigms with an eye toward distinguishing the functional paradigm from two common imperative paradigms. Our objective in this book is to explore the functional programming features of Python. We've noted that some parts of Python don't allow purely functional programming; we'll be using some hybrid techniques that meld the good features of succinct, expressive functional programming with some high-performance optimizations in Python.

In the next chapter, we'll look at five specific functional programming techniques in detail. These techniques will form the essential foundation for our hybridized functional programming in Python.

2

Introducing Some Functional Features

Most of the features of functional programming are already first-class parts of Python. Our goal in writing functional Python is to shift our focus away from imperative (procedural or object-oriented) techniques to the maximum extent possible.

We'll look at each of the following functional programming topics:

- First-class and higher-order functions, which are also known as pure functions.
- Immutable Data.
- Strict and non-strict evaluation. We can also call this eager vs. lazy evaluation.
- Recursion instead of an explicit loop state.
- Functional type systems.

This should reiterate some concepts from the first chapter. Firstly, that purely functional programming avoids the complexities of explicit state maintained via variable assignment. Secondly, that Python is not a purely functional language.

We don't offer a rigorous definition of functional programming. Instead, we'll locate some common features that are indisputably important. We'll steer clear of the blurry edges.

First-class functions

Functional programming is often succinct and expressive. One way to achieve this is by providing functions as arguments and return values for other functions. We'll look at numerous examples of manipulating functions.

For this to work, functions must be first-class objects in the runtime environment. In programming languages such as C, a function is not a runtime object. In Python, however, functions are objects that are created (usually) by the `def` statements and can be manipulated by other Python functions. We can also create a function as a callable object or by assigning `lambda` to a variable.

Here's how a function definition creates an object with attributes:

```
>>> def example(a, b, **kw):
...     return a*b
...
>>> type(example)
<class 'function'>
>>> example.__code__.co_varnames
('a', 'b', 'kw')
>>> example.__code__.co_argcount
2
```

We've created an object, `example`, that is of class `function()`. This object has numerous attributes. The `__code__` object associated with the function object has attributes of its own. The implementation details aren't important. What is important is that functions are first-class objects, and can be manipulated just like all other objects. We previously displayed the values of two of the many attributes of a function object.

Pure functions

To be expressive, a function used in a functional programming design will be free from the confusion created by side effects. Using pure functions can also allow some optimizations by changing evaluation order. The big win, however, stems from pure functions being conceptually simpler and much easier to test.

To write a pure function in Python, we have to write local-only code. This means we have to avoid the `global` statements. We need to look closely at any use of `nonlocal`; while it is a side effect in another scope, it's confined to a `nested` function definition. This is an easy standard to meet. Pure functions are a common feature of Python programs.

There isn't a trivial way to guarantee a Python function is free from side effects. It is easy to carelessly break the pure function rule. If we ever want to worry about our ability to follow this rule, we could write a function that uses the `dis` module to scan a given function's `__code__.co_code` compiled code for global references. It could report on use of internal closures, and the `__code__.co_freevars` tuple method as well. This is a rather complex solution to a rare problem; we won't pursue it further.

A Python `lambda` is a pure function. While this isn't a highly recommended style, it's certainly possible to create pure functions via `lambda` values.

Here's a function created by assigning `lambda` to a variable:

```
>>> mersenne = lambda x: 2**x-1
>>> mersenne(17)
131071
```

We created a pure function using `lambda` and assigned this to the variable `mersenne`. This is a callable object with a single argument value that returns a single value. Because lambda's can't have assignment statements, they're always pure functions and suitable for functional programming.

Higher-order functions

We can achieve expressive, succinct programs using higher-order functions. These are functions that accept a function as an argument or return a function as a value. We can use higher-order functions as a way to create composite functions from simpler functions.

Consider the Python `max()` function. We can provide a function as an argument and modify how the `max()` function behaves.

Here's some data we might want to process:

```
>>> year_cheese = [(2000, 29.87), (2001, 30.12), (2002, 30.6), (2003, 30.66),(2004, 31.33), (2005, 32.62), (2006, 32.73), (2007, 33.5), (2008, 32.84), (2009, 33.02), (2010, 32.92)]
```

We can apply the `max()` function as follows:

```
>>> max(year_cheese)
(2010, 32.92)
```

The default behavior is to simply compare each `tuple` in the sequence. This will return the `tuple` with the largest value on position 0.

Since the `max()` function is a higher-order function, we can provide another function as an argument. In this case, we'll use `lambda` as the function; this is used by the `max()` function, as follows:

```
>>> max(year_cheese, key=lambda yc: yc[1])
(2007, 33.5)
```

In this example, the `max()` function applies the supplied `lambda` and returns the tuple with the largest value in position 1.

Python provides a rich collection of higher-order functions. We'll see examples of each of Python's higher-order functions in later chapters, primarily in *Chapter 5*, *Higher-order Functions*. We'll also see how we can easily write our own higher-order functions.

Immutable data

Since we're not using variables to track the state of a computation, our focus needs to stay on immutable objects. We can make extensive use of `tuples` and `namedtuples` to provide more complex data structures that are immutable.

The idea of immutable objects is not foreign to Python. There can be a performance advantage to using immutable `tuples` instead of more complex mutable objects. In some cases, the benefits come from rethinking the algorithm to avoid the costs of object mutation.

We will avoid class definitions (almost) entirely. It can seem like it's anathema to avoid objects in an **Object-Oriented Programming (OOP)** language. Functional programming simply doesn't need stateful objects. We'll see this throughout this book. There are reasons for defining `callable` objects; it is a tidy way to provide `namespace` for closely-related functions, and it supports a pleasant level of configurability.

We'll look at a common design pattern that works well with immutable objects: the `wrapper()` function. A list of tuples is a fairly common data structure. We will often process this list of tuples in one of the two following ways:

- **Using Higher-order Functions**: As shown earlier, we provided `lambda` as an argument to the `max()` function: `max(year_cheese, key=lambda yc: yc[1])`

- **Using the Wrap-Process-Unwrap pattern**: In a functional context, we should call this the `unwrap(process(wrap(structure)))` pattern

For example, look at the following command snippet:

```
>>> max(map(lambda yc: (yc[1],yc), year_cheese))
(33.5, (2007, 33.5))
>>> _[1]
(2007, 33.5)
```

This fits the three-part pattern, although it might not be obvious how well it fits.

First, we wrap, using `map(lambda yc: (yc[1],yc), year_cheese)`. This will transform each item into a two tuple with a key followed by the original item. In this example, the comparison key is merely `yc[1]`.

Second, do the processing using the `max()` function. Since each piece of data has been simplified to a two tuple with position zero used for comparison, we don't really need the higher-order function feature of the `max()` function. The default behavior of the `max()` function is exactly what we require.

Finally, we unwrap using the subscript `[1]`. This will pick the second element of the two tuple selected by the `max()` function.

This kind of `wrap` and `unwrap` is so common that some languages have special functions with names like `fst()` and `snd()` that we can use as a function prefix instead of a syntactic suffix of `[0]` or `[1]`. We can use this idea to modify our wrap-process-unwrap example, as follows:

```
snd= lambda x: x[1]
snd( max(map(lambda yc: (yc[1],yc), year_cheese)))
```

We defined a `snd()` function to pick the second item from a `tuple`. This provides us with an easier-to-read version of `unwrap(process(wrap()))`. We used `map(lambda... , year_cheese)` to wrap our raw data items. We used `max()` function as the processing and, finally, the `snd()` function to extract the second item from the tuple.

In *Chapter 13, Conditional Expressions and the Operator Module*, we'll look at some alternatives to `lambda` functions like `fst()` and `snd()`.

Strict and non-strict evaluation

Functional programming's efficiency stems, in part, from being able to defer a computation until it's required. The idea of lazy or non-strict evaluation is very helpful. It's so helpful that Python already offers this feature.

In Python, the logical expression operators and, or, and if-then-else are all non-strict. We sometimes call them *short-circuit* operators because they don't need to evaluate all arguments to determine the resulting value.

The following command snippet shows the and operator's non-strict feature:

```
>>> 0 and print("right")
0
>>> True and print("right")
right
```

When we execute the preceding command snippet, the left-hand side of the and operator is equivalent to False; the right-hand side is not evaluated. When the left-hand side is equivalent to True, the right-hand side is evaluated.

Other parts of Python are strict. Outside the logical operators, an expression is evaluated eagerly from left-to-right. A sequence of statement lines is also evaluated strictly in order. Literal lists and tuples require eager evaluation.

When a class is created, the method functions are defined in a strict order. In the case of a class definition, the method functions are collected into a dictionary (by default) and order is not maintained after they're created. If we provide two methods with the same name, the second one is retained because of the strict evaluation order.

Python's generator expressions and generator functions, however, are lazy. These expressions don't create all possible results immediately. It's difficult to see this without explicitly logging the details of a calculation. Here is an example of the version of the range() function that has the side effect of showing the numbers it creates:

```
>>> def numbers():
...     for i in range(1024):
...         print( "=", i )
...         yield i
```

If this function were eager, it would create all 1,024 numbers. Since it's lazy, it only creates numbers as requested.

The older Python 2 range() function was eager and created an actual list of object with all of the requested numbers. Python 2 has an xrange() function that is lazy and matches the semantics of the Python 3 range() function.

We can use this noisy `numbers()` function in a way that will show lazy evaluation. We'll write a function that evaluates some, but not all, of the values from this iterator:

```
>>> def sum_to(n):
...     sum= 0
...     for i in numbers():
...         if i == n: break
...         sum += i
...     return sum
```

The `sum_to()` function will not evaluate the entire result of the `numbers()` function. It will break after only consuming a few values from the `numbers()` function. We can see this consumption of values in the following log:

```
>>> sum_to(5)
= 0
= 1
= 2
= 3
= 4
= 5
10
```

As we'll see later, Python generator functions have some properties that make them a little awkward for simple functional programming. Specifically, a generator can only be used once in Python. We have to be cautious how we use the lazy Python generator expressions.

Recursion instead of a explicit loop state

Functional programs don't rely on `loops` and the associated overhead of tracking the state of loops. Instead, functional programs try to rely on the much simpler approach of recursive functions. In some languages, the programs are written as recursions, but **Tail-Call Optimization (TCO)** by the compiler changes them to `loops`. We'll introduce some recursion here and examine it closely in *Chapter 6, Recursions and Reductions*.

We'll look at a simple iteration to test a number for being prime. A prime number is a natural number, evenly divisible by only 1 and itself. We can create a naïve and poorly performing algorithm to determine if a number has any factors between two and the number. This algorithm has the advantage of simplicity; it works acceptably for solving **Project Euler** problems. Read up on **Miller-Rabin** primality tests for a much better algorithm.

We'll use the term `coprime` to mean that two numbers have only 1 as their common factor. The numbers 2 and 3, for example, are `coprime`. The numbers 6 and 9, however, are not `coprime` because they have 3 as a common factor.

If we want to know if a number, n, is prime, we actually ask this: is the number n `coprime` to all prime numbers, p, such that $p^2 < n$. We can simplify this using all integers, p, such that $2 \le p^2 < n$.

Sometimes, it helps to formalize this as follows:

$$prime(n) = \forall x\left[\left(2 \le x < 1 + \sqrt{n}\right) and \left(n(\bmod\ x) \ne 0\right)\right]$$

The expression could look as follows in Python:

```
not any(n%p==0 for p in range(2,int(math.sqrt(n))+1))
```

A more direct conversion from mathematical formalism to Python would use `all(n%p != 0... )` but that requires strict evaluation of all values of p. The *not any* version can terminate early if a `True` value is found.

This simple expression has a `for` loop inside it: it's not a pure example of stateless functional programming. We can reframe this into a function that works with a collection of values. We can ask whether the number, n, is `coprime` within any value in the range $[2,1+\sqrt{n})$?". This uses the symbols, `[)`, to show a half-open interval: the lower values are included, and the upper value is not included. This is typical behavior of the Python `range()` function. We will also restrict ourselves to the domain of natural numbers. The square root values, for example, are implicitly truncated to `integers`.

We can think of the definition of prime as the following:

$$prime(n) = \neg coprime\left(n, \left[2, 1 + \sqrt{n}\right)\right), \text{given n > 1.}$$

When defining a recursive function over a simple range of values, the base case can be an empty range. A nonempty range is handled recursively by processing one value combined with a range that's narrower by one value. We might formalize it as follows:

$$\text{coprime}\big(n,[a,b)\big) = \begin{cases} \text{True} & \textbf{if } a=b \\ n \quad (\text{mod } a) \neq 0 \wedge \text{coprime}\big(n,[a+1,b)\big) & \textbf{if } a < b \end{cases}$$

This version is relatively easy to confirm by examining the two cases, which are given as follows:

- If the range is empty, $a = b$, we evaluate something like: $\text{coprime}\big(131071,[363,363)\big)$. The range contains no values, so the return is a trivial `True`.

- If the range is not empty, we ask something like $\text{coprime}\big(131071,[2,363)\big)$. This decomposes into $131071\,(\text{mod } 2) \neq 0 \wedge \text{coprime}\big(131071,[3,363)\big)$. For this example, we can see that the first clause is `True`, and we'll evaluate the second clause recursively.

As an exercise for the reader: this recursion can be redefined to count down instead of up, using `[a,b-1)` in the second case.

As a side note, some folks like to think of the empty interval as $a \geq b$, not $a=b$. This is needless, since a is incremented by 1 and we can easily guarantee that $a \leq b$, initially. There's no way for a to somehow leap past b by some error in the function; we don't need to over-specify the rules for an empty interval.

Here is a Python code snippet that implements this definition of prime:

```python
def isprimer(n):
    def isprime(k, coprime):
        """Is k relatively prime to the value coprime?"""
        if k < coprime*coprime: return True
        if k % coprime == 0: return False
        return isprime(k, coprime+2)
    if n < 2: return False
    if n == 2: return True
    if n % 2 == 0: return False
    return isprime(n, 3)
```

This shows a recursive definition of an `isprime()` function. The half-open interval $\left[2,1+\sqrt{n}\right)$ is reduced to just the low-end argument, a, which is renamed `coprime` in this function to clarify its purpose. The base case is implemented as `n < coprime*coprime`; the range of values from `coprime` to `1+math.sqrt(n)` would be empty.

The non-strict and operation is implemented by splitting it out into a separate `if` statement, `if n % coprime == 0`. The `return` statement is the recursive call with a different `coprime` test value.

Because the recursion is the tail end of the function, this is an example of **Tail recursion**.

This function is embedded in a function that establishes the boundary condition that *n* is an odd number greater than 2. There's no point in testing any even number for being prime, since 2 is the only even prime.

What's important in this example is that the two cases of this recursive function are quite simple to design. Making the range of values an explicit argument to the internal `isprime()` function allows us to call the function recursively with argument values that reflect a steadily shrinking interval.

While this is often extremely succinct and very expressive, we have to be a little cautious about using recursion in Python. There are two problems that arise. They are stated as follows:

- Python imposes a recursion limit to detect recursive functions with improperly defined base cases
- Python does have a compiler to do Tail-Call Optimization (TCO)

The default recursion limit is 1,000, which is adequate for many algorithms. It's possible to change this with the `sys.setrecursionlimit()` function. It's not wise to raise this arbitrarily since it might lead to exceeding the OS memory limitations and crashing the Python interpreter.

If we try a recursive `isprimer()` function on a number over 1,000,000, we'll run foul of the recursion limit. If we used a somehow smarter `isprimer()` function that only checked prime factors instead of all factors, we'd be stopped at the 1,000th prime number, 7,919, limiting our prime testing to numbers below 62,710,561.

Some functional programming languages can optimize simple recursive functions such as our `isprimer()` function. An optimizing compiler can transform the recursive evaluation of the `isprimer(n, coprime+1)` method into a low-overhead `loop`. The optimization tends to make a hash of call stacks; debugging optimized programs becomes difficult. Python doesn't perform this optimization. Performance and memory are sacrificed for clarity and simplicity.

In Python, when we use a generator expression instead of a recursive function, we essentially do the tail-call optimization manually. We don't rely on a compiler for some functional language to do this optimization.

Here is TCO done as a generator expression:

```
def isprime(p):
    if p < 2: return False
    if p == 2: return True
    if p % 2 == 0: return False
    return not any(p==0 for p in range(3,int(math.sqrt(n))+1,2))
```

This function includes many of the functional programming principles, but it uses a generator expression instead of a pure recursion.

 We'll often optimize a purely recursive function to use an explicit for loop in a generator expression.

This algorithm is slow for large primes. For composite numbers, the function often returns a value quickly. If used on a value such as $M_{61} = 2^{61} - 1$, it will take a few minutes to show that this is prime. Clearly, the slowness comes from checking 1,518,500,249 individual candidate factors.

Functional type systems

Some functional programming languages such as **Haskell** and **Scala** are statically compiled, and depend on declared types for functions and their arguments. In order to provide the kind of flexibility Python already has, these languages have sophisticated type matching rules so that a generic function can be written, which works for a variety of related types.

In Object-Oriented Python, we often use the class inheritance hierarchy instead of sophisticated function type matching. We rely on Python to dispatch an operator to a proper method based on simple name matching rules.

Since Python already has the desired levels of flexibility, the type matching rules for a compiled functional language aren't relevant. Indeed, we could argue that the sophisticated type matching is a workaround imposed by static compilation. Python doesn't need this workaround because it's a dynamic language.

In some cases, we might have to resort to using isinstance(a, tuple) to detect if an argument value is tuple or an individual value. This will be as rare in functional programs as it is in Object-Oriented Programs.

Familiar territory

One of the ideas that emerge from the previous list of topics is that most functional programming is already present in Python. Indeed, most functional programming is already a very typical and common part of Object-Oriented Programming.

As a very specific example, a fluent **Application Program Interface (API)** is a very clear example of functional programming. If we take time to create a class with `return self()` in each method function, we can use it as follows:

```
some_object.foo().bar().yet_more()
```

We can just as easily write several closely-related functions that work as follows:

```
yet_more(bar(foo(some_object)))
```

We've switched the syntax from traditional object-oriented suffix notation to a more functional prefix notation. Python uses both notations freely, often using a prefix version of a special method name. For example, the `len()` function is generally implemented by the class.`__len__()` special method.

Of course, the implementation of the class shown above might involve a highly stateful object. Even then, a small change in viewpoint might reveal a functional approach that can lead to more succinct or more expressive programming.

The point is not that imperative programming is broken in some way, or that functional programming offers such a vastly superior technology. The point is that functional programming leads to a change in viewpoint that can—in many cases—be very helpful.

Saving some advanced concepts

We will set some more advanced concepts aside for consideration in later chapters. These concepts are part of the implementation of a purely functional language. Since Python isn't purely functional, our hybrid approach won't require deep consideration of these topics.

We will identify these up-front for the benefit of folks who already know a functional language such as Haskell and are learning Python. The underlying concerns are present in all programming languages but we'll tackle them differently in Python. In many cases, we can and will drop into imperative programming rather than use a strictly functional approach.

The topics are as follows:

- **Referential transparency**: When looking at lazy evaluation and the various kinds of optimization that are possible in a compiled language, the idea of multiple routes to the same object is important. In Python, this isn't as important because there aren't any relevant compile-time optimizations.

- **Currying**: The type systems will employ currying to reduce multiple-argument functions to single-argument functions. We'll look at currying in some depth in *Chapter 11, Decorator Design Techniques*.

- **Monads**: These are purely functional constructs that allow us to structure a sequential pipeline of processing in a flexible way. In some cases, we'll resort to imperative Python to achieve the same end. We'll also leverage the elegant `PyMonad` library for this. We'll defer this to *Chapter 14, The PyMonad Library*.

Summary

In this chapter, we've identified a number of features that characterize the functional programming paradigm. We started with first-class and higher-order functions. The idea is that a function can be an argument to a function or the result of a function. When functions become the object of additional programming, we can write some extremely flexible and generic algorithms.

The idea of immutable data is sometimes odd in an imperative and object-oriented programming language such as Python. When we start to focus on functional programming, however, we see a number of ways that state changes can be confusing or unhelpful. Using immutable objects can be a helpful simplification.

Python focuses on strict evaluation: all sub-expressions are evaluated from left-to-right through the statement. Python, however, does perform some non-strict evaluation. The or, and, and `if-else` logical operators are non-strict: all subexpressions are not necessarily evaluated. Similarly, a generator function is also non-strict. We can also call this eager vs. lazy. Python is generally eager but we can leverage generator functions to create lazy evaluation.

While functional programming relies on recursion instead of explicit `loop` state, Python imposes some limitations here. Because of the stack limitation and the lack of an optimizing compiler, we're forced to manually optimize recursive functions. We'll return to this topic in *Chapter 6, Recursions and Reductions*.

Although many functional languages have sophisticated type systems, we'll rely on Python's dynamic type resolution. In some cases, it means we'll have to write manual coercion among types. It might also mean that we'll have to create class definitions to handle very complex situations. For the most part, however, Python's built-in rules will work very elegantly.

In the next chapter, we'll look at the core concepts of pure functions and how these fit with Python's built-in data structures. Given this foundation, we can look at higher-order functions available in Python and how we can define our own higher-order functions.

3
Functions, Iterators, and Generators

The core of functional programming is the use of pure functions to map values from the input domain to the output range. A pure function has no side effects, a relatively easy threshold for us to achieve in Python.

Avoiding side effects also means reducing our dependence on variable assignment to maintain the state of our computations. We can't purge the assignment statement from the Python language, but we can reduce our dependence on stateful objects. This means we need to choose among the available Python built-in data structures to select those that don't require stateful operations.

This chapter will present several Python features from a functional viewpoint, as follows:

- Pure Functions, free of side effects
- Functions as objects that can be passed as arguments or returned as results
- The use of Python strings using object-oriented suffix notation and prefix notation
- Using tuples and namedtuples as a way to create stateless objects
- Using iterable collections as our primary design tool for functional programming

We'll look at generators and generator expressions, since these are ways to work with collections of objects. As we noted in *Chapter 2, Introducing Some Functional Features*, there are some boundary issues while trying to replace all generator expressions with recursions. Python imposes a recursion limit, and doesn't automatically handle TCO: we must optimize recursions manually using a generator expression.

We'll write generator expressions that will perform the following tasks:

- Conversions
- Restructuring
- Complex calculations

We'll make a quick survey of many of the built-in Python collections, and how we can work with collections while pursuing a functional paradigm. This might change our approach to working with lists, dicts, and sets. Writing functional Python encourages us to focus on tuples and immutable collections. In the next chapter, we'll emphasize more functional ways to work with specific kinds of collections.

Writing pure functions

A pure function has no side effects: there are no global changes to variables. If we avoid the global statement, we will almost meet this threshold. We also need to avoid changing the state mutable objects. We'll look at a number of ways of ensuring these two aspects of pure functions. A reference to a value in the Python global using a free variable is something we can rework into a proper parameter. In most cases, it's quite easy.

Here is an example where the usage of the global statement is explained:

```
def some_function(a, b, t):
    return a+b*t+global_adjustment
```

We can refactor this function to make the global_adjustment variable into a proper parameter. We would need to change each reference to this function, which might have a large ripple effect through a complex application. A global reference will be visible as a free variable in the body of a function. There will be neither a parameter nor an assignment for this variable, making it reasonably clear that it's global.

There are many internal Python objects, which are stateful. Instances of the file class, and all file-like objects, are examples of stateful objects in common use. We observe that the most commonly used stateful objects in Python generally behave as context managers. Not all developers make use of the available context managers but many objects implement the required interface. In a few cases, stateful objects don't completely implement the context manager interface; in these cases, there's often a close() method. We can use the contextlib.closing() function to provide these objects with the proper context manager interface.

We can't easily eliminate all stateful Python objects, except from small programs. Therefore, we must manage state while still exploiting the strengths of functional design. Toward this end, we should always use the `with` statement to encapsulate stateful file objects into a well-defined scope.

 Always use file objects in a `with` context.

We should always avoid global file objects, global database connections, and the associated state issues. The global file object is a very common pattern for handling open files. We might have a function as shown in the following command snippet:

```
def open(iname, oname):
    global ifile, ofile
    ifile= open(iname, "r")
    ofile= open(oname, "w")
```

Given this context, numerous other functions can use the `ifile` and `ofile` variables, hoping they properly refer to the `global` files, which are left open for the application to use.

This is not a very good design, and we need to avoid it. The files should be proper parameters to functions, and the open files should be nested in a `with` statement to assure that their stateful behavior is handled properly.

This design pattern also applies to databases. A database connection object can generally be provided as a formal argument to the application's functions. This is contrary to the way some popular web frameworks work that rely on a global database connection in an effort to make the database a transparent feature of the application. Additionally, a multithreaded web server might not benefit from sharing a single database connection. This suggests that there are some benefits of a hybrid approach that uses functional design with a few isolated stateful features.

Functions as first-class objects

It shouldn't come as a surprise that Python functions are first-class objects. In Python, functions are objects with a number of attributes. The reference manual lists a number of special member names that apply to functions. Since functions are objects with attributes, we can extract the `docstring` function or the name of a function, using special attributes such as __doc__ or __name__. We can also extract the body of the function via the __code__ attribute. In compiled languages, this introspection is relatively complex because of the source information that needs to be retained. In Python, it's quite simple.

We can assign functions to variables, pass functions as arguments, and return functions as values. We can easily use these techniques to write higher-order functions.

Since functions are objects, Python already has many features required to be a functional programming language.

Additionally, a callable object also helps us to create functions, which are first-class objects. We can even consider the callable class definition as a higher-order function. We do need to be judicious in how we use the __init__() method of a callable object; we should avoid setting stateful class variables. One common application is to use an __init__() method to create objects that fit the **Strategy design pattern**.

A class following the Strategy design pattern depends on another object to provide an algorithm or parts of an algorithm. This allows us to inject algorithmic details at runtime, rather than compiling the details into the class.

Here is an example of a callable object with an embedded Strategy object:

```python
import collections
class Mersenne1(collections.Callable):
    def __init__(self, algorithm):
        self.pow2= algorithm
    def __call__(self, arg):
        return self.pow2(arg)-1
```

This class uses __init__() to save a reference to another function. We're not creating any stateful instance variables.

The function given as a Strategy object must raise 2 to the given power. The three candidate objects that we can plug into this class are as follows:

```python
def shifty(b):
    return 1 << b
def multy(b):
    if b == 0: return 1
    return 2*multy(b-1)
def faster(b):
    if b == 0: return 1
    if b%2 == 1: return 2*faster(b-1)
    t= faster(b//2)
    return t*t
```

The `shifty()` function raises 2 to the desired power using a left shift of the bits. The `multy()` function uses a naive recursive multiplication. The `faster()` function uses a divide and conquer strategy that will perform $\log_2(b)$ multiplications instead of b multiplications.

We can create instances of our `Mersenne1` class with an embedded strategy algorithm, as follows:

```
m1s= Mersenne1(shifty)
m1m= Mersenne1(multy)
m1f= Mersenne1(faster)
```

This shows how we can define alternative functions that produce the same result but use different algorithms.

> Python allows us to compute $M_{89} = 2^{89} - 1$, since this doesn't even come close to the recursion limits in Python. This is quite a large prime number, with 27 digits.

Using strings

Since Python strings are immutable, they're an excellent example of functional programming objects. A Python `string` module has a number of methods, all of which produce a new string as the result. These methods are pure functions with no side effects.

The syntax for `string` method functions is postfix, where most functions are prefix. This means that complex string operations can be hard to read when they're commingled with conventional functions.

When scraping data from a web page, we might have a cleaner function that applies a number of transformations to a string to clean up the punctuation and return a `Decimal` object for use by the rest of the application. This will involve a mixture of prefix and postfix syntax.

It might look like the following command snippet:

```
from decimal import *
def clean_decimal(text):
    if text is None: return text
    try:
        return Decimal(text.replace("$", "").replace(",", ""))
    except InvalidOperation:
        return text
```

This function does two replacements on the string to remove $ and , string values. The resulting string is used as an argument to the `Decimal` class constructor, which returns the desired object.

To make this more consistent, we can consider defining our own prefix functions for the `string` method functions, as follows:

```
def replace(data, a, b):
    return data.replace(a,b)
```

This can allow us to use `Decimal(replace(replace(text, "$", ""), ",", ""))` with consistent-looking prefix syntax. In this case, we simply rearrange the existing argument values, allowing us an additional technique. We can do this for trivial cases, such as the follows:

```
>>> replace=str.replace
>>> replace("$12.45","$","")
```

12.45

It's not clear if this kind of consistency is a significant improvement over the mixed prefix and postfix notation. The issue with functions of multiple arguments is that the arguments wind up in various places in the expression.

A slightly better approach might be to define a more meaningful prefix function to strip punctuation, such as the following command snippet:

```
def remove( str, chars ):
    if chars: return remove( str.replace(chars[0], ""), chars[1:] )
    return str
```

This function will recursively remove each of the characters from the `char` variable. We can use it as `Decimal(remove(text, "$,"))` to make the intent of our string cleanup more clear.

Using tuples and namedtuples

Since Python tuples are immutable objects, they're another excellent example of objects suitable for functional programming. A Python `tuple` has very few method functions, so almost everything is done through functions using prefix syntax. There are a number of use cases for tuples, particularly when working with list-of-tuple, tuple-of-tuple and generator-of-tuple constructs.

Of course, namedtuples add an essential feature to a tuple: a name that we can use instead of an index. We can exploit namedtuples to create objects that are accretions of data. This allows us to write pure functions based on stateless objects, yet keep data bound into tidy object-like packages.

We'll almost always use tuples (and namedtuples) in the context of a collection of values. If we're working with single values, or a tidy group of exactly two values, we'll usually use named parameters to a function. When working with collections, however, we might need to have iterable-of-tuples or iterable-of-namedtuple constructs.

The decision to use a `tuple` or `namedtuple` object is entirely a matter of convenience. We might be working with a sequence of values as a three tuple of the form (number, number, number) assuming that the triple is in red, green, and blue order.

We can use functions to pick a three-tuple apart, as shown in the following command snippet:

```
red = lambda color: color[0]
green = lambda color: color[1]
blue = lambda color: color[2]
```

Or, we might introduce the following command line:

```
Color = namedtuple("Color", ("red", "green", "blue", "name"))
```

This allows us to use `item.red` instead of `red(item)`.

The functional programming application of tuples centers on the iterable-of-tuple design pattern. We'll look closely at a few iterable-of-tuple techniques. We'll look at the namedtuple techniques in *Chapter 7, Additional Tuple Techniques*.

Using generator expressions

We've shown some examples of generator expressions already. We'll show many more later in the chapter. We'll introduce some more sophisticated generator techniques in this section.

We need to mention a small bit of Python syntax here. It's common to see generator expressions used to create the `list` or `dict` literals via a `list` comprehension or a `dict` comprehension. For our purposes, a list display (or comprehension) is just one use of generator expressions. We can try to make a distinction between generator expressions outside a display and generator expressions inside a display, but there's nothing to be gained by this. The syntax is the same except for the enclosing punctuation and the semantics are indistinguishable.

A display includes the enclosing literal syntax: `[x**2 for x in range(10)]`; this example is a list comprehension, which creates a list object from the enclosed generator expression. In this section, we're going to focus on the generator expression. We'll occasionally create a display as part of demonstrating how the generator works. Displays have the disadvantage of creating (potentially large) `collection` objects. A generator expression is lazy and creates objects only as required.

We have to provide two important caveats on generator expressions, as follows:

- Generators appear to be sequence-like except for a function such as the `len()` function that needs to know the size of the collection.

- Generators can be used only once. After that, they appear empty.

Here is a generator function that we'll use for some examples:

```
def pfactorsl(x):
    if x % 2 == 0:
        yield 2
        if x//2 > 1:
            yield from pfactorsl(x//2)
        return
    for i in range(3,int(math.sqrt(x)+.5)+1,2):
        if x % i == 0:
            yield i
            if x//i > 1:
                yield from pfactorsl(x//i)
            return
    yield x
```

We're locating the prime factors of a number. If the number, *x*, is even, we'll yield 2 and then recursively yield all factors of *x*÷2.

For odd numbers, we'll step through odd values greater than or equal to 3, to locate a candidate factor of the number. When we locate a factor, we'll yield that factor, *i*, and then recursively yield all factors of *x*÷*i*.

In the event that we can't locate a factor, the number must be prime, so we can yield that.

We handle 2 as a special case to cut the number of iterations in half. All prime numbers, except 2, are odd.

We've used one important `for` loop in addition to recursion. This allows us to easily handle numbers that have as many as 1,000 factors. This number is at least as large as $2^{1,000}$, a number with 300 digits. Since the `for` variable, `i`, is not used outside the indented body of the loop, the stateful nature of the `i` variable won't lead to confusion if we make any changes to the body of the loop.

In effect, we've done tail-call optimization, the recursive calls that count from 3 to $\sqrt{x}$. The `for` loop saves us from deeply recursive calls that test every single number in the range.

The other two `for` loops exist merely to consume the results of a recursive function that is iterable.

In a recursive generator function, be careful of the return statement. Do not use the following command line:

```
return recursive_iter(args)
```

It returns only a generator object; it doesn't evaluate the function to return the generated values. Use either of the following:

```
for result in recursive_iter(args):
yield result
```

OR `yield from recursive_iter(args)`

As an alternative, the following command is a more purely recursive version:

```
def pfactorsr(x):
    def factor_n(x, n):
        if n*n > x:
            yield x
            return
        if x % n == 0:
            yield n
            if x//n > 1:
                yield from factor_n(x//n, n)
        else:
            yield from factor_n(x, n+2)
    if x % 2 == 0:
        yield 2
        if x//2 > 1:
            yield from pfactorsr(x//2)
        return
    yield from factor_n(x, 3)
```

We defined an internal recursive function, `factor_n()`, to test factors, n, in the range $3 \le n \le \sqrt{x}$. If the candidate factor, n, is outside the range, then x is prime. Otherwise, we'll see if n is a factor of x. If so, we'll yield n and all factors of $\frac{x}{n}$. If n is not a factor, we'll evaluate the function recursively using $n+2$. This recursion to test each value of $(n+2, n+2+2, n+2+2+2, ...)$ can be optimized into a `for` loop, as shown in the previous example.

The outer function handles some edge cases. As with other prime-related processing, we handle 2 as a special case. For even numbers, we'll yield 2 and then evaluate `pfactorsr()` recursively for $x \div 2$. All other prime factors must be odd numbers greater than or equal to 3. We'll evaluate the `factors_n()` function starting with 3 to test these other candidate prime factors.

> The purely recursive function can only locate prime factors of numbers up to about 4,000,000. Above this, Python's recursion limit will be reached.

Exploring the limitations of generators

We noted that there are some limitations of generator expressions and generator functions. The limitations can be observed by executing the following command snippet:

```
>>> from ch02_ex4 import *
>>> pfactorsl( 1560 )
<generator object pfactorsl at 0x1007b74b0>
>>> list(pfactorsl(1560))
[2, 2, 2, 3, 5, 13]
>>> len(pfactorsl(1560))
Traceback (most recent call last):
  File "<stdin>", line 1, in <module>
TypeError: object of type 'generator' has no len()
```

In the first example, we saw that generator functions are not strict. They're lazy, and don't have a proper value until we consume the generator functions. This isn't a limitation, per se; this is the whole reason that generator expressions fit with functional programming in Python.

In the second example, we materialized a list object from the generator function. This is handy for seeing the output and writing unit test cases.

In the third example, we saw one limitation of generator functions: there's no `len()`.

The other limitation of generator functions is that they can only be used once. For example, look at the following command snippet:

```
>>> result= pfactorsl(1560)
>>> sum(result)
27
>>> sum(result)
0
```

The first evaluation of the `sum()` method performed evaluation of the generator. The second evaluation of the `sum()` method found that the generator was now empty. We can only consume the values once.

Generators have a stateful life in Python. While they're very nice for some aspects of functional programming, they're not quite perfect.

We can try to use the `itertools.tee()` method to overcome the once-only limitation. We'll look at this in depth in *Chapter 8, The Itertools Module*. Here is a quick example of its usage:

```
import itertools
def limits(iterable):
    max_tee, min_tee = itertools.tee(iterable, 2)
    return max(max_tee), min(min_tee)
```

We created two clones of the parameter generator expression, `max_tee()` and `min_tee()`. This leaves the original iterator untouched, a pleasant feature that allows us to do very flexible combinations of functions. We can consume these two clones to get `maxima` and `minima` from the iterable.

While appealing, we'll see that this doesn't work out well in the long run. Once consumed, an iterable will not provide any more values. When we want to compute multiple kinds of reductions—for example, `sums`, `counts`, `minimums`, `maximums`—we need to design with this one-pass-only limitation in mind.

Combining generator expressions

The essence of functional programming comes from the ways we can easily combine generator expressions and generator functions to create very sophisticated composite processing sequences. When working with generator expressions, we can combine generators in several ways.

One common way to combine generator functions is when we create a composite function. We might have a generator that computes `(f(x) for x in range())`. If we want to compute `g(f(x))`, we have several ways to combine two generators.

We can tweak the original generator expression as follows:

```
g_f_x = (g(f(x)) for x in range())
```

While technically correct, this defeats any idea of reuse. Rather than reusing an expression, we rewrite it.

We can also substitute one expression within another expression, as follows:

```
g_f_x = (g(y) for y in (f(x) for x in range()))
```

This has the advantage of allowing us to use simple substitution. We can revise this slightly to emphasize reuse, using the following commands:

```
f_x= (f(x) for x in range())
g_f_x= (g(y) for y in f_x)
```

This has the advantage of leaving the initial expression, `(f(x) for x in range())`, essentially untouched. All we did was assign the expression to a variable.

The resulting composite function is also a generator expression, which is also lazy. This means that extracting the next value from `g_f_x` will extract one value from `f_x`, which will extract one value from the source `range()` function.

Cleaning raw data with generator functions

One of the tasks that arise in exploratory data analysis is cleaning up raw source data. This is often done as a composite operation applying several scalar functions to each piece of input data to create a usable data set.

Let's look at a simplified set of data. This data is commonly used to show techniques in exploratory data analysis. It's called **Anscombe's Quartet**, and it comes from the article, **Graphs in Statistical Analysis**, by F. J. Anscombe that appeared in *American Statistician* in 1973. Following are the first few rows of a downloaded file with this dataset:

```
Anscombe's quartet
I   II   III   IV
x   y   x   y   x   y   x   y
10.0   8.04   10.0   9.14    10.0   7.46   8.0   6.58
8.06.95   8.0   8.14   8.0   6.77   8.0   5.76
13.0   7.58   13.0   8.74   13.0   12.74   8.0   7.71
```

Sadly, we can't trivially process this with the `csv` module. We have to do a little bit of parsing to extract the useful information from this file. Since the data is properly tab-delimited, we can use the `csv.reader()` function to iterate through the various rows. We can define a data iterator as follows:

```
import csv
def row_iter(source):
    return csv.reader(source, delimiter="\t")
```

We simply wrapped a file in a `csv.reader` function to create an iterator over rows. We can use this iterator in the following context:

```
with open("Anscombe.txt") as source:
    print( list(row_iter(source)) )
```

The problem with this is that the first three items in the resulting iterable aren't data. The Anacombe's quartet file looks as follows when opened:

```
[["Anscombe's quartet"], ['I', 'II', 'III', 'IV'],
['x', 'y', 'x', 'y', 'x', 'y', 'x', 'y'],
```

We need to filter these rows from the iterable. Here is a function that will neatly excise three expected title rows, and return an iterator over the remaining rows:

```
def head_split_fixed(row_iter):
    title= next(row_iter)
    assert len(title) == 1 and title[0] == "Anscombe's quartet"
    heading= next(row_iter)
    assert len(heading) == 4 and heading == ['I', 'II', 'III', 'IV']
    columns= next(row_iter)
    assert len(columns) == 8 and columns == ['x', 'y', 'x', 'y', 'x',
    'y', 'x', 'y']
    return row_iter
```

This function plucks three rows from the iterable. It asserts that each row has an expected value. If the file doesn't meet these basic expectations, it's a symptom that the file was damaged or perhaps our analysis is focused on the wrong file.

Since both the `row_iter()` and the `head_split_fixed()` functions expect an iterable as an argument value, they can be trivially combined as follows:

```
with open("Anscombe.txt") as source:
    print( list(head_split_fixed(row_iter(source))))
```

We've simply applied one iterator to the results of another iterator. In effect, this defines a composite function. We're not done, of course; we still need to convert the `strings` values to the `float` values and we also need to pick apart the four parallel series of data in each row.

The final conversions and data extractions are more easily done with higher-order functions such as map() and filter(). We'll return to those in *Chapter 5, Higher-order Functions*.

Using lists, dicts, and sets

A Python sequence object, like a list, is iterable. However, it has some additional features. We'll think of it as a materialized iterable. We've used the tuple() function in several examples to collect the output of a generator expression or generator function into a single tuple object. We can also materialize a sequence to create a list object.

In Python, a list display offers simple syntax to materialize a generator: we just add the [] brackets. This is ubiquitous to the point where the distinction between generator expression and list comprehension is a subtlety of little practical importance.

The following is an example to enumerate the cases:

```
>>> range(10)
range(0, 10)
>>> [range(10)]
[range(0, 10)]
>>> [x for x in range(10)]
[0, 1, 2, 3, 4, 5, 6, 7, 8, 9]
>>> list(range(10))
[0, 1, 2, 3, 4, 5, 6, 7, 8, 9]
```

The first example is a generator function.

 The range(10) function is lazy; it won't produce the 10 values until evaluated in a context that iterates through the values.

The second example shows a list composed of a single generator function. To evaluate this, we'll have to use nested loops. Something like this [x for gen in [range(10)] for x in gen].

The third example shows a list comprehension built from a generator expression that includes a generator function. The function, range(10), is evaluated by a generator expression, x for x in range(10). The resulting values are collected into a list object.

We can also use the list() function to build a list from an iterable or a generator expression. This also works for set(), tuple(), and dict().

> The `list(range(10))` function evaluated the generator expression. The `[range(10)]` list literal does not evaluate the generator function.

While there's shorthand syntax for `list`, `dict`, and `set` using `[]` and `{}`, there's no shorthand syntax for a tuple. To materialize a tuple, we must use the `tuple()` function. For this reason, it often seems most consistent to use the `list()`, `tuple()`, and `set()` functions as the preferred syntax.

In the data cleansing example, we used a composite function to create a list of four tuples. The function looked as follows:

```
with open("Anscombe.txt") as source:
    data = head_split_fixed(row_iter(source))
    print(list(data))
```

We assigned the results of the composite function to a name, `data`. The data looks as follows:

```
[['10.0', '8.04', '10.0', '9.14', '10.0', '7.46', '8.0', '6.58'],
['8.0', '6.95', '8.0', '8.14', '8.0', '6.77', '8.0', '5.76'], ...
['5.0', '5.68', '5.0', '4.74', '5.0', '5.73', '8.0', '6.89']]
```

We need to do a little bit more processing to make this useful. First, we need to pick pairs of columns from the eight tuple. We can select pair of columns with a function, as shown in the following command snippet:

```
from collections import namedtuple
Pair = namedtuple("Pair", ("x", "y"))
def series(n, row_iter):
    for row in row_iter:
        yield Pair(*row[n*2:n*2+2])
```

This function picks two adjacent columns based on a number between 0 and 3. It creates a `namedtuple` object from those two columns. This allows us to pick the *x* or *y* value from each row.

We can now create a tuple-of-tuples collection as follows:

```
with open("Anscombe.txt") as source:
    data = tuple(head_split_fixed(row_iter(source)))
    sample_I= tuple(series(0,data))
    sample_II= tuple(series(1,data))
    sample_III= tuple(series(2,data))
    sample_IV= tuple(series(3,data))
```

We applied the `tuple()` function to a composite function based on the `head_split_fixed()` and `row_iter()` methods. This will create an object that we can reuse in several other functions. If we don't materialize a `tuple` object, only the first sample will have any data. After that, the source iterator will be exhausted and all other attempts to access it would yield empty sequestionsnces.

The `series()` function will pick pairs of items to create the `Pair` objects. Again, we applied an overall `tuple()` function to materialize the resulting tuple-of-namedtuple sequences so that we can do further processing on each one.

The `sample_I` sequence looks like the following command snippet:

```
(Pair(x='10.0', y='8.04'), Pair(x='8.0', y='6.95'),
Pair(x='13.0', y='7.58'), Pair(x='9.0', y='8.81'),
Etc.
Pair(x='5.0', y='5.68'))
```

The other three sequences are similar in structure. The values, however, are quite different.

The final thing we'll need to do is create proper numeric values from the strings that we've accumulated so that we can compute some statistical summary values. We can apply the `float()` function conversion as the last step. There are many alternative places to apply the `float()` function, and we'll look at some choices in *Chapter 5, Higher-order Functions*.

Here is an example describing the usage of `float()` function:

```
mean = sum(float(pair.y) for pair in sample_I)/len(sample_I)
```

This will provide the mean of the `y` value in each `Pair` object. We can gather a number of statistics as follows:

```
for subset in sample_I, sample_II, sample_III, sample_III:
    mean = sum(float(pair.y) for pair in subset)/len(subset)
    print(mean)
```

We computed a mean for the `y` values in each `pair` built from the source database. We created a common tuple-of-namedtuple structure so that we can have reasonably clear references to members of the source dataset. Using `pair.y` is a bit less obscure than `pair[1]`.

To reduce memory use—and increase performance—we prefer to use generator expressions and functions as much as possible. These iterate through collections in a lazy (or non-strict) manner, computing values only when required. Since iterators can only be used once, we're sometimes forced to materialize a collection as a `tuple` (or `list`) object. Materializing a collection costs memory and time, so we do it reluctantly.

Programmers familiar with **Clojure** can match Python's lazy generators with the `lazy-seq` and `lazy-cat` functions. The idea is that we can specify a potentially infinite sequence, but only take values from it as needed.

Using stateful mappings

Python offers several stateful collections; the various mappings include the dict class and a number of related mappings defined in the `collections` module. We need to emphasize the stateful nature of these mappings and use them carefully.

For our purposes in learning functional programming techniques in Python, there are two use cases for `mapping`: a stateful dictionary that accumulates a mapping and a frozen dictionary. In the first example of this chapter, we showed a frozen dictionary that was used by the `ElementTree.findall()` method. Python doesn't provide an easy-to-use definition of an immutable mapping. The `collections.abc.Mapping` abstract class is immutable but it's not something we can use trivially. We'll dive into details in *Chapter 6, Recursions and Reductions*.

Instead of the formality of using the `collections.abc.Mapping` abstract class, we can fall back on confirming that the variable `ns_map` appears exactly once on the left side of an assignment statement, methods such as `ns_map.update()` or `ns_map.pop()` are never used, and the `del` statement isn't used with map items.

The stateful dictionary can be further decomposed into two typical use cases; they are as follows:

- A dictionary built once and never updated. In this case, we will exploit the hashed keys feature of the `dict` class to optimize performance. We can create a dictionary from any iterable sequence of (key, value) two tuples via `dict( sequence )`.

- A dictionary built incrementally. This is an optimization we can use to avoid materializing and sorting a list object. We'll look at this in *Chapter 6, Recursions and Reductions*. We'll look at the `collections.Counter` class as a sophisticated reduction. Incremental building is particularly helpful for memoization. We'll defer memoization until *Chapter 16, Optimizations and Improvements*.

The first example, building a dictionary once, stems from an application with three operating phases: gather some input, create a `dict` object, and then process input based on the mappings in the dictionary. As an example of this kind of application, we might be doing some image processing and have a specific palette of colors, represented by names and (R, G, B) tuples. If we use the **GNU Image Manipulation Program (GIMP) GNU General Public License (GPL)** file format, the color palette might look like the following command snippet:

```
GIMP Palette
Name: Small
Columns: 3
#
  0   0   0    Black
255 255 255    White
238  32  77    Red
28 172 120      Green
31 117 254      Blue
```

The details of parsing this file are the subject of *Chapter 6, Recursions and Reductions*. What's important is the results of the parsing.

First, we'll assume that we're using the following `Color` namedtuple:

```
from collections import namedtuple
Color = namedtuple("Color", ("red", "green", "blue", "name"))
```

Second, we'll assume that we have a parser that produces an iterable of `Color` objects. If we materialize it as a tuple, it would look like the following:

```
(Color(red=239, green=222, blue=205, name='Almond'),
Color(red=205, green=149, blue=117, name='Antique Brass'),
Color(red=253, green=217, blue=181, name='Apricot'),
Color(red=197, green=227, blue=132, name='Yellow Green'),
Color(red=255, green=174, blue=66, name='Yellow Orange'))
```

In order to locate a given color name quickly, we will create a frozen dictionary from this sequence. This is not the only way to get fast lookups of a color by name. We'll look at another option later.

To create a mapping from a tuple, we will use the `process(wrap(iterable))` design pattern. The following command shows how we can create the color name mapping:

```
name_map= dict( (c.name, c) for c in sequence )
```

Where the sequence variable is the iterable of the `Color` objects shown previously, the `wrap()` element of the design pattern simply transforms each `Color` object, c, into the two tuple (`c.name, c`). The `process()` element of the design uses `dict()` initialization to create a mapping from name to `Color`. The resulting dictionary looks as follows:

```
{'Caribbean Green': Color(red=28, green=211, blue=162,
name='Caribbean Green'),
'Peach': Color(red=255, green=207, blue=171, name='Peach'),
'Blizzard Blue': Color(red=172, green=229, blue=238, name='Blizzard
Blue'),
```

The order is not guaranteed, so you may not see Caribbean Green first.

Now that we've materialized the mapping, we can use this `dict()` object in some later processing for repeated transformations from color name to (R, G, B) color numbers. The lookup will be blazingly fast because a dictionary does a rapid transformation from key to hash value followed by lookup in the dictionary.

Using the bisect module to create a mapping

In the previous example, we created a `dict` mapping to achieve a fast mapping from a color name to a `Color` object. This isn't the only choice; we can use the `bisect` module instead. Using the `bisect` module means that we have to create a sorted object, which we can then search. To be perfectly compatible with the `dict` mapping, we can use `collections.abc.Mapping` as the base class.

The `dict` mapping uses a hash to locate items almost immediately. However, this requires allocating a fairly large block of memory. The `bisect` mapping does a search, which doesn't require as much memory, but performance can be described as immediate.

A `static` mapping class looks like the following command snippet:

```
import bisect
from collections.abc import Mapping
class StaticMapping(Mapping):
    def __init__( self, iterable ):
        self._data = tuple(iterable)
        self._keys = tuple(sorted(key for key, _ in self._data))

    def __getitem__(self, key):
        ix= bisect.bisect_left(self._keys, key)
        if ix != len(self._keys) and self._keys[ix] == key:
            return self._data[ix][1]
```

```
        raise ValueError("{0!r} not found".format(key))
    def __iter__(self):
        return iter(self._keys)
    def __len__(self):
        return len(self._keys)
```

This class extends the abstract superclass `collections.abc.Mapping`. It provides an initialization and implementations for three functions missing from the abstract definition. The `__getitem__()` method uses the `bisect.bisect_left()` function to search the collection of keys. If the key is found, the appropriate value is returned. The `__iter__()` method returns an iterator, as required by the superclass. The `__len__()` method, similarly, provides the required length of the collection.

Another option is to start with the source code for the `collections.OrderedDict` class, change the superclass to `Mapping` instead of `MutableMapping`, and remove all of the methods that implement mutability. For more details on which methods to keep and which to discard, refer to the *Python Standard Library*, section 8.4.1.

Visit the following link for more details:

`https://docs.python.org/3.3/library/collections.abc.html#collections-abstract-base-classes`

This class might not seem to embody too many functional programming principles. Our goal here is to support a larger application that minimizes the use of stateful variables. This class saves a static collection of key-value pairs. As an optimization, it materializes two objects.

An application that creates an instance of this class is using a materialized object to perform rapid lookups of the keys. The superclass does not support updates to the object. The collection, as a whole, is stateless. It's not as fast as the built-in `dict` class, but it uses less memory and, through the formality of being a subclass of `Mapping`, we can be assured that this object is not used to contain a processing state.

Using stateful sets

Python offers several stateful collections, including the set collection. For our purposes, there are two use cases for a set: a stateful set that accumulates items, and a frozenset that is used to optimize searches for an item.

We can create a frozenset from an iterable in the same way as we create a `tuple` object from an iterable `fronzenset(some_iterable)` method; this will create a structure that has the advantage of a very fast `in` operator. This can be used in an application that gatheres data, creates a set, and then uses that frozenset to process some other data items.

We might have a set of colors that we will use as a kind of **chroma-key**: we will use this color to create a mask that will be used to combine two images. Pragmatically, a single color isn't appropriate but a small set of very similar colors works best. In this case, we'll examine each pixel of an image file to see if the pixel is in the chroma-key set or not. For this kind of processing, the chroma-key colors are loaded into a frozenset before processing the target images. For more information, read about chroma-key processing from the following link:

```
http://en.wikipedia.org/wiki/Chroma_key
```

As with mappings—specifically the Counter class—there are some algorithms that can benefit from a memoized set of values. Some functions benefit from memoization because a function is a mapping between domain values and range values, a job for which a mapping works nicely. A few algorithms benefit from a memoized set, which is stateful and grows as data is processed.

We'll return to memoization in *Chapter 16, Optimizations and Improvements.*

Summary

In this chapter, we looked closely at writing pure functions: free of side effects. The bar is low here, since Python forces us to use the global statement to write impure functions. We looked at generator functions and how we can use these as the backbone of functional programming.

We also examined the built-in collection classes to show how they're used in the functional paradigm. While the general ideal behind functional programming is to limit the use of stateful variables, the collection objects are generally stateful and, for many algorithms, also essential. Our goal is to be judicious in our use of Python's nonfunctional features.

In the next two chapters, we'll look at higher-order functions: functions that accept functions as arguments as well as returning functions. We'll start with an exploration of the built-in higher-order functions. In later chapters, we'll look at techniques for defining our own higher-order functions. We'll also look at the itertools and functools modules and their higher-order functions in later chapters.

4

Working with Collections

Python offers a number of functions that process whole collections. They can be applied to sequences (lists or tuples), sets, mappings, and iterable results of generator expressions. We'll look at some of Python's collection-processing functions from a functional programming viewpoint.

We'll start out by looking at iterables and some simple functions that work with iterables. We'll look at some additional design patterns to handle iterables and sequences with recursion as well as explicit `for` loops. We'll look at how we can apply a `scalar()` function to a collection of data with a generator expression.

In this chapter, we'll show examples of how to use the following functions to work with collections:

- `any()` and `all()`
- `len()` and `sum()` and some higher-order statistical processing related to these functions
- `zip()` and some related techniques to structure and flatten lists of data
- `reversed()`
- `enumerate()`

The first four functions can all be called reductions; they reduce a collection to a single value. The other three functions (`zip()`, `reversed()`, and `enumerate()`) are mappings; they produce a new collection from an existing collection(s). In the next chapter, we'll look at some `mapping()` and `reduction()` functions that use an additional function as an argument to customize their processing.

In this chapter, we'll start out by looking at ways to process data using generator expressions. Then, we'll apply different kinds of collection-level functions to show how they can simplify the syntax of iterative processing. We'll also look at some different ways of restructuring data.

In the next chapter, we'll focus on using higher-order collection functions to do similar kinds of processing.

An overview of function varieties

We need to distinguish between two broad species of functions, as follows:

- Scalar functions apply to individual values and compute an individual result. Functions such as `abs()`, `pow()`, and the entire `math` module are examples of scalar functions.

- `Collection()` functions work with iterable collections.

We can further subdivide the collection functions into three subspecies:

- **Reduction**: This uses a function that is used to fold values in the collection together, resulting in a single final value. We can call this an aggregate function, as it produces a single aggregate value for an input collection.

- **Mapping**: This applies a function to all items of a collection; the result is a collection of the same size.

- **Filter**: This applies a function to all items of a collection that rejects some items and passes others. The result is a subset of the input. A filter might do nothing, which means that the output matches the input; this is an improper subset, but it still fits the broader definition of subset.

We'll use this conceptual framework to characterize ways in which we use the built-in collection functions.

Working with iterables

As we noted in the previous chapters, we'll often use Python's `for` loop to work with collections. When working with materialized collections such as tuples, lists, maps, and sets, the `for` loop involves an explicit management of state. While this strays from purely functional programming, it reflects a necessary optimization for Python. If we assure that state management is localized to an iterator object that's created as part of the `for` statement evaluation, we can leverage this feature without straying too far from pure, functional programming. For example, if we use the `for` loop variable outside the indented body of `loop`, we've strayed too far from purely functional programming.

We'll return to this in *Chapter 6, Recursion and Reduction*. It's an important topic, and we'll just scratch the surface here with a quick example of working with generators.

One common application of `for` loop iterable processing is the
`unwrap(process(wrap(iterable)))` design pattern. A `wrap()` function will first
transform each item of an iterable into a two tuples with a derived sort key or other
value and then the original immutable item. We can then process these two tuples
based on the wrapped value. Finally, we'll use an `unwrap()` function to discard the
value used to wrap, which recovers the original item.

This happens so often in a functional context that we have two functions that are
used heavily for this; they are as follows:

```
fst = lambda x: x[0]
snd = lambda x: x[1]
```

These two functions pick the first and second values from a tuple, and both are
handy for the `process()` and `unwrap()` functions.

Another common pattern is `wrap(wrap(wrap()))`. In this case, we're starting
with simple tuples and then wrapping them with additional results to build
up larger and more complex tuples. A common variation on this theme is
`extend(extend(extend()))` where the additional values build new, more
complex `namedtuple` instances without actually wrapping the original tuples.
We can summarize both of these as the Accretion design pattern.

We'll apply the Accretion design to work with a simple sequence of latitude and
longitude values. The first step will convert the simple points (`lat`, `lon`) on a path
into pairs of legs (`begin`, `end`). Each pair in the result will be ((`lat`, `lon`), (`lat`, `lon`)).

In the next sections, we'll show how to create a generator function that will iterate over
the content of a file. This iterable will contain the raw input data that we will process.

Once we have the data, later sections will show how to decorate each leg with the
haversine distance along the leg. The final result of the `wrap(wrap(iterable()))`
processing will be a sequence of three tuples: ((`lat`, `lon`), (`lat`, `lon`), `distance`). We
can then analyze the results for the longest, shortest distance, bounding rectangle,
and other summaries of the data.

Parsing an XML file

We'll start by parsing an **XML** (short for **Extensible Markup Language**) file to get
the raw latitude and longitude pairs. This will show how we can encapsulate some
not-quite functional features of Python to create an iterable sequence of values.
We'll make use of the `xml.etree` module. After parsing, the resulting `ElementTree`
object has a `findall()` method that will iterate through the available values.

We'll be looking for constructs such as the following code snippet:

```
<Placemark><Point>
<coordinates>-76.33029518659048,37.54901619777347,0</coordinates>
</Point></Placemark>
```

The file will have a number of `<Placemark>` tags, each of which has a point and coordinate structure within it. This is typical of **Keyhole Markup Language (KML)** files that contain geographic information.

Parsing an XML file can be approached at two levels of abstraction. At the lower level, we need to locate the various tags, attribute values, and content within the XML file. At a higher level, we want to make useful objects out of the text and attribute values.

The lower-level processing can be approached in the following way:

```
import xml.etree.ElementTree as XML
def row_iter_kml(file_obj):
    ns_map= {
        "ns0": "http://www.opengis.net/kml/2.2",
        "ns1": "http://www.google.com/kml/ext/2.2"}
    doc= XML.parse(file_obj)
    return (comma_split(coordinates.text)
            for coordinates in
            doc.findall("./ns0:Document/ns0:Folder/ns0:Placemark/
            ns0:Point/ns0:coordinates", ns_map))
```

This function requires a file that was already opened, usually via a `with` statement. However, it can also be any of the file-like objects that the XML parser can handle. The function includes a simple static `dict` object, `ns_map`, that provides the `namespace` mapping information for the XML tags we'll be searching. This dictionary will be used by the `XML ElementTree.findall()` method.

The essence of the parsing is a generator function that uses the sequence of tags located by `doc.findall()`. This sequence of tags is then processed by a `comma_split()` function to tease the text value into its comma-separated components.

The `comma_split()` function is the functional version of the `split()` method of a string, which is as follows:

```
def comma_split(text):
    return text.split(",")
```

We've used the functional wrapper to emphasize a slightly more uniform syntax.

The result of this function is an iterable sequence of rows of data. Each row will be a tuple composed of three strings: `latitude`, `longitude`, and `altitude` of a waypoint along this path. This isn't directly useful yet. We'll need to do some more processing to get `latitude` and `longitude` as well as converting these two numbers into useful floating-point values.

This idea of an iterable sequence of tuples as results of lower-level parsing allows us to process some kinds of data files in a simple and uniform way. In *Chapter 3, Functions, Iterators, and Generators*, we looked at how **Comma Separated Values (CSV)** files are easily handled as rows of tuples. In *Chapter 6, Recursions and Reductions*, we'll revisit the parsing idea to compare these various examples.

The output from the preceding function looks like the following code snippet:

```
[['-76.33029518659048', '37.54901619777347', '0'],
 ['-76.27383399999999', '37.840832', '0'],
 ['-76.459503', '38.331501', '0'],
 and so on
 ['-76.47350299999999', '38.976334', '0']]
```

Each row is the source text of the `<ns0:coordinates>` tag split using `,` that's part of the text content. The values are the East-West longitude, North-South latitude, and altitude. We'll apply some additional functions to the output of this function to create a usable set of data.

Parsing a file at a higher level

Once we've parsed the low-level syntax, we can restructure the raw data into something usable in our Python program. This kind of structuring applies to XML, **JavaScript Object Notation (JSON)**, CSV, and any of the wide variety of physical formats in which data is serialized.

We'll aim to write a small suite of generator functions that transforms the parsed data into a form our application can use. The generator functions include some simple transformations on the text that's found by the `row_iter_kml()` function, which are as follows:

- Discarding `altitude`, or perhaps keeping only `latitude` and `longitude`
- Changing the order from (`longitude`, `latitude`) to (`latitude`, `longitude`)

We can make these two transformations have more syntactic uniformity by defining a utility function as follows:

```
def pick_lat_lon(lon, lat, alt):
    return lat, lon
```

We can use this function as follows:

```
def lat_lon_kml(row_iter):
    return (pick_lat_lon(*row) for row in row_iter)
```

This function will apply the `pick_lat_lon()` function to each row. We've used `*row` to assign each element of the row three tuple to separate parameters of the `pick_lat_lon()` function. The function can then extract and reorder the two relevant values from each three tuple.

It's important to note that a good functional design allows us to freely replace any function with its equivalent, which makes refactoring quite simple. We've tried to achieve this goal when we provide alternative implementations of the various functions. In principle, a clever functional language compiler might do some replacements as part of an optimization pass.

We'll use the following kind of processing to parse the file and build a structure we can use, such as the following code snippet:

```
with urllib.request.urlopen("file:./Winter%202012-2013.kml") as
source:
    v1= tuple(lat_lon_kml(row_iter_kml(source)))
print(v1)
```

We've used the `urllib` command to open a source. In this case, it's a local file. However, we can also open a KML file on a remote server. Our objective with using this kind of file opening is to assure that our processing is uniform no matter what the source of the data is.

We've shown the two functions that do low-level parsing of the KML source. The `row_iter_kml(source)` expression produces a sequence of text columns. The `lat_lon_kml()` function will extract and reorder the `latitude` and `longitude` values. This creates an intermediate result that sets the stage for further processing. The subsequent processing is independent of the original format.

When we run this, we see results like the following:

```
(('37.54901619777347', '-76.33029518659048'),
('37.840832', '-76.27383399999999'), ('38.331501', '-76.459503'),
('38.330166', '-76.458504'), ('38.976334', '-76.47350299999999'))
```

We've extracted just the `latitude` and `longitude` values from a complex XML file using an almost purely functional approach. As the result is an iterable, we can continue to use functional programming techniques to process each point that we retrieve from the file.

We've explicitly separated low-level XML parsing from higher-level reorganization of the data. The XML parsing produced a generic tuple of string structure. This is compatible with the output from the CSV parser. When working with **SQL** databases, we'll have a similar iterable of tuple structures. This allows us to write code for higher-level processing that can work with data from a variety of sources.

We'll show a series of transformations to rearrange this data from a collection of strings to a collection of waypoints along a route. This will involve a number of transformations. We'll need to restructure the data as well as convert from strings to floating-point values. We'll also look at a few ways to simplify and clarify the subsequent processing steps. We'll use this data set in later chapters because it's reasonably complex.

Pairing up items from a sequence

A common restructuring requirement is to make start-stop pairs out of points in a sequence. Given a sequence, $S = \{s_0, s_1, s_2, ..., s_n\}$, we want to create a paired sequence $\hat{S} = \{(s_0, s_1), (s_1, s_2), ..., (s_{n-1}, s_n)\}$. When doing time-series analysis, we might be combining more widely separated values. In this example, it's adjacent values.

A paired sequence will allow us to use each pair to compute distances from point to point using a trivial application of a `haversine` function. This technique is also used to convert a path of points into a series of line segments in a graphics application.

Why pair up items? Why not do something like this?

```
begin= next(iterable)
for end in iterable:
    compute_something(begin, end)
    begin = end
```

This, clearly, will process each leg of the data as a begin-end pair. However, the processing function and the loop that restructures the data are tightly bound, making reuse more complex than necessary. The algorithm for pairing is hard to test in isolation because it's bound to the `compute_something()` function.

This combined function also limits our ability to reconfigure the application. There's no easy way to inject an alternative implementation of the `compute_something()` function. Additionally, we've got a piece of explicit state, the `begin` variable, which makes life potentially complex. If we try to add features to the body of `loop`, we can easily fail to set the `begin` variable correctly if a point is dropped from consideration. A `filter()` function introduces an `if` statement that can lead to an error in updating the `begin` variable.

We achieve better reuse by separating this simple pairing function. This, in the long run, is one of our goals. If we build up a library of helpful primitives such as this pairing function, we can tackle problems more quickly and confidently.

There are many ways to pair up the points along the route to create start and stop information for each leg. We'll look at a few here and then revisit this in *Chapter 5, Higher-order Functions* and again in *Chapter 8, The Itertools Module*.

Creating pairs can be done in a purely functional way using a recursion. The following is one version of a function to pair up the points along a route:

```
def pairs(iterable):
    def pair_from( head, iterable_tail ):
        nxt= next(iterable_tail)
        yield head, nxt
        yield from pair_from( nxt, iterable_tail )
    try:
        return pair_from( next(iterable), iterable )
    except StopIteration:
        return
```

The essential function is the internal `pair_from()` function. This works with the item at the head of an iterable plus the iterable itself. It yields the first pair, pops the next item from the iterable, and then invokes itself recursively to yield any additional pairs.

We've invoked this function from the `pairs()` function. The `pairs()` function ensures that the initialization is handled properly and the terminating exception is silenced properly.

> Python iterable recursion involves a `for` loop to properly consume and yield the results from the recursion. If we try to use a simpler-looking `return pair_from(nxt, iterable_tail)` method, we'll see that it does not properly consume the iterable and yield all of the values.
>
> Recursion in a generator function requires `yield` from a statement to consume the resulting iterable. For this, use `yield from recursive_iter(args)`.
>
> Something like `return recursive_iter(args)` will return only a generator object; it doesn't evaluate the function to return the generated values.

Our strategy for performing tail-call optimization is to replace the recursion with a generator expression. We can clearly optimize this recursion into a simple `for` loop. The following is another version of a function to pair up the points along a route:

```
def legs(lat_lon_iter):
    begin= next(lat_lon_iter)
    for end in lat_lon_iter:
        yield begin, end
        begin= end
```

The version is quite fast and free from stack limits. It's independent of any particular type of sequence, as it will pair up anything emitted by a sequence generator. As there's no processing function inside loop, we can reuse the `legs()` function as needed.

We can think of this function as one that yields the following kind of sequence of pairs:

```
list[0:1], list[1:2], list[2:3], ..., list[-2:]
```

Another view of this function is as follows:

```
zip(list, list[1:])
```

While informative, these other two formulations only work for sequence objects. The `legs()` and `pairs()` functions work for any iterable, including sequence objects.

Using the iter() function explicitly

The purely functional viewpoint is that all of our iterables can be processed with recursive functions, where the state is merely the recursive call stack. Pragmatically, Python iterables will often involve evaluation of other `for` loops. There are two common situations: collections and iterables. When working with a collection, an iterator object is created by the `for` statement. When working with a generator function, the generator function is the iterator and maintains its own internal state. Often, these are equivalent from a Python programming perspective. In rare cases, generally those situations where we have to use an explicit `next()` function, the two won't be precisely equivalent.

Our `legs()` function shown previously has an explicit `next()` function call to get the first value from the iterable. This works wonderfully well with generator functions, expressions, and other iterables. It doesn't work with sequence objects such as tuples or `list`s.

The following are three examples to clarify the use of the `next()` and `iter()` functions:

```
>>> list(legs(x for x in range(3)))
[(0, 1), (1, 2)]
>>> list(legs([0,1,2]))
Traceback (most recent call last):
  File "<stdin>", line 1, in <module>
  File "<stdin>", line 2, in legs
TypeError: 'list' object is not an iterator
>>> list(legs( iter([0,1,2])))
[(0, 1), (1, 2)]
```

In the first case, we applied the `legs()` function to an iterable. In this case, the iterable was a generator expression. This is the expected behavior based on our previous examples in this chapter. The items are properly paired up to create two legs from three waypoints.

In the second case, we tried to apply the `legs()` function to a sequence. This resulted in an error. While a `list` object and an iterable are equivalent when used in a `for` statement, they aren't equivalent everywhere. A sequence isn't an iterator; it doesn't implement the `next()` function. The `for` statement handles this gracefully, however, by creating an iterator from a sequence automatically.

To make the second case work, we need to explicitly create an iterator from a `list` object. This permits the `legs()` function to get the first item from the iterator over the `list` items.

Extending a simple loop

We have two kinds of extensions we might factor into a simple loop. We'll look first at a `filter` extension. In this case, we might be rejecting values from further consideration. They might be data outliers, or perhaps source data that's improperly formatted. Then, we'll look at mapping source data by performing a simple transformation to create new objects from the original objects. In our case, we'll be transforming `strings` to `floating-point` numbers. The idea of extending a simple `loop` with a mapping, however, applies to situations. We'll look at refactoring the above `pairs()` function. What if we need to adjust the sequence of points to discard a value? This will introduce a `filter` extension that rejects some data values.

As the loop we're designing simply returns pairs without performing any additional application-related processing, the complexity is minimal. Simplicity means we're somewhat less likely to confuse the processing state.

Adding a `filter` extension to this design might look something like the following code snippet:

```
def legs_filter(lat_lon_iter):
    begin= next(lat_lon_iter)
    for end in lat_lon_iter:
        if #some rule for rejecting:
            continue
        yield begin, end
        begin= end
```

We have plugged in a processing rule to reject certain values. As the `loop` remains succinct and expressive, we are confident that the processing will be done properly. Also, we can easily write a test for this function, as the results work for any iterable, irrespective of the long-term destination of the pairs.

The next refactoring will introduce additional mapping to a loop. Adding mappings is common when a design is evolving. In our case, we have a sequence of `string` values. We need to convert these to `floating-point` values for later use. This is a relatively simple mapping that shows the design pattern.

The following is one way to handle this data mapping, through a generator expression that wraps a generator function:

```
print(tuple(legs((float(lat), float(lon))
for lat,lon in lat_lon_kml()))))
```

We've applied the `legs()` function to a generator expression that creates `float` values from the output of the `lat_lon_kml()` function. We can read this in the opposite order as well. The `lat_lon_kml()` function's output is transformed into a pair of `float` values, which is then transformed into a sequence of `legs`.

This is starting to get complex. We've got a large number of nested functions here. We're applying `float()`, `legs()`, and `tuple()` to a data generator. One common refactoring of complex expressions is to separate the generator expression from any materialized collection. We can do the following to simplify the expression:

```
flt= ((float(lat), float(lon)) for lat,lon in lat_lon_kml())
print(tuple(legs(flt)))
```

We've assigned the generator function to a variable named `flt`. This variable isn't a collection object; we're not using a `list` comprehension to create an object. We've merely assigned the generator expression to a variable name. We've then used the `flt` variable in another expression.

The evaluation of the `tuple()` method actually leads to a proper object being built so that we can print the output. The `flt` variable's objects are created only as needed.

There are other refactoring's we might like to do. In general, the source of the data is something we often want to change. In our example, the `lat_lon_kml()` function is tightly bound in the rest of the expression. This makes reuse difficult when we have a different data source.

In the case where the `float()` operation is something we'd like to parameterize so that we can reuse it, we can define a function around the generator expression. We'll extract some of the processing into a separate function merely to group the operations. In our case, the string-pair to float-pair is unique to a particular source data. We can rewrite a complex float-from-string expression into a simpler function such as follows:

```
def float_from_pair( lat_lon_iter ):
    return ((float(lat), float(lon)) for lat,lon in lat_lon_iter)
```

The `float_from_pair()` function applies the `float()` function to the first and second values of each item in the iterable, yielding a two tuple of floats created from an input value. We've relied on Python's `for` statement to decompose the two tuple.

We can use this function in the following context:

```
legs( float_from_pair(lat_lon_kml()))
```

We're going to create `legs` that are built from `float` values that come from a KML file. It's fairly easy to visualize the processing, as each stage in the process is a simple prefix function.

When parsing, we often have sequences of `string` values. For numeric applications, we'll need to convert `strings` to `float`, `int`, or `Decimal` values. This often involves inserting a function such as the `float_from_pair()` function into a sequence of expressions that clean up the source data.

Our previous output was all strings; it looked like the following code snippet:

```
(('37.54901619777347', '-76.33029518659048'),
('37.840832', '-76.27383399999999'), ...
('38.976334', '-76.47350299999999'))
```

We'll want data like the following code snippet, where we have floats:

```
(((37.54901619777347, -76.33029518659048),
(37.840832, -76.273834)), ((37.840832, -76.273834), ...
((38.330166, -76.458504), (38.976334, -76.473503)))
```

We'll need to create a pipeline of simpler transformation functions. Above, we arrived at `flt= ((float(lat), float(lon)) for lat,lon in lat_lon_kml())`. We can exploit the substitution rule for functions and replace a complex expression such as `(float(lat), float(lon)) for lat,lon in lat_lon_kml()` with a function that has the same value, in this case, `float_from_pair(lat_lon_kml())`. This kind of refactoring allows us to be sure that a simplification has the same effect as a more complex expression.

There are some simplifications that we'll look at in *Chapter 5, Higher-order Functions*. We will revisit this in *Chapter 6, Recursions and Reductions* to see how to apply these simplifications to the file-parsing problem.

Applying generator expressions to scalar functions

We'll look cat a more complex kind of generator expression to map data values from one kind of data to another. In this case, we'll apply a fairly complex function to individual data values created by a generator.

We'll call these non-generator functions *scalar*, as they work with simple `scalar` values. To work with collections of data, a scalar function will be embedded in a generator expression.

To continue the example started earlier, we'll provide a `haversine` function and then use a generator expression to apply a scalar `haversine()` function to a sequence of pairs from our KML file.

The `haversine()` function looks like following:

```
from math import radians, sin, cos, sqrt, asin

MI= 3959
NM= 3440
KM= 6371

def haversine( point1, point2, R=NM ):
    lat_1, lon_1= point1
    lat_2, lon_2= point2

    Δ_lat = radians(lat_2 - lat_1)
    Δ_lon = radians(lon_2 - lon_1)
    lat_1 = radians(lat_1)
    lat_2 = radians(lat_2)
```

```
    a = sin(Δ_lat/2)**2 + cos(lat_1)*cos(lat_2)*sin(Δ_lon/2)**2
    c = 2*asin(sqrt(a))

    return R * c
```

This is a relatively simple implementation copied from the **World Wide Web**.

The following is how we might use our collection of functions to examine some KML data and produce a sequence of distances:

```
trip= ((start, end, round(haversine(start, end),4))
    for start,end in legs(float_from_pair(lat_lon_kml())))
for start, end, dist in trip:
    print(start, end, dist)
```

The essence of the processing is the generator expression assigned to the `trip` variable. We've assembled three tuples with a start, end, and the distance from start to end. The start and end pairs come from the `legs()` function. The `legs()` function works with `floating-point` data built from the `latitude-longitude` pairs extracted from a KML file.

The output looks like the following command snippet:

```
(37.54901619777347, -76.33029518659048) (37.840832, -76.273834)
17.7246
(37.840832, -76.273834) (38.331501, -76.459503) 30.7382
(38.331501, -76.459503) (38.845501, -76.537331) 31.0756
(36.843334, -76.298668) (37.549, -76.331169) 42.3962
(37.549, -76.331169) (38.330166, -76.458504) 47.2866
(38.330166, -76.458504) (38.976334, -76.473503) 38.8019
```

Each individual processing step has been defined succinctly. The overview, similarly, can be expressed succinctly as a composition of functions and generator expressions.

Clearly, there are several further processing steps we might like to apply to this data. First, of course, is to use the `format()` method of a string to produce better-looking output.

More importantly, there are a number of aggregate values we'd like to extract from this data. We'll call these values reductions of the available data. We'd like to reduce the data to get the maximum and minimum latitude—for example, to show the extreme North and South ends of this route. We'd like to reduce the data to get the maximum distance in one leg as well as the total distance for all `legs`.

The problem we'll have using Python is that the output generator in the `trip` variable can only be used once. We can't easily perform several reductions of this detailed data. We can use `itertools.tee()` to work with the iterable several times. It seems wasteful, however, to read and parse the KML file for each reduction.

We can make our processing more efficient by materializing intermediate results. We'll look at this in the next section. Then, we can see how to compute multiple reductions of the available data.

Using any() and all() as reductions

The `any()` and `all()` functions provide `boolean` reduction capabilities. Both functions reduce a collection of values to a single `True` or `False`. The `all()` function assures that all values are `True`. The `any()` function assures that at least one value is `True`.

These functions are closely related to a universal quantifier and an existential quantifier used to express mathematical logic. We might, for example, want to assert that all elements in a given collection have some property. One formalism for this might look like following:

$$\left(\forall x \in SomeSet \right) Prime\left(x \right)$$

We'd read this as: *for all x in SomeSet, the function Prime(x) is true*. We've put a quantifier in front of the logical expression.

In Python, we switch the order of the items slightly to transcribe the logic expression as follows:

```
all(isprime(x) for x in someset)
```

This will evaluate each argument value (`isprime(x)`) and reduce the collection of values to a single `True` or `False`.

The `any()` function is related to the existential quantifier. If we want to assert that no value in a collection is prime, we might have something like one of the two equivalent expressions:

$$\neg\left(\forall x \in SomeSet \right) Prime\left(x \right) \equiv \left(\exists x \in SomeSet \right) \neg Prime\left(x \right)$$

The first states that *it is not the case that all elements in SomeSet are prime*. The second version asserts that *there exists one element in SomeSet that is not prime*. These two are equivalent—that is, *if not all elements are prime, then one element must be non-prime*.

In Python, we can switch the order of the terms and transcribe these to working code as follows:

```
not all(isprime(x) for x in someset)
any(not isprime(x) for x in someset)
```

As they're equivalent, there are two reasons for preferring one over the other: performance and clarity. The performance is nearly identical, so it boils down to clarity. Which of these states the condition the most clearly?

The `all()` function can be described as an and reduction of a set of values. The result is similar to folding the and operator between the given sequence of values. The `any()` function, similarly, can be described as an or reduction. We'll return to this kind of general-purpose reduce when we look at the `reduce()` function in *Chapter 10, The Functools Module*.

We also need to look at the degenerate case of these functions. What if the sequence has 0 elements? What are the values of `all(())` or `all([])`?

If we ask, "Are all elements in an empty set prime?", then what's the answer? As there are no elements, the question is a bit difficult to answer.

If we ask "Are all elements in an empty set prime and all elements in `SomeSet` prime?", we have a hint as to how we have to proceed. We're performing an and reduction of an empty set and an and reduction of `SomeSet`.

$$(\forall x \in \varnothing)\,\mathrm{Prime}(x) \wedge (\forall x \in SomeSet)\,\mathrm{Prime}(x)$$

It turns out that the and operator can be distributed freely. We can rewrite this to a union of the two sets, which is then evaluated for being prime:

$$(\forall x \in \varnothing \cup SomeSet)\,\mathrm{Prime}(x)$$

Clearly, $S \cup \varnothing \equiv S$. If we union an empty set, we get the original set. The empty set can be called the **union identify element**. This parallels the way 0 is the additive identity element: $a + 0 = a$.

Similarly, `any(())` must be the or identity element, which is `False`. If we think of the multiplicative identify element, 1, where $b \times 1 = b$, then `all(())` must be `True`.

We can demonstrate that Python follows these rules:

```
>>> all(())
True
>>> any(())
False
```

Python gives us some very nice tools to perform processing that involves logic. We have the built-in and, or, and not operators. However, we also have these collection-oriented any() and all() functions.

Using len() and sum()

The len() and sum() functions provide two simple reductions: a count of the elements and the sum of the elements in a sequence. These two functions are mathematically similar, but their Python implementation is quite different.

Mathematically, we can observe this cool parallelism. The len() function returns the sum of 1's for each value in a collection, X: $\sum_{x \in X} 1 = \sum_{x \in X} x^0$.

The sum() function returns the sum of x for each value in a collection, X:

$$\sum_{x \in X} x = \sum_{x \in X} x^1$$

The sum() function works for any iterable. The len() function doesn't apply to iterables; it only applies to sequences. This little asymmetry in the implementation of these functions is a little awkward around the edges of statistical algorithms.

For empty sequences, both of these functions return a proper additive identity element of 0.

```
>>> sum(())
0
```

Of course, sum(()) returns an integer 0. When other numeric types are used, the integer 0 will be coerced to the proper type for the available data.

Using sums and counts for statistics

The definitions of the arithmetic mean have an appealingly trivial definition based on `sum()` and `len()`, which is as follows:

```
def mean( iterable ):
    return sum(iterable)/len(iterable)
```

While elegant, this doesn't actually work for iterables. This definition only works for sequences.

Indeed, we have a hard time performing a simple computation of mean or standard deviation based on iterables. In Python, we must either materialize a sequence object, or resort to somewhat more complex operations.

We have a fairly elegant expression of mean and standard deviation in the following definitions:

```
import math
s0= len(data) # sum(1 for x in data) # x**0
s1= sum(data) # sum(x for x in data) # x**1
s2= sum(x*x for x in data)

mean= s1/s0
stdev= math.sqrt(s2/s0 - (s1/s0)**2)
```

These three sums, `s0`, `s1`, and `s2`, have a tidy, parallel structure. We can easily compute the mean from two of the sums. The standard deviation is a bit more complex, but it's still based on the three sums.

This kind of pleasant symmetry also works for more complex statistical functions such as correlation and even least-squares linear regression.

The moment of correlation between two sets of samples can be computed from their standardized value. The following is a function to compute the standardized value:

```
def z( x, μ_x, σ_x ):
    return (x-μ_x)/σ_x
```

The calculation is simply to subtract the mean, $μ\_x$, from each sample, x, and divide by the standard deviation, $σ\_x$. This gives as a value measured in units of sigma, $σ$. A value ± 1 $σ$ is expected about two-thirds of the time. Larger values should be less common. A value outside ± 3 $σ$ should happen less than 1 percent of the time.

We can use this scalar function as follows:

```
>>> d = [2, 4, 4, 4, 5, 5, 7, 9]
>>> list(z(x, mean(d), stdev(d)) for x in d)
[-1.5, -0.5, -0.5, -0.5, 0.0, 0.0, 1.0, 2.0]
```

We've materialized `list` that consists of normalized scores based on some raw data in the variable, d. We used a generator expression to apply the scalar function, z(), to the sequence object.

The mean() and stdev() functions are simply based on the examples shown above:

```
def mean(x):
    return s1(x)/s0(x)
def stdev(x):
    return math.sqrt(s2(x)/s0(x) - (s1(x)/s0(x))**2)
```

The three sum functions, similarly, are based on the examples above:

```
def s0(data):
    return sum(1 for x in data) # or len(data)
def s1(data):
    return sum(x for x in data) # or sum(data)
def s2(data):
    return sum(x*x for x in data)
```

While this is very expressive and succinct, it's a little frustrating because we can't simply use an iterable here. We're computing a mean, which requires a sum of the iterable, plus a count. We're also computing a standard deviation that requires two sums and a count from the iterable. For this kind of statistical processing, we must materialize a sequence object so that we can examine the data multiple times.

The following is how we can compute the correlation between two sets of samples:

```
def corr( sample1, sample2 ):
    μ_1, σ_1 = mean(sample1), stdev(sample1)
    μ_2, σ_2 = mean(sample2), stdev(sample2)
    z_1 = (z(x, μ_1, σ_1) for x in sample1)
    z_2 = (z(x, μ_2, σ_2) for x in sample2)
    r = sum(zx1*zx2 for zx1, zx2 in zip(z_1, z_2) )/s0(sample1)
    return r
```

This correlation function gathers basic statistical summaries of the two sets of samples: the mean and standard deviation. Given these summaries, we defined two generator functions that will create normalized values for each set of samples. We can then use the `zip()` function (see the next example) to pair up items from the two sequences of normalized values and compute the product of those two normalized values. The average of the product of the normalized scores is the correlation.

The following is an example of gathering the correlation between two sets of samples:

```
>>> xi= [1.47, 1.50, 1.52, 1.55, 1.57, 1.60, 1.63, 1.65,
...     1.68, 1.70, 1.73, 1.75, 1.78, 1.80, 1.83,] # Height (m)
>>> yi= [52.21, 53.12, 54.48, 55.84, 57.20, 58.57, 59.93, 61.29,
...     63.11, 64.47, 66.28, 68.10, 69.92, 72.19, 74.46,] #
...     Mass (kg)
>>> round(corr( xi, yi ), 5)
0.99458
```

We've shown two sequences of data points, `xi` and `yi`. The correlation is over .99, which shows a very strong relationship between the two sequences.

This shows one of the strengths of functional programming. We've created a handy statistical module using a half-dozen functions with definitions that are single expressions. The counterexample is the `corr()` function that can be reduced to a single very long expression. Each internal variable in this function is used just once; a local variable can be replaced with a copy-and-paste of the expression that created it. This shows us that the `corr()` function has a functional design even though it's written out in six separate lines of Python.

Using zip() to structure and flatten sequences

The `zip()` function interleaves values from several iterators or sequences. It will create *n* tuples from the values in each of the *n* input iterables or sequences. We used it in the previous section to interleave data points from two sets of samples, creating two tuples.

[The `zip()` function is a generator. It does not materialize a resulting collection.]

The following is an example that shows what the `zip()` function does:

```
>>> xi= [1.47, 1.50, 1.52, 1.55, 1.57, 1.60, 1.63, 1.65,
... 1.68, 1.70, 1.73, 1.75, 1.78, 1.80, 1.83,]
>>> yi= [52.21, 53.12, 54.48, 55.84, 57.20, 58.57, 59.93, 61.29,
... 63.11, 64.47, 66.28, 68.10, 69.92, 72.19, 74.46,]
>>> zip( xi, yi )
<zip object at 0x101d62ab8>
>>> list(zip( xi, yi ))
[(1.47, 52.21), (1.5, 53.12), (1.52, 54.48), (1.55, 55.84),
(1.57, 57.2), (1.6, 58.57), (1.63, 59.93), (1.65, 61.29),
(1.68, 63.11), (1.7, 64.47), (1.73, 66.28), (1.75, 68.1),
(1.78, 69.92), (1.8, 72.19), (1.83, 74.46)]
```

There are a number of edge cases for the `zip()` function. We must ask the following questions about its behavior:

- What happens where then are no arguments at all?
- What happens where there's only one argument?
- What happens when the sequences are different lengths?

For reductions (`any()`, `all()`, `len()`, `sum()`), we want an identity element from reducing an empty sequence.

Clearly, each of these edge cases must produce some kind of iterable output. Here are some examples to clarify the behaviors. First, the empty argument list:

```
>>> zip()
<zip object at 0x101d62ab8>
>>> list(_)
[]
```

We can see that the `zip()` function with no arguments is a generator function, but there won't be any items. This fits the requirement that the output is iterable.

Next, we'll try a single iterable:

```
>>> zip( (1,2,3) )
<zip object at 0x101d62ab8>
>>> list(_)
[(1,), (2,), (3,)]
```

In this case, the `zip()` function emitted one tuple from each input value. This too makes considerable sense.

Finally, we'll look at the different-length `list` approach used by the `zip()` function:

```
>>> list(zip((1, 2, 3), ('a', 'b')))
[(1, 'a'), (2, 'b')]
```

This result is debatable. Why truncate? Why not pad the shorter list with None values? This alternate definition of `zip()` function is available in the `itertools` module as the `zip_longest()` function. We'll look at this in *Chapter 8, The Itertools Module*.

Unzipping a zipped sequence

`zip()` mapping can be inverted. We'll look at several ways to unzip a collection of tuples.

> We can't fully unzip an iterable of tuples, since we might want to make multiple passes over the data. Depending on our needs, we might need to materialize the iterable to extract multiple values.

The first way is something we've seen many times; we can use a generator function to unzip a sequence of tuples. For example, assume that the following pairs are a sequence object with two tuples:

```
p0= (x[0] for x in pairs)
p1= (x[1] for x in pairs)
```

This will create two sequences. The `p0` sequence has the first element of each two tuple; the `p1` sequence has the second element of each two tuple.

Under some circumstances, we can use the multiple ssignment of a `for` loop to decompose the tuples. The following is an example that computes the sum of products:

```
sum(p0*p1 for for p0, p1 in pairs)
```

We used the `for` statement to decompose each two tuple into `p0` and `p1`.

Flattening sequences

Sometimes, we'll have zipped data that needs to be flattened. For example, our input might be a file that looks like this:

2	3	5	7	11	13	17	19	23	29
31	37	41	43	47	53	59	61	67	71

...

We can easily use `((line.split() for line in file)` to create a sequence of ten tuples.

We might heave data in blocks that looks as follows:

```
blocked = [['2', '3', '5', '7', '11', '13', '17', '19', '23',
'29'], ['31', '37', '41', '43', '47', '53', '59', '61', '67',
'71'],
...
```

This isn't really what we want, though. We want to get the numbers into a single, flat sequence. Each item in the input is a ten tuple; we'd rather not wrangle with decomposing this one item at a time.

We can use a two-level generator expression, as shown in the following code snippet, for this kind of flattening:

```
>>> (x for line in blocked for x in line)
<generator object <genexpr> at 0x101cead70>
>>> list(_)
['2', '3', '5', '7', '11', '13', '17', '19', '23', '29', '31',
'37', '41', '43', '47', '53', '59', '61', '67', '71', … ]
```

The two-level generator is confusing at first. We can understand this through a simple rewrite as follows:

```
for line in data:
    for x in line:
        yield x
```

This transformation shows us how the generator expression works. The first for clause (`for line in data`) steps through each ten tuple in the data. The second for clause (`for x in line`) steps through each item in the first for clause.

This expression flattens a sequence-of-sequence structure into a single sequence.

Structuring flat sequences

Sometimes, we'll have raw data that is a flat list of values that we'd like to bunch up into subgroups. This is a bit more complex. We can use the `itertools` module's `groupby()` function to implement this. This will have to wait until *Chapter 8, The Iterools Module*.

Let's say we have a simple flat `list` as follows:

```
flat= ['2', '3', '5', '7', '11', '13', '17', '19', '23', '29',
'31', '37', '41', '43', '47', '53', '59', '61', '67', '71', ... ]
```

We can write nested generator functions to build a sequence-of-sequence structure from flat data. In order to do this, we'll need a single iterator that we can use multiple times. The expression looks like the following code snippet:

```
>>> flat_iter=iter(flat)
>>> (tuple(next(flat_iter) for i in range(5)) for row in
range(len(flat)//5))
<generator object <genexpr> at 0x101cead70>
>>> list(_)
[('2', '3', '5', '7', '11'), ('13', '17', '19', '23', '29'),
('31', '37', '41', '43', '47'), ('53', '59', '61', '67', '71'),
('73', '79', '83', '89', '97'), ('101', '103', '107', '109',
'113'), ('127', '131', '137', '139', '149'), ('151', '157', '163',
'167', '173'), ('179', '181', '191', '193', '197'), ('199', '211',
'223', '227', '229')]
```

First, we created an iterator that exists outside either of the two loops that we'll use to create our sequence-of-sequences. The generator expression uses `tuple(next(flat_iter) for i in range(5))` to create five tuples from the iterable values in the `flat_iter` variable. This expression is `nested` inside another generator that repeats the inner loop the proper number of times to create the required sequence of values.

This works only when the flat list is divided evenly. If the last row has partial elements, we'll need to process them separately.

We can use this kind of function to group data into same-sized tuples, with an odd sized tuple at the end using the following definitions:

```
def group_by_seq(n, sequence):
    flat_iter=iter(sequence)
    full_sized_items = list( tuple(next(flat_iter)
        for i in range(n))
            for row in range(len(sequence)//n))
    trailer = tuple(flat_iter)
    if trailer:
        return full_sized_items + [trailer]
    else:
        return full_sized_items
```

We've created an initial `list` where each `tuple` is of the size n. If there are leftovers, we'll have a trailer `tuple` with a non-zero length that we can append to the `list` of full-sized items. If the trailer `tuple` is of the length 0, we'll ignore it.

This isn't as delightfully simple and functional-looking as other algorithms we've looked at. We can rework this into a pleasant-enough generator function. The following code uses a `while` loop as part of tail-recursion optimization:

```
def group_by_iter( n, iterable ):
    row= tuple(next(iterable) for i in range(n))
    while row:
        yield row
        row= tuple(next(iterable) for i in range(n))
```

We've created a row of the required length from the input iterable. When we get to the end of the input iterable, the value of `tuple(next(iterable) for i in range(n))` will be a zero-length tuple. This is the base case of a recursion, which we've written as the terminating condition for a `while` loop.

Structuring flat sequences—an alternative approach

Let's say we have a simple, flat `list` and we want to create pairs from this list. The following is the required data:

```
flat= ['2', '3', '5', '7', '11', '13', '17', '19', '23', '29',
'31', '37', '41', '43', '47', '53', '59', '61', '67', '71',... ]
```

We can create pairs using list slices as follows:

```
zip(flat[0::2], flat[1::2])
```

The slice `flat[0::2]` is all of the even positions. The slice `flat[1::2]` is all of the odd positions. If we zip these together, we get a two tuple of `(0)`, the value from the first even position, and `(1)`, the value from the first odd position. If the number of elements is even, this will produce pairs nicely.

This has the advantage of being quite short. The functions shown in the previous section are longer ways to solve the same problem.

This approach can be generalized. We can use the `*(args)` approach to generate a sequence-of-sequences that must be zipped together. It looks like the following:

```
zip(*(flat[i::n] for i in range(n)))
```

This will generate n slices: `flat[0::n]`, `flat[1::n]`, `flat[2::n]`, ..., `flat[n-1::n]`. This collection of slices becomes the arguments to `zip()`, which then interleaves values from each slice.

Recall that `zip()` truncates the sequence at the shortest `list`. This means that, if the `list` is not an even multiple of the grouping factor n, (`len(flat)%n != 0`), which is the final slice, won't be the same length as the others and the others will all be truncated. This is rarely what we want.

If we use the `itertools.zip_longest()` method, then we'll see that the final tuple will be padded with enough `None` values to make it have a length of n. In some cases, this padding is acceptable. In other cases, the extra values are undesirable.

The `list` slicing approach to grouping data is another way to approach the problem of structuring a flat sequence of data into blocks. As it is a general solution, it doesn't seem to offer too many advantages over the functions in the previous section. As a solution specialized for making two tuples from a flat last, it's elegantly simple.

Using reversed() to change the order

There are times when we need a sequence reversed. Python offers us two approaches to this: the `reversed()` function and slices with reversed indices.

For an example, consider performing a base conversion to hexadecimal or binary. The following is a simple conversion function:

```
def digits(x, b):
    if x == 0: return
    yield x % b
    for d in to_base(x//b, b):
        yield d
```

This function uses a recursion to yield the digits from the least significant to the most significant. The value of `x%b` will be the least significant digits of x in the base b.

We can formalize it as following:

$$\text{digits}(x,b) = \begin{cases} [] & \text{if } x = 0 \\ \left[x(\mod b)\right] + \text{digits}\left(\dfrac{x}{b}, b\right) & \text{if } x > 0 \end{cases}$$

In many cases, we'd prefer the digits to be yielded in the reverse order. We can wrap this function with the `reversed()` function to swap the order of the digits:

```
def to_base(x, b):
    return reversed(tuple(digits(x, b)))
```

The reversed() function produces an iterable, but the argument value must be a sequence object. The function then yields the items from that object in the reverse order.

We can do a similar kind of thing also with a slice such as tuple(digits(x, b)) [::-1]. The slice, however, is not an iterator. A slice is a materialized object built from another materialized object. In this case, for such small collections of values, the distinction is minor. As the reversed() function uses less memory, it might be advantageous for larger collections.

Using enumerate() to include a sequence number

Python offers the enumerate() function to apply index information to values in a sequence or iterable. It performs a specialized kind of wrap that can be used as part of an unwrap(process(wrap(data))) design pattern.

It looks like the following code snippet:

```
>>> xi
[1.47, 1.5, 1.52, 1.55, 1.57, 1.6, 1.63, 1.65, 1.68, 1.7, 1.73,
1.75, 1.78, 1.8, 1.83]
>>> list(enumerate(xi))
[(0, 1.47), (1, 1.5), (2, 1.52), (3, 1.55), (4, 1.57), (5, 1.6),
(6, 1.63), (7, 1.65), (8, 1.68), (9, 1.7), (10, 1.73), (11, 1.75),
(12, 1.78), (13, 1.8), (14, 1.83)]
```

The enumerate() function transformed each input item into a pair with a sequence number and the original item. It's vaguely similar to something as follows:

```
zip(range(len(source)), source)
```

An important feature of enumerate() is that the result is an iterable and it works with any iterable input.

When looking at statistical processing, for example, the enumerate() function comes in handy to transform a single sequence of values into a more proper time series by prefixing each sample with a number.

Summary

In this chapter, we saw detailed ways to use a number of built-in reductions.

We've used `any()` and `all()` to do essential logic processing. These are tidy examples of reductions using a simple operator such as `or` or `and`.

We've also looked at numeric reductions such as `len()` and `sum()`. We've applied these functions to create some higher-order statistical processing. We'll return to these reductions in *Chapter 6, Recursions and Reductions*.

We've also looked at some of the built-in mappings.

The `zip()` function merges multiple sequences. This leads us to look at using this in the context of structuring and flattening more complex data structures. As we'll see in examples in later chapters, nested data is helpful in some situations and flat data is helpful in others.

The `enumerate()` function maps an iterable to a sequence of two tuples. Each two tuple has `(0)` as the sequence number and `(1)` as the original item.

The `reversed()` function iterates over the items in a sequence object with their original order reversed. Some algorithms are more efficient at producing results in one order, but we'd like to present these results in the opposite order.

In the next chapter, we'll look at the `mapping` and `reduction` functions that use an additional function as an argument to customize their processing. Functions that accept a function as an argument are our first examples of higher-order functions. We'll also touch on functions that return functions as a result.

5
Higher-order Functions

A very important feature of the functional programming paradigm is higher-order functions. These are functions that accept functions as arguments or return functions as results. Python offers several of these kinds of functions. We'll look at them and some logical extensions.

As we can see, there are three varieties of higher-order functions, which are as follows:

- Functions that accept a function as one of its arguments
- Functions that return a function
- Functions that accept a function and return a function

Python offers several higher-order functions of the first variety. We'll look at these built-in higher-order functions in this chapter. We'll look at a few of the library modules that offer higher-order functions in later chapters.

The idea of a function that emits functions can seem a bit odd. However, when we look at a Callable class object, we see a function that returns a Callable object. This is one example of a function that creates another function.

Functions that accept functions and create functions include complex Callable classes as well as function decorators. We'll introduce decorators in this chapter, but defer deeper consideration of decorators until *Chapter 11, Decorator Design Techniques*.

Sometimes we wish that Python had higher-order versions of the collection functions from the previous chapter. In this chapter, we'll show the reduce(extract()) design pattern to perform a reduction on specific fields extracted from a larger tuple. We'll also look at defining our own version of these common collection-processing functions.

In this chapter, we'll look at the following functions:

- `max()` and `min()`
- `Lambda` forms that we can use to simplify using higher-order functions
- `map()`
- `filter()`
- `iter()`
- `sorted()`

There are a number of higher-order functions in the `itertools` module. We'll look at this module in *Chapter 8, The Itertools Module* and *Chapter 9, More Itertools Techniques*.

Additionally, the `functools` module provides a general-purpose `reduce()` function. We'll look at this in *Chapter 10, The Functools Module*. We'll defer this because it's not as generally applicable as the other higher-order functions in this chapter.

The `max()` and `min()` functions are reductions; they create a single value from a collection. The other functions are mappings. They don't reduce the input to a single value.

 The `max()`, `min()`, and `sorted()` functions have a default behavior as well as a higher-order function behavior. The function is provided via the `key=` argument. The `map()` and `filter()` functions take the function as the first positional argument.

Using max() and min() to find extrema

The `max()` and `min()` functions have a dual life. They are simple functions that apply to collections. They are also higher-order functions. We can see their default behavior as follows:

```
>>> max(1, 2, 3)
3
>>> max((1,2,3,4))
4
```

Both functions will accept an indefinite number of arguments. The functions are designed to also accept a sequence or an iterable as the only argument and locate the max (or min) of that iterable.

They also do something more sophisticated. Let's say we have our trip data from the examples in *Chapter 4, Working with Collections*. We have a function that will generate a sequence of tuples that looks as follows:

```
(((37.54901619777347, -76.33029518659048), (37.840832, -76.273834),
17.7246), ((37.840832, -76.273834), (38.331501, -76.459503),
30.7382), ((38.331501, -76.459503), (38.845501, -76.537331),
31.0756), ((36.843334, -76.298668), (37.549, -76.331169), 42.3962),
((37.549, -76.331169), (38.330166, -76.458504), 47.2866),
((38.330166, -76.458504), (38.976334, -76.473503), 38.8019))
```

Each `tuple` has three values: a starting location, an ending location, and a distance. The locations are given in latitude and longitude pairs. The East latitude is positive, so these are points along the US East Coast, about 76° West. The distances are in nautical miles.

We have three ways of getting the maximum and minimum distances from this sequence of values. They are as follows:

- Extract the distance with a generator function. This will give us only the distances, as we've discarded the other two attributes of each leg. This won't work out well if we have any additional processing requirements.
- Use the `unwrap(process(wrap()))` pattern. This will give us the legs with the longest and shortest distances. From these, we can extract just the distance, if that's all that's needed. The other two will give us the leg that contains the maximum and minimum distances.
- Use the `max()` and `min()` functions as higher-order functions.

To provide context, we'll show the first two solutions. The following is a script that builds the trip and then uses the first two approaches to locate the longest and shortest distances traveled:

```
from ch02_ex3 import float_from_pair, lat_lon_kml, limits,
haversine, legs
path= float_from_pair(lat_lon_kml())
trip= tuple((start, end, round(haversine(start, end),4))
  for start,end in legs(iter(path)))
```

This section creates the `trip` object as a `tuple` based on `haversine` distances of each `leg` built from a `path` read from a KML file.

Once we have the `trip` object, we can extract distances and compute the maximum and minimum of those distances. The code looks as follows:

```
long, short = max(dist for start,end,dist in trip),
min(dist for start,end,dist in trip)
print(long, short)
```

We've used a generator function to extract the relevant item from each leg of the `trip` tuple. We've had to repeat the generator function because each generator expression can be consumed only once.

The following are the results:

```
129.7748 0.1731
```

The following is a version with the unwrap(process(wrap())) pattern. We've actually declared functions with the names wrap() and unwrap() to make it clear how this pattern works:

```
def wrap(leg_iter):
    return ((leg[2],leg) for leg in leg_iter)


def unwrap(dist_leg):
    distance, leg = dist_leg
    return leg
long, short = unwrap(max(wrap(trip))), unwrap(min(wrap(trip)))
print(long, short)
```

Unlike the previous version, this locates all attributes of the legs with the longest and shortest distances. Rather than simply extracting the distances, we put the distances first in each wrapped tuple. We can then use the default forms of the min() and max() functions to process the two tuples that contain the distance and leg details. After processing, we can strip the first element, leaving just the leg details.

The results look as follows:

```
((27.154167, -80.195663), (29.195168, -81.002998), 129.7748)
((35.505665, -76.653664), (35.508335, -76.654999), 0.1731)
```

The final and most important form uses the higher-order function feature of the max() and min() functions. We'll define a helper function first and then use it to reduce the collection of legs to the desired summaries by executing the following code snippet:

```
def by_dist(leg):
    lat, lon, dist= leg
    return dist
long, short = max(trip, key=by_dist), min(trip, key=by_dist)
print(long, short)
```

The `by_dist()` function picks apart the three items in each `leg` tuple and returns the distance item. We'll use this with the `max()` and `min()` functions.

The `max()` and `min()` functions both accept an iterable and a function as arguments. The keyword parameter `key=` is used by all of Python's higher-order functions to provide a function that will be used to extract the necessary key value.

We can use the following to help conceptualize how the `max()` function uses the `key` function:

```
wrap= ((key(leg),leg) for leg in trip)
return max(wrap)[1]
```

The `max()` and `min()` functions behave as if the given `key` function is being used to wrap each item in the sequence into a two tuple, process the two tuple, and then decompose the two tuple to return the original value.

Using Python lambda forms

In many cases, the definition of a `helper` function requires too much code. Often, we can digest the `key` function to a single expression. It can seem wasteful to have to write both `def` and `return` statements to wrap a single expression.

Python offers the lambda form as a way to simplify using higher-order functions. A lambda form allows us to define a small, anonymous function. The function's body is limited to a single expression.

The following is an example of using a simple `lambda` expression as the key:

```
long, short = max(trip, key=lambda leg: leg[2]),
min(trip, key=lambda leg: leg[2])
print(long, short)
```

The `lambda` we've used will be given an item from the sequence; in this case, each leg three tuple will be given to the `lambda`. The `lambda` argument variable, `leg`, is assigned and the expression, `leg[2]`, is evaluated, plucking the distance from the three tuple.

In the rare case that a `lambda` is never reused, this form is ideal. It's common, however, to need to reuse the `lambda` objects. Since copy-and-paste is such a bad idea, what's the alternative?

We can always define a function.

We can also assign lambdas to variables, by doing something like this:

```
start= lambda x: x[0]
end = lambda x: x[1]
dist = lambda x: x[2]
```

A `lambda` is a `callable` object and can be used like a function. The following is an example at the interactive prompt:

```
>>> leg = ((27.154167, -80.195663), (29.195168, -81.002998),
129.7748)
>>> start= lambda x: x[0]
>>> end   = lambda x: x[1]
>>> dist  = lambda x: x[2]
>>> dist(leg)
129.7748
```

Python offers us two ways to assign meaningful names to elements of tuples: namedtuples and a collection of lambdas. Both are equivalent.

To extend this example, we'll look at how we get the `latitude` or `longitude` value of the starting or ending point. This is done by defining some additional lambdas.

The following is a continuation of the interactive session:

```
>>> start(leg)
(27.154167, -80.195663)
>>>
>>> lat = lambda x: x[0]
>>> lon = lambda x: x[1]
>>> lat(start(leg))
27.154167
```

There's no clear advantage to lambdas over namedtuples. A set of `lambdas` to extract fields requires more lines of code to define than a namedtuple. On the other hand, we can use a prefix function notation, which might be easier to read in a functional programing context. More importantly, as we'll see in the `sorted()` example later, the `lambdas` can be used more effectively than `namedtuple` attribute names by `sorted()`, `min()`, and `max()`.

Lambdas and the lambda calculus

In a book on a purely functional programming language, it would be necessary to explain lambda calculus, and the technique invented by Haskell Curry that we call **currying**. Python, however, doesn't stick closely to this kind of lambda calculus. Functions are not curried to reduce them to single-argument lambda forms.

We can, using the functools.partial function, implement currying. We'll save this for *Chapter 10, The Functools Module*.

Using the map() function to apply a function to a collection

A scalar function maps values from a domain to a range. When we look at the math. sqrt() function, as an example, we're looking at a mapping from the float value, *x*, to another float value, $y = sqrt(x)$ such that $y^2 = x$. The domain is limited to positive values. The mapping can be done via a calculation or table interpolation.

The map() function expresses a similar concept; it maps one collection to another collection. It assures that a given function is used to map each individual item from the domain collection to the range collection—the ideal way to apply a built-in function to a collection of data.

Our first example involves parsing a block of text to get the sequence of numbers. Let's say we have the following chunk of text:

```
>>> text= """\
...         2       3       5       7       11      13      17      19      23
29
...         31      37      41      43      47      53      59      61      67
71
...         73      79      83      89      97      101     103     107     109
113
...         127     131     137     139     149     151     157     163     167
173
...         179     181     191     193     197     199     211     223     227
229
... """
```

We can restructure this text using the following generator function:

```
>>> data= list(v for line in text.splitlines() for v in line.split())
```

This will split the text into lines. For each line, it will split the line into space-delimited words and iterate through each of the resulting strings. The results look as follows:

```
['2', '3', '5', '7', '11', '13', '17', '19', '23', '29',
'31', '37', '41', '43', '47', '53', '59', '61', '67', '71',
'73', '79', '83', '89', '97', '101', '103', '107', '109', '113',
'127', '131', '137', '139', '149', '151', '157', '163', '167',
'173', '179', '181', '191', '193', '197', '199', '211', '223',
'227', '229']
```

We still need to apply the `int()` function to each of the `string` values. This is where the `map()` function excels. Take a look at the following code snippet:

```
>>> list(map(int,data))

[2, 3, 5, 7, 11, 13, 17, 19, 23, 29, 31, 37, 41, 43, 47, 53, 59,
61, 67, 71, 73, 79, 83, 89, 97, 101, 103, 107, 109, 113, 127, 131,
137, 139, 149, 151, 157, 163, 167, 173, 179, 181, 191, 193, 197,
199, 211, 223, 227, 229]
```

The `map()` function applied the `int()` function to each value in the collection. The result is a sequence of numbers instead of a sequence of strings.

The `map()` function's results are iterable. The `map()` function can process any type of iterable.

The idea here is that any Python function can be applied to the items of a collection using the `map()` function. There are a lot of built-in functions that can be used in this map-processing context.

Working with lambda forms and map()

Let's say we want to convert our trip distances from nautical miles to statute miles. We want to multiply each leg's distance by 6076.12/5280, which is 1.150780.

We can do this calculation with the `map()` function as follows:

```
map(lambda x: (start(x),end(x),dist(x)*6076.12/5280), trip)
```

We've defined a `lambda` that will be applied to each leg in the trip by the `map()` function. The `lambda` will use other `lambda`s to separate the start, end, and distance values from each leg. It will compute a revised distance and assemble a new leg tuple from the start, end, and statute mile distance.

This is precisely like the following generator expression:

```
((start(x),end(x),dist(x)*6076.12/5280) for x in trip)
```

We've done the same processing on each item in the generator expression.

The important difference between the map() function and a generator expression is that the map() function tends to be faster than the generator expression. The speedup is in the order of 20 percent less time.

Using map() with multiple sequences

Sometimes, we'll have two collections of data that need to parallel each other. In *Chapter 4*, *Working with Collections*, we saw how the zip() function can interleave two sequences to create a sequence of pairs. In many cases, we're really trying to do something like this:

```
map(function, zip(one_iterable, another_iterable))
```

We're creating argument tuples from two (or more) parallel iterables and applying a function to the argument tuple. We can also look at it like this:

```
(function(x,y) for x,y in zip(one_iterable, another_iterable))
```

Here, we've replaced the map() function with an equivalent generator expression.

We might have the idea of generalizing the whole thing to this:

```
def star_map(function, *iterables)
    return (function(*args) for args in zip(*iterables))
```

There is a better approach that is already available to us. We don't actually need these techniques. Let's look at a concrete example of the alternate approach.

In *Chapter 4*, *Working with Collections*, we looked at trip data that we extracted from an XML file as a series of waypoints. We needed to create legs from this list of waypoints that show the start and end of each leg.

The following is a simplified version that uses the zip() function applied to a special kind of iterable:

```
>>> waypoints= range(4)
>>> zip(waypoints, waypoints[1:])
<zip object at 0x101a38c20>
>>> list(_)
[(0, 1), (1, 2), (2, 3)]
```

We've created a sequence of pairs drawn from a single flat list. Each pair will have two adjacent values. The `zip()` function properly stops when the shorter list is exhausted. This `zip( x, x[1:])` pattern only works for materialized sequences and the iterable created by the `range()` function.

We created pairs so that we can apply the `haversine()` function to each pair to compute the distance between the two points on the path. The following is how it looks in one sequence of steps:

```
from ch02_ex3 import lat_lon_kml, float_from_pair, haversine
path= tuple(float_from_pair(lat_lon_kml()))
distances1= map( lambda s_e: (s_e[0], s_e[1], haversine(*s_e)),
    zip(path, path[1:]))
```

We've loaded the essential sequence of waypoints into the `path` variable. This is an ordered sequence of latitude-longitude pairs. As we're going to use the `zip(path, path[1:])` design pattern, we must have a materialized sequence and not a simple iterable.

The results of the `zip()` function will be pairs that have a start and end. We want our output to be a triple with the start, end, and distance. The `lambda` we're using will decompose the original two tuple and create a new three tuple from the start, end, and distance.

As noted previously, we can simplify this by using a clever feature of the `map()` function, which is as follows:

```
distances2= map(lambda s, e: (s, e, haversine(s, e)), path, path[1:])
```

Note that we've provided a function and two iterables to the `map()` function. The `map()` function will take the next item from each iterable and apply those two values as the arguments to the given function. In this case, the given function is a `lambda` that creates the desired three tuple from the start, end, and distance.

The formal definition for the `map()` function states that it will do **star-map** processing with an indefinite number of iterables. It will take items from each iterable to create a tuple of argument values for the given function.

Using the filter() function to pass or reject data

The job of the `filter()` function is to use and apply a decision function called a predicate to each value in a collection. A decision of `True` means that the value is passed; otherwise, the value is rejected. The `itertools` module includes `filterfalse()` as variations on this theme. Refer to *Chapter 8, The Itertools Module* to understand the usage of the `itertools` module's `filterfalse()` function.

We might apply this to our trip data to create a subset of legs that are over 50 nautical miles long, as follows:

```
long= list(filter(lambda leg: dist(leg) >= 50, trip)))
```

The predicate `lambda` will be `True` for long legs, which will be passed. Short legs will be rejected. The output is the 14 legs that pass this distance test.

This kind of processing clearly segregates the filter rule (`lambda leg: dist(leg) >= 50`) from any other processing that creates the `trip` object or analyzes the long legs.

For another simple example, look at the following code snippet:

```
>>> filter(lambda x: x%3==0 or x%5==0, range(10))
<filter object at 0x101d5de50>
>>> sum(_)
23
```

We've defined a simple `lambda` to check whether a number is a multiple of three or a multiple of five. We've applied that function to an iterable, `range(10)`. The result is an iterable sequence of numbers that are passed by the decision rule.

The numbers for which the `lambda` is `True` are `[0, 3, 5, 6, 9]`, so these values are passed. As the `lambda` is `False` for all other numbers, they are rejected.

This can also be done with a generator expression by executing the following code:

```
>>> list(x for x in range(10) if x%3==0 or x%5==0)
[0, 3, 5, 6, 9]
```

We can formalize this using the following set comprehension notation:

$$\left\{ x \mid 0 \le x < 10 \wedge \left(x (\bmod 3) = 0 \vee x (\bmod 5) = 0 \right) \right\}$$

This says that we're building a collection of x values such that x is in `range(10)` and `x%3==0 or x%5==0`. There's a very elegant symmetry between the `filter()` function and formal mathematical set comprehensions.

We often want to use the `filter()` function with defined functions instead of `lambda` forms. The following is an example of reusing a predicate defined earlier:

```
>>> from ch01_ex1 import isprimeg
>>> list(filter(isprimeg, range(100)))
[2, 3, 5, 7, 11, 13, 17, 19, 23, 29, 31, 37, 41, 43, 47, 53, 59, 61,
67, 71, 73, 79, 83, 89, 97]
```

In this example, we imported a function from another module called `isprimeg()`. We then applied this function to a collection of values to pass the prime numbers and reject any non-prime numbers from the collection.

This can be a remarkably inefficient way to generate a table of prime numbers. The superficial simplicity of this is the kind of thing lawyers call an *attractive nuisance*. It looks like it might be fun, but it doesn't scale well at all. A better algorithm is the **Sieve of Eratosthenes**; this algorithm retains the previously located prime numbers and uses them to prevent a lot of inefficient recalculation.

Using filter() to identify outliers

In the previous chapter, we defined some useful statistical functions to compute mean and standard deviation and normalize a value. We can use these functions to locate outliers in our trip data. What we can do is apply the `mean()` and `stdev()` functions to the distance value in each `leg` of a trip to get the population mean and standard deviation.

We can then use the `z()` function to compute a normalized value for each `leg`. If the normalized value is more than 3, the data is extremely far from the mean. If we reject this outliers, we have a more uniform set of data that's less likely to harbor reporting or measurement errors.

The following is how we can tackle this:

```
from stats import mean, stdev, z
dist_data = list(map(dist, trip))
µ_d = mean(dist_data)
σ_d = stdev(dist_data)
outlier = lambda leg: z(dist(leg),µ_d,σ_d) > 3
print("Outliers", list(filter(outlier, trip)))
```

We've mapped the distance function to each `leg` in the `trip` collection. As we'll do several things with the result, we must materialize a `list` object. We can't rely on the iterator as the first function will consume it. We can then use this extraction to compute population statistics µ_d and σ_d with the mean and standard deviation.

Given the statistics, we used the outlier lambda to `filter` our data. If the normalized value is too large, the data is an outlier.

The result of `list(filter(outlier, trip))` is a list of two legs that are quite long compared to the rest of the legs in the population. The average distance is about 34 nm, with a standard deviation of 24 nm. No trip can have a normalized distance of less than -1.407.

We're able to decompose a fairly complex problem into a number of independent functions, each one of which can be easily tested in isolation. Our processing is a composition of simpler functions. This can lead to succinct, expressive functional programming.

The iter() function with a sentinel value

The built-in `iter()` function creates an iterator over a `collection` object. We can use this to wrap an `iterator` object around a `collection`. In many cases, we'll allow the `for` statement to handle this implicitly. In a few cases, we might want to create an iterator explicitly so that we can separate the head from the tail of a `collection`. This function can also iterate through the values created by a `callable` or function until a `sentinel` value is found. This feature is sometimes used with the `read()` function of a file to consume rows until some `sentinel` value is found. In this case, the given function might be some file's `readline()` method. Providing a `callable` function to `iter()` is a bit hard for us because this function must maintain state internally. This hidden state is a feature of an open file, for example, each `read()` or `readline()` function advances some internal state to the next character or next line.

Another example of this is the way that a mutable collection object's `pop()` method makes a stateful change in the object. The following is an example of using the `pop()` method:

```
>>> tail= iter([1, 2, 3, None, 4, 5, 6].pop, None)
>>> list(tail)
[6, 5, 4]
```

The `tail` variable was set to an iterator over the list `[1, 2, 3, None, 4, 5, 6]` that will be traversed by the `pop()` function. The default behavior of `pop()` is pop `(-1)`, that is, the elements are popped in the reverse order. When the `sentinel` value is found, the `iterator` stops returning values.

This kind of internal state is something we'd like to avoid as much as possible. Consequently, we won't try to contrive a use for this feature.

Using sorted() to put data in order

When we need to produce results in a defined order, Python gives us two choices. We can create a `list` object and use the `list.sort()` method to put items in an order. An alternative is to use the `sorted()` function. This function works with any iterable, but it creates a final `list` object as part of the sorting operation.

The `sorted()` function can be used in two ways. It can be simply applied to collections. It can also be used as a higher-order function using the `key=` argument.

Let's say we have our trip data from the examples in *Chapter 4, Working with Collections*. We have a function that will generate a sequence of tuples with start, end, and distance for each `leg` of a `trip`. The data looks as follows:

```
(((37.54901619777347, -76.33029518659048), (37.840832, -76.273834),
17.7246), ((37.840832, -76.273834), (38.331501, -76.459503),
30.7382), ((38.331501, -76.459503), (38.845501, -76.537331),
31.0756), ((36.843334, -76.298668), (37.549, -76.331169), 42.3962),
((37.549, -76.331169), (38.330166, -76.458504), 47.2866),
((38.330166, -76.458504), (38.976334, -76.473503), 38.8019))
```

We can see the default behavior of the `sorted()` function using the following interaction:

```
>>> sorted(dist(x) for x in trip)
[0.1731, 0.1898, 1.4235, 4.3155, ... 86.2095, 115.1751, 129.7748]
```

We used a generator expression (`dist(x) for x in trip`) to extract the distances from our trip data. We then sorted this iterable collection of numbers to get the distances from 0.17 nm to 129.77 nm.

If we want to keep the legs and distances together in their original three tuples, we can have the `sorted()` function apply a `key()` function to determine how to sort the tuples, as shown in the following code snippet:

```
>>> sorted(trip, key=dist)
[((35.505665, -76.653664), (35.508335, -76.654999), 0.1731),
((35.028175, -76.682495), (35.031334, -76.682663), 0.1898),
((27.154167, -80.195663), (29.195168, -81.002998), 129.7748)]
```

We've sorted the trip data, using a `dist` lambda to extract the distance from each tuple. The `dist` function is simply as follows:

```
dist = lambda leg: leg[2]
```

This shows the power of using simple `lambda` to decompose a complex tuple into constituent elements.

Writing higher-order functions

We can identify three varieties of higher-order functions; they are as follows:

- Functions that accept a function as one of its arguments.

- Functions that return a function. A `Callable` class is a common example of this. A function that returns a generator expression can be thought of as a higher-order function.

- Functions that accept and return a function. The `functools.partial()` function is a common example of this. We'll save this for *Chapter 10, The Functools Module*. A decorator is different; we'll save this for *Chapter 11, Decorator Design Techinques.*

We'll expand on these simple patterns using a higher-order function to also transform the structure of the data. We can do several common transformations such as the following:

- Wrap objects to create more complex objects

- Unwrap complex objects into their components

- Flatten a structure

- Structure a flat sequence

A `Callable` class object is a commonly used example of a function that returns a `callable` object. We'll look at this as a way to write flexible functions into which configuration parameters can be injected.

We'll also introduce simple decorators in this chapter. We'll defer deeper consideration of decorators until *Chapter 11, Decorator Design Techniques*.

Writing higher-order mappings and filters

Python's two built-in higher-order functions, `map()` and `filter()`, generally handle almost everything we might want to throw at them. It's difficult to optimize them in a general way to achieve higher performance. We'll look at functions of Python 3.4, such as `imap()`, `ifilter()`, and `ifilterfalse()`, in *Chapter 8, The Itertools Module*.

We have three largely equivalent ways to express a mapping. Assume that we have some function, `f(x)`, and some collection of objects, `C`. We have three entirely equivalent ways to express a mapping; they are as follows:

- The `map()` function:

  ```
  map(f, C)
  ```

- The generator expression:

```
(f(x) for x in C)
```

- The generator function:

```
def mymap(f, C):
    for x in C:
        yield f(x)
mymap(f, C)
```

Similarly, we have three ways to apply a `filter` function to a `collection`, all of which are equivalent:

- The `filter()` function:

```
filter(f, C)
```

- The generator expression:

```
(x for x in C if f(x))
```

- The generator function:

```
def myfilter(f, C):
    for x in C:
        if f(x):
            yield x
myfilter(f, C)
```

There are some performance differences; the `map()` and `filter()` functions are fastest. More importantly, there are different kinds of extensions that fit these mapping and filtering designs, which are as follows:

- We can create a more sophisticated function, `g(x)`, that is applied to each element, or we can apply a function to the collection, `C`, prior to processing. This is the most general approach and applies to all three designs. This is where the bulk of our functional design energy is invested.

- We can tweak the `for` loop. One obvious tweak is to combine mapping and filtering into a single operation by extending the generator expression with an `if` clause. We can also merge the `mymap()` and `myfilter()` functions to combine mapping and filtering.

The profound change we can make is to alter the structure of the data handled by the loop. We have a number of design patterns, including wrapping, unwrapping (or extracting), flattening, and structuring. We've looked at a few of these techniques in previous chapters.

We need to exercise some caution when designing mappings that combine too many transformations in a single function. As far as possible, we want to avoid creating functions that fail to be succinct or expressive of a single idea. As Python doesn't have an optimizing compiler, we might be forced to manually optimize slow applications by combining functions. We need to do this kind of optimization reluctantly, only after profiling a poorly performing program.

Unwrapping data while mapping

When we use a construct such as (f(x) for x, y in C), we've used multiple assignment in the for statement to unwrap a multi-valued tuple and then apply a function. The whole expression is a mapping. This is a common Python optimization to change the structure and apply a function.

We'll use our trip data from *Chapter 4, Working with Collections*. The following is a concrete example of unwrapping while mapping:

```
def convert(conversion, trip):
    return (conversion(distance) for start, end, distance in trip)
```

This higher-order function would be supported by conversion functions that we can apply to our raw data as follows:

```
to_miles = lambda nm: nm*5280/6076.12
to_km = lambda nm: nm*1.852
to_nm = lambda nm: nm
```

This function would then be used as follows to extract distance and apply a conversion function:

```
convert(to_miles, trip)
```

As we're unwrapping, the result will be a sequence of floating-point values. The results are as follows:

```
[20.397120559090908, 35.37291511060606, ..., 44.652462240151515]
```

This convert() function is highly specific to our start-end-distance trip data structure, as the for loop decomposes that three tuple.

We can build a more general solution for this kind of unwrapping while mapping a design pattern. It suffers from being a bit more complex. First, we need general-purpose decomposition functions like the following code snippet:

```
fst= lambda x: x[0]
snd= lambda x: x[1]
sel2= lambda x: x[2]
```

We'd like to be able to express `f(sel2(s_e_d))` for s_e_d in trip. This involves functional composition; we're combining a function like `to_miles()` and a selector like `sel2()`. We can express functional composition in Python using yet another lambda, as follows:

```
to_miles= lambda s_e_d: to_miles(sel2(s_e_d))
```

This gives us a longer but more general version of unwrapping, as follows:

```
to_miles(s_e_d) for s_e_d in trip
```

While this second version is somewhat more general, it doesn't seem wonderfully helpful. When used with particularly complex tuples, however, it can be handy.

What's important to note about our higher-order `convert()` function is that we're accepting a function as an argument and returning a function as a result. The `convert()` function is not a generator function; it doesn't `yield` anything. The result of the `convert()` function is a generator expression that must be evaluated to accumulate the individual values.

The same design principle works to create hybrid filters instead of mappings. We'd apply the filter in an `if` clause of the generator expression that was returned.

Of course, we can combine mapping and filtering to create yet more complex functions. It might seem like a good idea to create more complex functions to limit the amount of processing. This isn't always true; a complex function might not beat the performance of a nested use of simple `map()` and `filter()` functions. Generally, we only want to create a more complex function if it encapsulates a concept and makes the software easier to understand.

Wrapping additional data while mapping

When we use a construct such as `((f(x), x) for x in C)`, we've done a wrapping to create a multi-valued tuple while also applying a mapping. This is a common technique to save derived results to create constructs that have the benefits of avoiding recalculation without the liability of complex state-changing objects.

This is part of the example shown in *Chapter 4, Working with Collections*, to create the trip data from the path of points. The code looks like this:

```
from ch02_ex3 import float_from_pair, lat_lon_kml, limits, haversine, legs

path= float_from_pair(lat_lon_kml())

trip= tuple((start, end, round(haversine(start, end),4)) for start,end in legs(iter(path)))
```

We can revise this slightly to create a higher-order function that separates the `wrapping` from the other functions. We can define a function like this:

```
def cons_distance(distance, legs_iter):
    return ((start, end, round(distance(start,end),4)) for start,
    end in legs_iter)
```

This function will decompose each leg into two variables, `start` and `end`. These will be used with the given `distance()` function to compute the distance between the points. The result will build a more complex three tuple that includes the original two legs and also the calculated result.

We can then rewrite our trip assignment to apply the `haversine()` function to compute distances as follows:

```
path= float_from_pair(lat_lon_kml())
trip2= tuple(cons_distance(haversine, legs(iter(path))))
```

We've replaced a generator expression with a higher-order function, `cons_distance()`. The function not only accepts a function as an argument, but it also returns a generator expression.

A slightly different formulation of this is as follows:

```
def cons_distance3(distance, legs_iter):
    return ( leg+(round(distance(*leg),4),) for leg in legs_iter)
```

This version makes the construction of a new object built up from an old object a bit clearer. We're iterating through legs of a trip. We're computing the distance along a `leg`. We're building new structures with the `leg` and the distance concatenated.

As both of these `cons_distance()` functions accept a function as an argument, we can use this feature to provide an alternative distance formula. For example, we can use the `math.hypot(lat(start)-lat(end), lon(start)-lon(end))` method to compute a less-correct plane distance along each `leg`.

In *Chapter 10, The Functools Module*, we'll show how to use the `partial()` function to set a value for the R parameter of the `haversine()` function, which changes the units in which the distance is calculated.

Flattening data while mapping

In *Chapter 4, Working with Collections,* we looked at algorithms that flattened a nested tuple-of-tuples structure into single iterable. Our goal at the time was simply to restructure some data, without doing any real processing. We can create hybrid solutions that combine a function with a flattening operation.

Let's assume that we have a block of text that we want to convert to a flat sequence of numbers. The text looks as follows:

```
text= """\
     2      3      5      7     11     13     17     19     23
29
    31     37     41     43     47     53     59     61     67
71
    73     79     83     89     97    101    103    107    109
113
   127    131    137    139    149    151    157    163    167
173
   179    181    191    193    197    199    211    223    227
229
"""
```

Each line is a block of 10 numbers. We need to unblock the rows to create a flat sequence of numbers.

This is done with a two part generator function as follows:

```
data= list(v for line in text.splitlines() for v in line.split())
```

This will split the text into lines and iterate through each line. It will split each line into words and iterate through each word. The output from this is a list of strings, as follows:

```
['2', '3', '5', '7', '11', '13', '17', '19', '23', '29', '31', '37',
'41', '43', '47', '53', '59', '61', '67', '71', '73', '79', '83',
'89', '97', '101', '103', '107', '109', '113', '127', '131', '137',
'139', '149', '151', '157', '163', '167', '173', '179', '181', '191',
'193', '197', '199', '211', '223', '227', '229']
```

To convert the strings to numbers, we must apply a conversion function as well as unwind the blocked structure from its original format, using the following code snippet:

```
def numbers_from_rows(conversion, text):
    return (conversion(v) for line in text.splitlines() for v in
    line.split())
```

This function has a `conversion` argument, which is a function that is applied to each value that will be emitted. The values are created by flattening using the algorithm shown above.

We can use this `numbers_from_rows()` function in the following kind of expression:

```
print(list(numbers_from_rows(float, text)))
```

Here we've used the built-in `float()` to create a list of `floating-point` values from the block of text.

We have many alternatives using mixtures of higher-order functions and generator expressions. For example, we might express this as follows:

```
map(float, v for line in text.splitlines() for v in line.split())
```

This might be helpful if it helps us understand the overall structure of the algorithm. The principle is called **chunking**; the details of a function with a meaningful name can be abstracted and we can work with the function in a new context. While we often use higher-order functions, there are times when a generator expression can be more clear.

Structuring data while filtering

The previous three examples combined additional processing with mapping. Combining processing with filtering doesn't seem to be quite as expressive as combining with mapping. We'll look at an example in detail to show that, although it is useful, it doesn't seem to have as compelling a use case as combining mapping and processing.

In *Chapter 4*, *Working with Collections*, we looked at structuring algorithms. We can easily combine a filter with the structuring algorithm into a single, complex function. The following is a version of our preferred function to group the output from an iterable:

```
def group_by_iter(n, iterable):
    row= tuple(next(iterable) for i in range(n))
    while row:
        yield row
        row= tuple(next(iterable) for i in range(n))
```

This will try to assemble a tuple of n items taken from an iterable. If there are any items in the tuple, they are yielded as part of the resulting iterable. In principle, the function then operates recursively on the remaining items from the original iterable. As the recursion is relatively inefficient in Python, we've optimized it into an explicit `while` loop.

We can use this function as follows:

```
group_by_iter(7, filter( lambda x: x%3==0 or x%5==0, range(100)))
```

This will group the results of applying a `filter()` function to an iterable created by the `range()` function.

We can merge grouping and filtering into a single function that does both operations in a single function body. The modification to `group_by_iter()` looks as follows:

```
def group_filter_iter(n, predicate, iterable):
    data = filter(predicate, iterable)
    row= tuple(next(data) for i in range(n))
    while row:
        yield row
        row= tuple(next(data) for i in range(n))
```

This function applies the filter predicate function to the source iterable. As the filter output is itself a non-strict iterable, the `data` variable isn't computed in advance; the values for data are created as needed. The bulk of this function is identical to the version shown above.

We can slightly simplify the context in which we use this function as follows:

```
group_filter_iter(7, lambda x: x%3==0 or x%5==0, range(1,100))
```

Here, we've applied the filter predicate and grouped the results in a single function invocation. In the case of the `filter()` function, it's rarely a clear advantage to apply the filter in conjunction with other processing. It seems as if a separate, visible `filter()` function is more helpful than a combined function.

Writing generator functions

Many functions can be expressed neatly as generator expressions. Indeed, we've seen that almost any kind of mapping or filtering can be done as a generator expression. They can also be done with a built-in higher-order function such as `map()` or `filter()` or as a generator function. When considering multiple statement generator functions, we need to be cautious that we don't stray from the guiding principles of functional programming: stateless function evaluation.

Using Python for functional programming means walking on a knife edge between purely functional programming and imperative programming. We need to identify and isolate the places where we must resort to imperative Python code because there isn't a purely functional alternative available.

We're obligated to write generator functions when we need statement features of Python. Features like the following aren't available in generator expressions:

- A `with` context to work with external resources. We'll look at this in *Chapter 6, Recursions and Reductions*, where we address file parsing.

- A `while` statement to iterate somewhat more flexibly than a `for` statement. The example of this is shown previously in the *Flattening data while mapping* section.

- A `break` or `return` statement to implement a search that terminates a loop early.

- The `try-except` construct to handle exceptions.

- An internal function definition. We've looked at this in several examples in *Chapter 1, Introducing Functional Programming* and *Chapter 2, Introducing Some Functional Features*. We'll also revisit it in *Chapter 6, Recursions and Reductions*.

- A really complex `if-elif` sequence. Trying to express more than one alternatives via `if-else` conditional expressions can become complex-looking.

- At the edge of the envelope, we have less-used features of Python such as `for-else`, `while-else`, `try-else`, and `try-else-finally`. These are all statement-level features that aren't available in generator expressions.

The `break` statement is most commonly used to end processing of a collection early. We can end processing after the first item that satisfies some criteria. This is a version of the `any()` function we're looking at to find the existence of a value with a given property. We can also end after processing some larger numbers of items, but not all of them.

Finding a single value can be expressed succinctly as `min(some-big-expression)` or `max(something big)`. In these cases, we're committed to examining all of the values to assure that we've properly found the minimum or the maximum.

In a few cases, we can stand to have a `first(function, collection)` function where the first value that is `True` is sufficient. We'd like the processing to terminate as early as possible, saving needless calculation.

We can define a function as follows:

```
def first(predicate, collection):
    for x in collection:
        if predicate(x): return x
```

We've iterated through the `collection`, applying the given predicate function. If the predicate is `True`, we'll return the associated value. If we exhaust the `collection`, the default value of `None` will be returned.

We can also download a version of this from `PyPi`. The first module contains a variation on this idea. For more details visit: `https://pypi.python.org/pypi/first`.

This can act as a helper when trying to determine whether a number is a prime number or not. The following is a function that tests a number for being prime:

```
import math
def isprimeh(x):
    if x == 2: return True
    if x % 2 == 0: return False
    factor= first( lambda n: x%n==0,
    range(3,int(math.sqrt(x)+.5)+1,2))
    return factor is None
```

This function handles a few of the edge cases regarding the number 2 being a prime number and every other even number being composite. Then, it uses the `first()` function defined above to locate the first factor in the given collection.

When the `first()` function will return the factor, the actual number doesn't matter. Its existence is all that matters for this particular example. Therefore, the `isprimeh()` function returns `True` if no factor was found.

We can do something similar to handle data exceptions. The following is a version of the `map()` function that also filters bad data:

```
def map_not_none(function, iterable):
    for x in iterable:
        try:
            yield function(x)
        except Exception as e:
            pass # print(e)
```

This function steps through the items in the iterable. It attempts to apply the function to the item; if no exception is raised, this new value is yielded. If an exception is raised, the offending value is silently dropped.

This can be handy when dealing with data that include values that are not applicable or missing. Rather than working out complex filters to exclude these values, we attempt to process them and drop the ones that aren't valid.

We might use the map() function for mapping not-None values as follows:

```
data = map_not_none(int, some_source)
```

We'll apply the int() function to each value in some_source. When the some_source parameter is an iterable collection of strings, this can be a handy way to reject strings that don't represent a number.

Building higher-order functions with Callables

We can define higher-order functions as instances of the Callable class. This builds on the idea of writing generator functions; we'll write callables because we need statement features of Python. In addition to using statements, we can also apply a static configuration when creating the higher-order function.

What's important about a Callable class definition is that the class object, created by the class statement, defines essentially a function that emits a function. Commonly, we'll use a callable object to create a composite function that combines two other functions into something relatively complex.

To emphasize this, consider the following class:

```
from collections.abc import Callable
class NullAware(Callable):
    def __init__(self, some_func):
        self.some_func= some_func
    def __call__(self, arg):
        return None if arg is None else self.some_func(arg)
```

This class creates a function named NullAware() that is a higher-order function that is used to create a new function. When we evaluate the NullAware(math.log) expression, we're creating a new function that can be applied to argument values. The __init__() method will save the given function in the resulting object.

The __call__() method is how the resulting function is evaluated. In this case, the function that was created will gracefully tolerate None values without raising exceptions.

The common approach is to create the new function and save it for future use by assigning it a name as follows:

```
null_log_scale= NullAware(math.log)
```

This creates a new function and assigns the name null_log_scale(). We can then use the function in another context. Take a look at the following example:

```
>>> some_data = [10, 100, None, 50, 60]
>>> scaled = map(null_log_scale, some_data)
>>> list(scaled)
[2.302585092994046, 4.605170185988092, None, 3.912023005428146,
4.0943445622221]
```

A less common approach is to create and use the emitted function in one expression as follows:

```
>>> scaled= map(NullAware( math.log ), some_data)
>>> list(scaled)
[2.302585092994046, 4.605170185988092, None, 3.912023005428146,
4.0943445622221]
```

The evaluation of NullAware(math.log) created a function. This anonymous function was then used by the map() function to process an iterable, some_data.

This example's __call__() method relies entirely on expression evaluation. It's an elegant and tidy way to define composite functions built up from lower-level component functions. When working with scalar functions, there are a few complex design considerations. When we work with iterable collections, we have to be a bit more careful.

Assuring good functional design

The idea of stateless functional programming requires some care when using Python objects. Objects are typically stateful. Indeed, one can argue that the entire purpose of object-oriented programming is to encapsulate state change into class definition. Because of this, we find ourselves pulled in opposing directions between functional programming and imperative programming when using Python class definitions to process collections.

The benefit of using a `Callable` to create a composite function gives us slightly simpler syntax when the resulting composite function is used. When we start working with iterable mappings or reductions, we have to be aware of how and why we introduce stateful objects.

We'll return to our `sum_filter_f()` composite function shown above. Here is a version built from a `Callable` class definition:

```
from collections.abc import Callable
class Sum_Filter(Callable):
    __slots__ = ["filter", "function"]
    def __init__(self, filter, function):
        self.filter= filter
        self.function= function
    def __call__(self, iterable):
        return sum(self.function(x) for x in iterable if
        self.filter(x))
```

We've imported the abstract superclass `Callable` and used this as the basis for our class. We've defined precisely two slots in this object; this puts a few constraints on our ability to use the function as a stateful object. It doesn't prevent all modifications to the resulting object, but it limits us to just two attributes. Attempting to add attributes results in an exception.

The initialization method, `__init__()`, stows the two function names, `filter` and `function`, in the object's instance variables. The `__call__()` method returns a value based on a generator expression that uses the two internal function definitions. The `self.filter()` function is used to pass or reject items. The `self.function()` function is used to transform objects that are passed by the `filter()` function.

An instance of this class is a function that has two strategy functions built into it. We create an instance as follows:

```
count_not_none = Sum_Filter(lambda x: x is not None, lambda x: 1)
```

We've built a function named `count_not_none()` that counts the non-None values in a sequence. It does this by using a `lambda` to pass non-None values and a function that uses a constant 1 instead of the actual values present.

Generally, this `count_not_none()` object will behave like any other Python function. The use is somewhat simpler than our previous example of `sum_filter_f()`.

We can use the `count_not_None()` function as follows:

```
N= count_not_none(data)
```

Instead of using `sum_filter_f()` funtion:

```
N= sum_filter_f(valid, count_, data)
```

The `count_not_none()` function, based on a `Callable`, doesn't require quite so many arguments as a conventional function. This makes it superficially simpler to use. However, it can also make it somewhat more obscure because the details of how the function works are in two places in the source code: where the function was created as an instance of the `Callable` class and where the function was used.

Looking at some of the design patterns

The `max()`, `min()`, and `sorted()` functions have a default behavior without a `key=` function. They can be customized by providing a function that defines how to compute a key from the available data. For many of our examples, the `key()` function has been a simple extraction of available data. This isn't a requirement; the `key()` function can do anything.

Imagine the following method: `max(trip, key=random.randint())`. Generally, we try not to have have `key()` functions that do something obscure.

The use of a `key=` function is a common design pattern. Our functions can easily follow this pattern.

We've also looked at `lambda forms` that we can use to simplify using higher-order functions. One significant advantage of using `lambda forms` is that it follows the functional paradigm very closely. When writing more conventional functions, we can create imperative programs that might clutter an otherwise succinct and expressive functional design.

We've looked at several kinds of higher-order functions that work with a collection of values. Throughout the previous chapters, we've hinted around at several different design patterns for higher-order `collection` and `scalar` functions. The following is a broad classification:

- Return a Generator. A higher-order function can return a generator expression. We consider the function higher-order because it didn't return `scalar` values or `collections` of values. Some of these higher-order functions also accept functions as arguments.

- Act as a Generator. Some function examples use the `yield` statement to make them first-class generator functions. The value of a generator function is an iterable collection of values that are evaluated lazily. We suggest that a generator function is essentially indistinguishable from a function that returns a generator expression. Both are non-strict. Both can yield a sequence of values. For this reason, we'll also consider generator functions as higher order. Built-in functions such as `map()` and `filter()` fall into this category.

- Materialize a Collection. Some functions must return a materialized collection object: `list`, `tuple`, `set`, or `mapping`. These kinds of functions can be of a higher order if they have a function as part of the arguments. Otherwise, they're ordinary functions that happen to work with `collections`.

- Reduce a Collection. Some functions work with an iterable (or a `collection` object) and create a `scalar` result. The `len()` and `sum()` functions are examples of this. We can create higher-order reductions when we accept a function as an argument. We'll return to this in the next chapter.

- Scalar. Some functions act on individual data items. These can be higher-order functions if they accept another function as an argument.

As we design our own software, we can pick and choose among these established design patterns.

Summary

In this chapter, we have seen two reductions that are higher-order functions: `max()` and `min()`. We also looked at the two central higher-order functions, `map()` and `filter()`. We also looked at `sorted()`.

We also looked at how to use a higher-order function to also transform the structure of data. We can perform several common transformations, including wrapping, unwrapping, flattening, and structure sequences of different kinds.

We looked at three ways to define our own higher-order functions, which are as follows:

- The `def` statement. Similar to this is a `lambda form` that we assign to a variable.

- Defining a `Callable` class as a kind of function that emits composite functions.

- We can also use decorators to emit composite functions. We'll return to this in *Chapter 11, Decorator Design Techniques*.

In the next chapter, we'll look at the idea of purely functional iteration via recursion. We'll use Pythonic structures to make several common improvements over purely functional techniques. We'll also look at the associated problem of performing reductions from collections to individual values.

6

Recursions and Reductions

In previous chapters, we've looked at several related kinds of processing designs; some of them are as follows:

- Mapping and filtering that create collections from collections
- Reductions that create a scalar value from a collection

The distinction is exemplified by functions such as `map()` and `filter()` that accomplish the first kind of collection processing. There are several specialized reduction functions, which include `min()`, `max()`, `len()`, and `sum()`. There's a general-purpose reduction function, also, `functools.reduce()`.

We'll also consider a `collections.Counter()` function as a kind of reduction operator. It doesn't produce a single scalar value per se, but it does create a new organization of the data that eliminates some of the original structure. At its heart, it's a kind of count-group-by operation that has more in common with a counting reduction than with a mapping.

In this chapter, we'll look at reduction functions in more detail. From a purely functional perspective, a reduction is defined recursively. For this reason, we'll look at recursion first before we look at reduction algorithms.

Generally, a functional programming language compiler will optimize a recursive function to transform a call in the tail of the function to a loop. This will dramatically improve performance. From a Python perspective, pure recursion is limited, so we must do the tail-call optimization manually. The tail-call optimization technique available in Python is to use an explicit `for` loop.

We'll look at a number of reduction algorithms including `sum()`, `count()`, `max()`, and `min()`. We'll also look at the `collections.Counter()` function and related `groupby()` reductions. We'll also look at how parsing (and lexical scanning) are proper reductions since they transform sequences of tokens (or sequences of characters) into higher-order collections with more complex properties.

Simple numerical recursions

We can consider all numeric operations to be defined by recursions. For more depth, read about the **Peano axioms** that define the essential features of numbers. http://en.wikipedia.org/wiki/Peano_axioms is one place to start.

From these axioms, we can see that addition is defined recursively using more primitive notions of the next number, or successor of a number, n, $S(n)$.

To simplify the presentation, we'll assume that we can define a predecessor function, $P(n)$, such that $n = S(P(n)) = P(S(n))$, as long as $n \neq 0$

Addition between two natural numbers could be defined recursively as follows:

$$\text{add}(a, b) = \begin{cases} b & \text{if } a = 0 \\ \text{add}(P(a), S(b)) & \text{if } a \neq 0 \end{cases}$$

If we use more common $n+1$ and $n-1$ instead of $S(n)$ and $P(n)$, we can see that $\text{add}(a, b) = \text{add}(a-1, b+1)$.

This translates neatly in Python, as shown in the following command snippet:

```
def add(a,b):
    if a == 0: return b
    else: return add(a-1, b+1)
```

We've simply rearranged common mathematical notation into Python. The `if` clauses are placed to the left instead of the right.

Generally, we don't provide our own functions in Python to do simple addition. We rely on Python's underlying implementation to properly handle arithmetic of various kinds. Our point here is that fundamental scalar arithmetic can be defined recursively.

All of these recursive definitions include at least two cases: the nonrecursive cases where the value of the function is defined directly and recursive cases where the value of the function is computed from a recursive evaluation of the function with different values.

In order to be sure the recursion will terminate, it's important to see how the recursive case computes values that approach the defined nonrecursive case. There are often constraints on the argument values that we've omitted from the functions here. The `add()` function in the preceding command snippet, for example, can include `assert a>=` and `b>=0` to establish the constraints on the input values.

Without these constraints. `a-1` can't be guaranteed to approach the nonrecursive case of `a == 0`.

In most cases, this is obvious. In a few rare cases, it might be difficult to prove. One example is the Syracuse function. This is one of the pathological cases where termination is unclear.

Implementing tail-call optimization

In the case of some functions, the recursive definition is the one often stated because it is succinct and expressive. One of the most common examples is the `factorial()` function.

We can see how this is rewritten as a simple recursive function in Python from the following formula:

$$n! = \begin{cases} 1 & \textbf{if } n = 0 \\ n \times (n-1)! & \textbf{if } n > 0 \end{cases}$$

The preceding formula can be executed in Python by using the following commands:

```
def fact(n):
    if n == 0: return 1
    else: return n*fact(n-1)
```

This has the advantage of simplicity. The recursion limits in Python artificially constrain us; we can't do anything larger than about fact(997). The value of 1000! has 2,568 digits and generally exceeds our floating-point capacity; on some systems this is about 10^{300} Pragmatically, it's common to switch to a `log gamma` function, which works well with large floating-point values.

This function demonstrates a typical tail recursion. The last expression in the function is a call to the function with a new argument value. An optimizing compiler can replace the function call stack management with a loop that executes very quickly.

Since Python doesn't have an optimizing compiler, we're obliged to look at scalar recursions with an eye toward optimizing them. In this case, the function involves an incremental change from *n* to *n-1*. This means that we're generating a sequence of numbers and then doing a reduction to compute their product.

Stepping outside purely functional processing, we can define an imperative `facti()` calculation as follows:

```
def facti(n):
    if n == 0: return 1
    f= 1
    for i in range(2,n):
        f= f*i
    return f
```

This version of the factorial function will compute values beyond 1000! (2000!, for example, has 5733 digits). It isn't purely functional. We've optimized the tail recursion into a stateful loop depending on the `i` variable to maintain the state of the computation.

In general, we're obliged to do this in Python because Python can't automatically do the tail-call optimization. There are situations, however, where this kind of optimization isn't actually helpful. We'll look at a few situations.

Leaving recursion in place

In some cases, the recursive definition is actually optimal. Some recursions involve a divide and conquer strategy that minimizes the work from $O(n)$ to $O(\log_2 n)$. One example of this is the exponentiation by the squaring algorithm. We can state it formally like this:

$$a^n = \begin{cases} 1 & \text{if } n = 0 \\ a \times a^{n-1} & \text{if } n \text{ is odd} \\ \left(a^{n/2}\right)^2 & \text{if } n \text{ is even} \end{cases}$$

We've broken the process into three cases, easily written in Python as a recursion. Look at the following command snippet:

```
def fastexp(a, n):
    if n == 0: return 1
    elif n % 2 == 1: return a*fastexp(a,n-1)
    else:
        t= fastexp(a,n//2)
        return t*t
```

This function has three cases. The base case, the `fastexp(a, 0)` method is defined as having a value of 1. The other two cases take two different approaches. For odd numbers, the `fastexp()` method is defined recursively. The exponent, *n*, is reduced by 1. A simple tail-recursion optimization would work for this case.

For even numbers, however, the `fastexp()` recursion uses `n/2`, chopping the problem into half of its original size. Since the problem size is reduced by a factor of 2, this case results in a significant speed-up of the processing.

We can't trivially reframe this kind of function into a tail-call optimization loop. Since it's already optimal, we don't really need to optimize this further. The recursion limit in Python would impose the constraint of $n \leq 2^{1000}$, a generous upper bound.

Handling difficult tail-call optimization

We can look at the definition of **Fibonacci** numbers recursively. Following is one widely used definition for the *nth* Fibonacci number:

$$F_n = \begin{cases} 0 & \text{if } n = 0 \\ 1 & \text{if } n = 1 \\ F_{n-1} + F_{n-2} & \text{if } n \geq 2 \end{cases}$$

A given Fibonacci number, F_n, is defined as the sum of the previous two numbers, $F_{n-1} + F_{n-2}$. This is an example of multiple recursion: it can't be trivially optimized as a simple tail-recursion. However, if we don't optimize it to a tail-recursion, we'll find it to be too slow to be useful.

The following is a naïve implementation:

```
def fib(n):
    if n == 0: return 0
    if n == 1: return 1
    return fib(n-1) + fib(n-2)
```

This suffers from the multiple recursion problem. When computing the `fib(n)` method, we must compute `fib(n-1)` and `fib(n-2)` methods. The computation of `fib(n-1)` method involves a duplicate calculation of `fib(n-2)` method. The two recursive uses of the Fibonacci function will duplicate the amount of computation being done.

Because of the left-to-right Python evaluation rules, we can evaluate values up to about `fib(1000)`. However, we have to be patient. Very patient.

Following is an alternative which restates the entire algorithm to use stateful variables instead of a simple recursion:

```
def fibi(n):
    if n == 0: return 0
    if n == 1: return 1
    f_n2, f_n1 = 1, 1
    for i in range(3, n+1):
        f_n2, f_n1 = f_n1, f_n2+f_n1
    return f_n1
```

 Our stateful version of this function counts up from 0, unlike the recursion, which counts down from the initial value of *n*. It saves the values of F_{n-2} and F_{n-1} that will be used to compute F_n. This version is considerably faster than the recursive version.

What's important here is that we couldn't trivially optimize the recursion with an obvious rewrite. In order to replace the recursion with an imperative version, we had to look closely at the algorithm to determine how many stateful intermediate variables were required.

Processing collections via recursion

When working with a collection, we can also define the processing recursively. We can, for example, define the map () function recursively. The formalism looks as follows:

$$map(f,C) = \begin{cases} [] & \textbf{if len}(C) = 0 \\ map(f,C[:-1]) append(f(C[-1])) & \textbf{if len}(C) \neq 0 \end{cases}$$

We've defined the mapping of a function to an empty collection as an empty sequence. We've also specified that applying a function to a collection can be defined recursively with a three step expression. First, apply the function to all of the collection except the last element, creating a sequence object. Then apply the function to the last element. Finally, append the last calculation to the previously built sequence.

Following is a purely recursive function version of the older `map()` function:

```
def mapr(f, collection):
    if len(collection) == 0: return []
    return mapr(f, collection[:-1]) + [f(collection[-1])]
```

The value of the `mapr(f, [])` method is defined to be an empty `list` object. The value of the `mapr()` function with a non-empty list will apply the function to the last element in the `list` and append this to the list built recursively from the `mapr()` function applied to the head of the list.

We have to emphasize that this `mapr()` function actually creates a `list` object, similar to the older `map()` function in Python. The Python 3 `map()` function is an iterable, and isn't as good an example of tail-call optimization.

While this is an elegant formalism, it still lacks the tail-call optimization required. The tail-call optimization allows us to exceed the recursion depth of 1000 and also performs much more quickly than this naïve recursion.

Tail-call optimization for collections

We have two general ways to handle collections: we can use a higher-order function which returns a generator expression or we can create a function which uses a `for` loop to process each item in a collection. The two essential patterns are very similar.

Following is a higher-order function that behaves like the built-in `map()` function:

```
def mapf(f, C):
    return (f(x) for x in C)
```

We've returned a generator expression which produces the required mapping. This uses an explicit `for` loop as a kind of tail-call optimization.

Following is a generator function with the same value:

```
def mapg(f, C):
    for x in C:
        yield f(x)
```

This uses a complete `for` statement for the required optimization.

In both cases, the result is iterable. We must do something following this to materialize a sequence object:

```
>>> list(mapg(lambda x:2**x, [0, 1, 2, 3, 4]))
[1, 2, 4, 8, 16]
```

For performance and scalability, this kind of tail-call optimization is essentially required in Python programs. It makes the code less than purely functional. However, the benefit far outweighs the lack of purity. In order to reap the benefits of succinct and expression functional design, it is helpful to treat these less-than-pure functions as if they were proper recursions.

What this means, pragmatically, is that we must avoid cluttering up a collection processing function with additional stateful processing. The central tenets of functional programming are still valid even if some elements of our programs are less than purely functional.

Reductions and folding – from many to one

We can consider the `sum()` function to have the following kind of definition:

We could say that the sum of a collection is 0 for an empty collection. For a non-empty collection the sum is the first element plus the sum of the remaining elements.

$$\text{sum}(C) = \begin{cases} 0 & \text{if } \textbf{len}(C) = 0 \\ C[0] + \text{sum}(C[1:]) & \text{if } \textbf{len}(C) > 0 \end{cases}$$

Similarly, we can compute the product of a collection of numbers recursively using two cases:

$$\text{prod}(C) = \begin{cases} 1 & \text{if } \textbf{len}(C) = 0 \\ C[0] \times \text{prod}(C[1:]) & \text{if } \textbf{len}(C) > 0 \end{cases}$$

The base case defines the product of an empty sequence as 1. The recursive case defines the product as the first item times the product of the remaining items.

We've effectively folded in × or + operators between each item of the sequence. Further, we've grouped the items so that processing will be done right-to-left. This could be called a fold-right way of reducing a collection to a single value.

In Python, the product function can be defined recursively as follows:

```
def prodrc(collection):
    if len(collection) == 0: return 1
    return collection[0] * prodrc(collection[1:])
```

This is technically correct. It's a trivial rewrite from mathematical notation to Python. However, it is less than optimal because it tends to create a large number of intermediate `list` objects. It's also limited to only working with explicit collections; it can't work easily with `iterable` objects.

We can revise this slightly to work with an iterable, which avoids creating any intermediate `collection` objects. Following is a properly recursive product function which works with an iterable source of data:

```
def prodri(iterable):
    try:
        head= next(iterable)
    except StopIteration:
        return 1
    return head*prodri(iterable)
```

We can't interrogate an iterable with the `len()` function to see how many elements it has. All we can do is attempt to extract the head of the `iterable` sequence. If there are no items in the sequence, then any attempt to get the head will raise the `StopIteration` exception. If there is an item, then we can multiply this item by the product of the remaining items in the sequence. For a demo, we must explicitly create an iterable from a materialized `sequence` object, using the `iter()` function. In other contexts, we might have an iterable result that we can use. Following is an example:

```
>>> prodri(iter([1,2,3,4,5,6,7]))
5040
```

This recursive definition does not rely on explicit state or other imperative features of Python. While it's more purely functional, it is still limited to working with collections of under 1000 items. Pragmatically, we can use the following kind of imperative structure for reduction functions:

```
def prodi(iterable):
    p= 1
    for n in iterable:
        p *= n
    return p
```

This lacks the recursion limits. It includes the required tail-call optimization. Further, this will work equally well with either a `sequence` object or an iterable.

In other functional languages, this is called a `foldl` operation: the operators are folded into the iterable collection of values from left-to-right. This is unlike the recursive formulations which are generally called `foldr` operations because the evaluations are done from right-to-left in the collection.

For languages with optimizing compilers and lazy evaluation, the fold-left and fold-right distinction determines how intermediate results are created. This may have profound performance implications, but the distinction might not be obvious. A fold-left, for example, could immediately consume and process the first elements in a sequence. A fold-right, however, might consume the head of the sequence, but not do any processing until the entire sequence was consumed.

Group-by reductions – from many to fewer

A very common operation is a reduction that groups values by some key or indicator. In **SQL**, this is often called the `SELECT GROUP BY` operation. The raw data is grouped by some columns value and reductions (sometimes aggregate functions) are applied to other columns. The SQL aggregate functions include `SUM`, `COUNT`, `MAX`, and `MIN`.

The statistical summary called the mode is a count that's grouped by some independent variable. Python offers us several ways to group data before computing a reduction of the grouped values. We'll start by looking at two ways to get simple counts of grouped data. Then we'll look at ways to compute different summaries of grouped data.

We'll use the trip data that we computed in *Chapter 4, Working with Collections*. This data started as a sequence of latitude-longitude waypoints. We restructured it to create legs represented by three tuples of start, end, and distance for the `leg`. The data looks as follows:

```
(((37.5490162, -76.330295), (37.840832, -76.273834), 17.7246),
 ((37.840832, -76.273834), (38.331501, -76.459503), 30.7382),
 ((38.331501, -76.459503), (38.845501, -76.537331), 31.0756), ...
 ((38.330166, -76.458504), (38.976334, -76.473503), 38.8019))
```

A common operation that can be approached either as a stateful map or as a materialized, sorted object is computing the mode of a set of data values. When we look at our trip data, the variables are all continuous. To compute a mode, we'll need to quantize the distances covered. This is also called **binning**: we'll group the data into different bins. Binning is common in data visualization applications, also. In this case, we'll use 5 nautical miles as the size of each bin.

The quantized distances can be produced with a generator expression:

```
quantized= (5*(dist//5) for start,stop,dist in trip)
```

This will divide each distance by 5 – discarding any fractions – and then multiply by 5 to compute a number that represents the distance rounded down to the nearest 5 nautical miles.

Building a mapping with Counter

A mapping like the `collections.Counter` method is a great optimization for doing reductions that create counts (or totals) grouped by some value in the collection. A more typical functional programming solution to grouping data is to sort the original collection, and then use a recursive loop to identify when each group begins. This involves materializing the raw data, performing a $O(n \log n)$ sort, and then doing a reduction to get the sums or counts for each key.

We'll use the following generator to create an simple sequence of distances transformed into bins:

```
quantized= (5*(dist//5) for start,stop,dist in trip)
```

We divided each distance by 5 using truncated integer division, and then multiplied by 5 to create a value that's rounded down to the nearest 5 miles.

The following expression creates a `mapping` from distance to frequency:

```
from collections import Counter

Counter(quantized)
```

This is a stateful object, that was created by – technically – imperative object-oriented programming. Since it looks like a function, however, it seems a good fit for a design based on functional programming ideas.

If we print `Counter(quantized).most_common()` function, we'll see the following results:

```
[(30.0, 15), (15.0, 9), (35.0, 5), (5.0, 5), (10.0, 5), (20.0, 5),
(25.0, 5), (0.0, 4), (40.0, 3), (45.0, 3), (50.0, 3), (60.0, 3),
(70.0, 2), (65.0, 1), (80.0, 1), (115.0, 1), (85.0, 1), (55.0, 1),
(125.0, 1)]
```

The most common distance was about 30 nautical miles. The shortest recorded `leg` was four instances of 0. The longest leg was 125 nautical miles.

Note that your output may vary slightly from this. The results of the `most_common()` function are in order by frequency; equal-frequency bins may be in any order. These 5 lengths may not always be in the order shown:

```
(35.0, 5), (5.0, 5), (10.0, 5), (20.0, 5), (25.0, 5)
```

Building a mapping by sorting

If we want to implement this without using the `Counter` class, we can use a more functional approach of sorting and grouping. Following is a common algorithm:

```python
def group_sort(trip):
    def group(data):
        previous, count = None, 0
        for d in sorted(data):
            if d == previous:
                count += 1
            elif previous is not None: # and d != previous
                yield previous, count
                previous, count = d, 1
            elif previous is None:
                previous, count = d, 1
            else:
                raise Exception("Bad bad design problem.")
        yield previous, count
    quantized= (5*(dist//5) for start,stop,dist in trip)
    return dict(group(quantized))
```

The internal `group()` function steps through the sorted sequence of data items. If a given item has already been seen – it matches the value in `previous` – then the counter can be incremented. If a given item does not match the previous value and the previous value is `not-None`, then we've had a change in value; we can emit the previous value and the count, and begin a new accumulation of counts for the new value. The third condition only applies once: if the previous value has never been set, then this is the first value, and we should save it.

The final line of the function creates a dictionary from the grouped items. This dictionary will be similar to a Counter dictionary. The primary difference is that a `Counter()` function will have a `most_common()` method function which a default dictionary lacks.

The `elif previous is None` method case is an irksome overhead. Getting rid of this `elif` clause (and seeing a slight performance improvement) isn't terribly difficult.

To remove the extra `elif` clause, we need to use a slightly more elaborate initialization in the internal `group()` function:

```
def group(data):
    sorted_data= iter(sorted(data))
    previous, count = next(sorted_data), 1
    for d in sorted_data:
        if d == previous:
            count += 1
        elif previous is not None: # and d != previous
            yield previous, count
            previous, count = d, 1
        else:
            raise Exception("Bad bad design problem.")
    yield previous, count
```

This picks the first item out of the set of data to initialize the `previous` variable. The remaining items are then processed through the loop. This design shows a loose parallel with recursive designs where we initialize the recursion with the first item, and each recursive call provides either a next item or `None` to indicate that no items are left to process.

We can also do this with `itertools.groupby()`. We'll look at this function closely in *Chapter 8, The Itertools Module*.

Grouping or partitioning data by key values

There are no limits to the kinds of reductions we might want to apply to grouped data. We might have data with a number of independent and dependent variables. We can consider partitioning the data by an independent variable and computing summaries like maximum, minimum, average, and standard deviation of the values in each partition.

The essential trick to doing more sophisticated reductions is to collect all of the data values into each group. The `Counter()` function merely collects counts of identical items. We want to create sequences of the original items based on a key value.

Looked at in a more general way, each 5-mile bin will contain the entire collection of legs of that distance, not merely a count of the legs. We can consider the partitioning as a recursion or as a stateful application of `defaultdict(list)` object. We'll look at the recursive definition of a `groupby()` function, since it's easy to design.

Clearly, the `groupby(C, key)` method for an empty collection, `C`, is the empty dictionary, `dict()`. Or, more usefully, the empty `defaultdict(list)` object.

For a non-empty collection, we need to work with item `C[0]`, the head, and recursively process sequence `C[1:]`, the tail. We can use `head, *tail = C` command to do this parsing of the collection, as follows:

```
>>> C= [1,2,3,4,5]
>>> head, *tail= C
>>> head
1
>>> tail
[2, 3, 4, 5]
```

We need to do the `dict[key(head)].append(head)` method to include the head element in the resulting dictionary. And then we need to do the `groupby(tail,key)` method to process the remaining elements.

We can create a function as follows:

```
def group_by(key, data):
    def group_into(key, collection, dictionary):
        if len(collection) == 0:
            return dictionary
        head, *tail= collection
        dictionary[key(head)].append(head)
        return group_into(key, tail, dictionary)
    return group_into(key, data, defaultdict(list))
```

The interior function handles our essential recursive definition. An empty collection returns the provided dictionary. A non-empty collection is parsed into a head and tail. The head is used to update the dictionary. The tail is then used, recursively, to update the dictionary with all remaining elements.

We can't easily use Python's default values to collapse this into a single function. We cannot use the following command snippet:

```
def group_by(key, data, dictionary=defaultdict(list)):
```

If we try this, all uses of the `group_by()` function share one common `defaultdict(list)` object. Python builds default values just once. Mutable objects as default values rarely do what we want. Rather than try to include more sophisticated decision-making to handle an immutable default value (like `None`), we prefer to use a nested function definition. The `wrapper()` function properly initializes the arguments to the interior function.

We can group the data by distance as follows:

```
binned_distance = lambda leg: 5*(leg[2]//5)
by_distance= group_by(binned_distance, trip)
```

We've defined simple, reusable `lambda` which puts our distances into 5 nm bins. We then grouped the data using the provided `lambda`.

We can examine the binned data as follows:

```
import pprint
for distance in sorted(by_distance):
    print(distance)
    pprint.pprint(by_distance[distance])
```

Following is what the output looks like:

```
0.0
[((35.505665, -76.653664), (35.508335, -76.654999), 0.1731),
((35.028175, -76.682495), (35.031334, -76.682663), 0.1898),
((25.4095, -77.910164), (25.425833, -77.832664), 4.3155),
((25.0765, -77.308167), (25.080334, -77.334), 1.4235)]
5.0
[((38.845501, -76.537331), (38.992832, -76.451332), 9.7151),
((34.972332, -76.585167), (35.028175, -76.682495), 5.8441),
((30.717167, -81.552498), (30.766333, -81.471832), 5.103),
((25.471333, -78.408165), (25.504833, -78.232834), 9.7128),
((23.9555, -76.31633), (24.099667, -76.401833), 9.844)] ...
125.0
[((27.154167, -80.195663), (29.195168, -81.002998), 129.7748)]
```

This can also be written as an iteration as follows:

```
def partition(key, data):
    dictionary= defaultdict(list)
    for head in data:
        dictionary[key(head)].append(head)
    return dictionary
```

When doing the tail-call optimization, the essential line of the code in the imperative version will match the recursive definition. We've highlighted that line to emphasize that the rewrite is intended to have the same outcome. The rest of the structure represents the tail-call optimization we've adopted as a common way to work around the Python limitations.

Writing more general group-by reductions

Once we have partitioned the raw data, we can compute various kinds of reductions on the data elements in each partition. We might, for example, want the northern-most point for the start of each leg in the distance bins.

We'll introduce some helper functions to decompose the tuple as follows:

```
start = lambda s, e, d: s
end = lambda s, e, d: e
dist = lambda s, e, d: d
latitude = lambda lat, lon: lat
longitude = lambda lat, lon: lon
```

Each of these helper functions expects a `tuple` object to be provided using the `*` operator to map each element of the tuple to a separate parameter of the `lambda`. Once the tuple is expanded into the s, e, and p parameters, it's reasonably obvious to return the proper parameter by name. It's much more clear than trying to interpret the `tuple_arg[2]` method.

Following is how we use these helper functions:

```
>>> point = ((35.505665, -76.653664), (35.508335, -76.654999),
0.1731)
>>> start(*point)
(35.505665, -76.653664)
>>> end(*point)
(35.508335, -76.654999)
>>> dist(*point)
```

```
0.1731
>>> latitude(*start(*point))
35.505665
```

Our initial point object is a nested three tuple with (0) - a starting position, (1) - the ending position, and (2) - the distance. We extracted various fields using our helper functions.

Given these helpers, we can locate the northern-most starting position for the legs in each bin:

```
for distance in sorted(by_distance):
    print(distance, max(by_distance[distance],
    key=lambda pt: latitude(*start(*pt))))
```

The data that we grouped by distance included each leg of the given distance. We supplied all of the legs in each bin to the max() function. The key function we provided to the max() function extracted just the latitude of the starting point of the leg.

This gives us a short list of the northern-most legs of each distance as follows:

```
0.0 ((35.505665, -76.653664), (35.508335, -76.654999), 0.1731)
5.0 ((38.845501, -76.537331), (38.992832, -76.451332), 9.7151)
10.0 ((36.444168, -76.3265), (36.297501, -76.217834), 10.2537)
...
125.0 ((27.154167, -80.195663), (29.195168, -81.002998), 129.7748)
```

Writing higher-order reductions

We'll look at an example of a higher-order reduction algorithm here. This will introduce a rather complex topic. The simplest kind of reduction develops a single value from a collection of values. Python has a number of built-in reductions, including any(), all(), max(), min(), sum(), and len().

As we noted in *Chapter 4, Working with Collections*, we can do a great deal of statistical calculation if we start with a few simple reductions such as the following:

```
def s0(data):
    return sum(1 for x in data) # or len(data)
def s1(data):
    return sum(x for x in data) # or sum(data)
def s2(data):
    return sum(x*x for x in data)
```

This allows us to define mean, standard deviation, normalized values, correction, and even least-squares linear regression using a few simple functions.

The last of our simple reductions, `s2()`, shows how we can apply existing reductions to create higher-order functions. We might change our approach to be more like the following:

```
def sum_f(function, data):
    return sum(function(x) for x in data)
```

We've added a function that we'll use to transform the data. We'll compute the sum of the transformed values.

Now we can apply this function in three different ways to compute the three essential sums as follows:

```
N= sum_f(lambda x: 1, data) # x**0
S= sum_f(lambda x: x, data) # x**1
S2= sum_f( lambda x: x*x, data ) # x**2
```

We've plugged in a small `lambda` to compute $\sum_{x \in X}(x^0) = \sum_{x \in X} 1$, which is the count, $\sum_{x \in X}(x^1) = \sum_{x \in X} x$, the sum, and $\sum_{x \in X} x^2$, the sum of the squares, which we can use to compute standard deviation.

A common extension to this includes a filter to reject raw data which is unknown or unsuitable in some way. We might use the following command to reject bad data:

```
def sum_filter_f(filter, function, data):
    return sum(function(x) for x in data if filter(x))
```

Execution of the following command snippet allows us to do things like reject None values in a simple way:

```
count_ = lambda x: 1
sum_   = lambda x: x
valid = lambda x: x is not None
N = sum_filter_f(valid, count_, data)
```

This shows how we can provide two distinct `lambda` to our `sum_filter_f()` function. The `filter` argument is a `lambda` that rejects None values, we've called it `valid` to emphasize its meaning. The `function` argument is a `lambda` that implements a `count` or a `sum` method. We can easily add a `lambda` to compute a sum of squares.

It's important to note that this function is similar to other examples in that it actually returns a function rather than a value. This is one of the defining characteristics of higher-order functions, and is pleasantly simple to implement in Python.

Writing file parsers

We can often consider a file parser to be a kind of reduction. Many languages have two levels of definition: the lower-level tokens in the language and the higher-level structures built from those tokens. When looking at an XML file, the tags, tag names, and attribute names form this lower-level syntax; the structures which are described by XML form a higher-level syntax.

The lower-level lexical scanning is a kind of reduction that takes individual characters and groups them into tokens. This fits well with Python's generator function design pattern. We can often write functions that look as follows:

```
Def lexical_scan( some_source ):
    for char in some_source:
        if some_pattern completed: yield token
        else: accumulate token
```

For our purposes, we'll rely on lower-level file parsers to handle this for us. We'll use the CSV, JSON, and XML packages to manage these details. We'll write higher-level parsers based on these packages.

We'll still rely on a two-level design pattern. A lower-level parser will produce a useful canonical representation of the raw data. It will be an iterator over tuples of text. This is compatible with many kinds of data files. The higher-level parser will produce objects useful for our specific application. These might be tuples of numbers, or namedtuples, or perhaps some other class of immutable Python objects.

We provided one example of a lower-level parser in *Chapter 4, Working with Collections*. The input was a KML file; KML is an XML representation of geographic information. The essential features of the parser look similar to the following command snippet:

```
def comma_split(text):
    return text.split(",")
def row_iter_kml(file_obj):
    ns_map={
        "ns0": "http://www.opengis.net/kml/2.2",
        "ns1": "http://www.google.com/kml/ext/2.2"}
    doc= XML.parse(file_obj)
```

```
    return (comma_split(coordinates.text)
            for coordinates in
            doc.findall("./ns0:Document/ns0:Folder/ns0:Placemark
            /ns0:Point/ns0:coordinates", ns_map)
```

The bulk of the `row_iter_kml()` function is the XML parsing that allows us to use the `doc.findall()` function to iterate through the `<ns0:coordinates>` tags in the document. We've used a function named `comma_split()` to parse the text of this tag into a three tuple of values.

This is focused on working with the normalized XML structure. The document mostly fits the database designer's definitions of **First Normal Form**, that is, each attribute is atomic and only a single value. Each row in the XML data had the same columns with data of a consistent type. The data values weren't properly atomic; we had to split the points on a "," to separate longitude, latitude, and altitude into atomic string values.

A large volume of data – xml tags, attributes, and other punctuation – was reduced to a somewhat smaller volume including just floating-point latitude and longitude values. For this reason, we can think of parsers as a kind of reduction.

We'll need a higher-level set of conversions to map the tuples of text into floating-point numbers. Also, we'd like to discard altitude, and reorder longitude and latitude. This will produce the application-specific tuple we need. We can use functions as follows for this conversion:

```
def pick_lat_lon(lon, lat, alt):
    return lat, lon
def float_lat_lon(row_iter):
    return (tuple(map(float, pick_lat_lon(*row)))
        for row in row_iter)
```

The essential tool is the `float_lat_lon()` function. This is a higher-order function which returns a generator expression. The generator uses `map()` function to apply the `float()` function conversion to the results of `pick_lat_lon()` class. We've used the `*row` parameter to assign each member of the row `tuple` to a different parameter of the `pick_lat_lon()` function. This function then returns a tuple of the selected items in the required order.

We can use this parser as follows:

```
with urllib.request.urlopen("file:./Winter%202012-2013.kml") as
source:
    trip = tuple(float_lat_lon(row_iter_kml(source)))
```

This will build a tuple-of-tuple representation of each waypoint along the path in the original KML file. It uses a low-level parser to extract rows of text data from the original representation. It uses a high-level parser to transform the text items into more useful tuples of floating-point values. In this case, we have not implemented any validation.

Parsing CSV files

In *Chapter 3, Functions, Iterators and Generators*, we saw another example where we parsed a CSV file that was not in a normalized form: we had to discard header rows to make it useful. To do this, we used a simple function that extracted the header and returned an iterator over the remaining rows.

The data looks as follows:

```
Anscombe's quartet
I    II   III   IV
x   y   x   y   x   y   x   y
10.0   8.04   10.0   9.14   10.0   7.46   8.0   6.58
8.0   6.95   8.0   8.14   8.0   6.77   8.0   5.76
...
5.0   5.68   5.0   4.74   5.0   5.73   8.0   6.89
```

The columns are separated by tab characters. Plus there are three rows of headers that we can discard.

Here's another version of that CSV-based parser. We've broken it into three functions. The first, row_iter() function, returns the iterator over the rows in a tab-delimited file. The function looks as follows:

```
def row_iter_csv(source):
    rdr= csv.reader(source, delimiter="\t")
    return rdr
```

This is a simple wrapper around the CSV parsing process. When we look back at the previous parsers for XML and plain text, this was the kind of thing that was missing from those parsers. Producing an iterable over row tuples can be a common feature of parsers for normalized data.

Once we have a row of tuples, we can pass rows that contain usable data and reject rows that contain other metadata, like titles and column names. We'll introduce a helper function that we can use to do some of the parsing, plus a filter() function to validate a row of data.

Following is the conversion:

```
def float_none(data):
    try:
        data_f= float(data)
        return data_f
    except ValueError:
        return None
```

This function handles the conversion of a single `string` to `float` values, converting bad data to `None` value. We can embed this function in a mapping so that we convert all columns of a row to a `float` or `None` value. The `lambda` looks as follows:

```
float_row = lambda row: list(map(float_none, row))
```

Following is a row-level validator based on the use of the `all()` function to assure that all values are `float` (or none of the values are `None`):

```
all_numeric = lambda row: all(row) and len(row) == 8
```

Following is a higher-order function which combines the row-level conversion and filtering:

```
def head_filter_map(validator, converter, validator, row_iter):
    return filter(all_validator, map(converter, row_iter))
```

This function gives us a slightly more complete pattern for parsing an input file. The foundation is a lower-level function that iterates over tuples of text. We can then wrap this in functions to convert and validate the converted data. For the cases where files are either in first normal form (all rows are the same) or a simple validator can reject the other rows, this design works out nicely.

All parsing problems aren't quite this simple, however. Some files have important data in header or trailer rows that must be preserved, even though it doesn't match the format of the rest of the file. These non-normalized files will require a more sophisticated parser design.

Parsing plain text files with headers

In *Chapter 3, Functions, Iterators, and Generators*, the `Crayola.GPL` file was presented without showing the parser. This file looks as follows:

```
GIMP Palette
Name: Crayola
Columns: 16
```

```
#
239 222 205    Almond
205 149 117    Antique Brass
```

We can parse a text file using regular expressions. We need to use a filter to read (and parse) header rows. We also want to return an iterable sequence of data rows. This rather complex two-part parsing is based entirely on the two-part – head and tail – file structure.

Following is a low-level parser that handles both head and tail:

```
def row_iter_gpl(file_obj):
    header_pat= re.compile(r"GIMP
    Palette\nName:\s*(.*?)\nColumns:\s*(.*?)\n#\n", re.M)

    def read_head(file_obj):
        match= header_pat.match("".join( file_obj.readline() for _ in
        range(4)))
        return (match.group(1), match.group(2)), file_obj

    def read_tail(headers, file_obj):
        return headers, (next_line.split() for next_line in file_obj)

    return read_tail(*read_head(file_obj))
```

We've defined a regular expression that parses all four lines of the header, and assigned this to the header_pat variable. There are two internal functions for parsing different parts of the file. The read_head() function parses the header lines. It does this by reading four lines and merging them into a single long string. This is then parsed with the regular expression. The results include the two data items from the header plus an iterator ready to process additional lines.

The read_tail() function accepts the output from the read_head() function and parses the iterator over the remaining lines. The parsed information from the header rows forms a two tuple that is given to the read_tail() function along with the iterator over the remaining lines. The remaining lines are merely split on spaces, since that fits the description of the GPL file format.

For more information, visit the following link:
https://code.google.com/p/grafx2/issues/detail?id=518.

Once we've transformed each line of the file into a canonical tuple-of-strings format, we can apply the higher level of parsing to this data. This involves conversion and (if necessary) validation.

Following is a higher-level parser command snippet:

```
def color_palette(headers, row_iter):
    name, columns = headers
    colors = tuple(Color(int(r), int(g), int(b), " ".join(name))
        for r,g,b,*name in row_iter)
    return name, columns, colors
```

This function will work with the output of the lower-level `row_iter_gpl()` parser: it requires the headers and the iterator. This function will use the multiple assignment to separate the `color` numbers and the remaining words into four variables, `r`, `g`, `b`, and `name`. The use of the `*name` parameter assures that all remaining values will be assigned to names as a `tuple`. The `" ".join(name)` method then concatenates the words into a single space-separated string.

Following is how we can use this two-tier parser:

```
with open("crayola.gpl") as source:
    name, columns, colors = color_palette(*row_iter_gpl(source))
    print(name, columns, colors)
```

We've applied the higher-level parser to the results of the lower-level parser. This will return the headers and a tuple built from the sequence of `Color` objects.

Summary

In this chapter, we've looked at two significant functional programming topics. We've looked at recursions in some detail. Many functional programming language compilers will optimize a recursive function to transform a call in the tail of the function to a loop. In Python, we must do the tail-call optimization manually by using an explicit `for` loop instead of a purely function recursion.

We've also looked at reduction algorithms including `sum()`, `count()`, `max()`, and `min()` functions. We looked at the `collections.Counter()` function and related `groupby()` reductions.

We've also looked at how parsing (and lexical scanning) are similar to reductions since they transform sequences of tokens (or sequences of characters) into higher-order collections with more complex properties. We've examined a design pattern that decomposes parsing into a lower level that tries to produce tuples of raw strings and a higher level that creates more useful application objects.

In the next chapter, we'll look at some techniques appropriate to working with namedtuples and other immutable data structures. We'll look at techniques that make stateful objects unnecessary. While stateful objects aren't purely functional, the idea of a class hierarchy can be used to package related method function definitions.

7
Additional Tuple Techniques

Many of the examples we've looked at have either been `scalar` functions, or relatively simple structures built from small tuples. We can often exploit Python's immutable `namedtuple` as a way to build complex data structures. We'll look at how we use and how we create `namedtuples`. We'll also look at ways that immutable `namedtuples` can be used instead of stateful object classes.

One of the beneficial features of object-oriented programming is the ability to create complex data structures incrementally. In some respects, an object is simply a cache for results of functions; this will often fit well with functional design patterns. In other cases, the object paradigm provides for property methods that include sophisticated calculations. This is an even better fit for functional design ideas.

In some cases, however, object class definitions are used statefully to create complex objects. We'll look at a number of alternatives that provide similar features without the complexities of stateful objects. We can identify stateful class definitions and then include meta-properties for valid or required ordering of method function calls. Statements such as *If X.p() is called before X.q(), the results are undefined* are outside the formalism of the language and are meta-properties of a class. Sometimes, stateful classes include the overhead of explicit assertions and error checking to assure that methods are used in the proper order. If we avoid stateful classes, we eliminate these kinds of overheads.

We'll also look at some techniques to write generic functions outside any polymorphic class definition. Clearly, we can rely on `Callable` classes to create a polymorphic class hierarchy. In some cases, this might be a needless overhead in a functional design.

Using an immutable namedtuple as a record

In *Chapter 3, Functions, Iterators, and Generators,* we showed two common techniques to work with tuples. We've also hinted at a third way to handle complex structures. We can do any of the following, depending on the circumstances:

- Use `lambdas` (or functions) to select a named item using the index
- Use `lambdas` (or functions) with `*parameter` to select an item by parameter name, which maps to an index
- Use `namedtuples` to select an item by attribute name or index

Our trip data, introduced in *Chapter 4, Working with Collections,* has a rather complex structure. The data started as an ordinary time series of position reports. To compute the distances covered, we transposed the data into a sequence of legs with a start position, end position, and distance as a nested three-tuple.

Each item in the sequence of legs looks as follows as a three-tuple:

```
first_leg= ((37.54901619777347, -76.33029518659048), (37.840832,
-76.273834), 17.7246)
```

This is a short trip between two points on the Chesapeake Bay.

A nested tuple of tuples can be rather difficult to read; for example, expressions such as `first_leg[0][0]` aren't very informative.

Let's look at the three alternatives for selected values out of a `tuple`. The first technique involves defining some simple selection functions that can pick items from a `tuple` by index position:

```
start= lambda leg: leg[0]

end= lambda leg: leg[1]

distance= lambda leg: leg[2]

latitude= lambda pt: pt[0]

longitude= lambda pt: pt[1]
```

With these definitions, we can use `latitude(start(first_leg))` to refer to a specific piece of data.

These definitions don't provide much guidance on the data types involved. We can use a simple naming convention to make this a bit more clear. The following are some examples of selection functions that use a suffix:

```
start_point = lambda leg: leg[0]
distance_nm= lambda leg: leg[2]
latitude_value= lambda point: point[0]
```

When used judiciously, this can be helpful. It can also degenerate into an elaborately complex Hungarian notation as a prefix (or suffix) of each variable.

The second technique uses the `*parameter` notation to conceal some details of the index positions. The following are some selection functions that use the `*` notation:

```
start= lambda start, end, distance: start
end= lambda start, end, distance: end
distance= lambda start, end, distance: distance
latitude= lambda lat, lon: lat
longitude= lambda lat, lon: lon
```

With these definitions, we can use `latitude(*start(*first_leg))` to refer to a specific piece of data. This has the advantage of clarity. It can look a little odd to see the `*` operator in front of the `tuple` arguments to these selection functions.

The third technique is the `namedtuple` function. In this case, we have nested namedtuple functions such as the following:

```
Leg = namedtuple("Leg", ("start", "end", "distance"))
Point = namedtuple("Point", ("latitude", "longitude"))
```

This allows us to use `first_leg.start.latitude` to fetch a particular piece of data. The change from prefix function names to postfix attribute names can be seen as a helpful emphasis. It can also be seen as a confusing shift in the syntax.

We will also replace `tuple()` functions with appropriate `Leg()` or `Point()` function calls in our process that builds the raw data. We will also have to locate some `return` and `yield` statements that implicitly create tuples.

For example, take a look at the following code snippet:

```
def float_lat_lon(row_iter):
    return (tuple(map(float, pick_lat_lon(*row)))
    for row in row_iter)
```

The preceding code would be changed to the following code snippet:

```
def float_lat_lon(row_iter):
    return (Point(*map(float, pick_lat_lon(*row)))
    for row in row_iter)
```

This would build `Point` objects instead of anonymous tuples of `floating-point` coordinates.

Similarly, we can introduce the following to build the complete trip of `Leg` objects:

```
with urllib.request.urlopen("file:./Winter%202012-2013.kml") as
source:
    path_iter = float_lat_lon(row_iter_kml(source))
    pair_iter = legs(path_iter)
    trip_iter = (Leg(start, end, round(haversine(start, end),4))
    for start,end in pair_iter)
    trip= tuple(trip_iter)
```

This will iterate through the basic path of points, pairing them up to make `start` and `end` for each `Leg` object. These pairs are then used to build `Leg` instances using the start point, end point, and the `haversine()` function from *Chapter 4, Working with Collections*.

The `trip` object will look as follows when we try to print it:

```
(Leg(start=Point(latitude=37.54901619777347, longitude=
-76.33029518659048), end=Point(latitude=37.840832, longitude=
-76.273834), distance=17.7246),
Leg(start=Point(latitude=37.840832, longitude=-76.273834),
end=Point(latitude=38.331501, longitude=-76.459503),
distance=30.7382),
...

Leg(start=Point(latitude=38.330166, longitude=-76.458504),
end=Point(latitude=38.976334, longitude=-76.473503),
distance=38.8019))
```

 It's important to note that the `haversine()` function was written to use simple tuples. We've reused this function with `namedtuples`. As we carefully preserved the order the arguments, this small change in representation was handled gracefully by Python.

In some cases, the `namedtuple` function adds clarity. In other cases, the `namedtuple` is a needless change in syntax from prefix to suffix.

Building namedtuples with functional constructors

There are three ways we can build `namedtuple` instances. The choice of technique we use is generally based on how much additional information is available at the time of object construction.

We've shown two of the three techniques in the examples in the previous section. We'll emphasize the design considerations here. It includes the following choices:

- We can provide the parameter values according to their positions. This works out well when there are one or more expressions that we were evaluating. We used it when applying the `haversine()` function to the `start` and `end` points to create a `Leg` object.

  ```
  Leg(start, end, round(haversine(start, end),4))
  ```

- We can use the `*argument` notation to assign parameters according to their positions in a tuple. This works out well when we're getting the arguments from another iterable or an existing tuple. We used it when using `map()` to apply the `float()` function to the `latitude` and `longitude` values.

  ```
  Point(*map(float, pick_lat_lon(*row)))
  ```

- We can use explicit keyword assignment. While not used in the previous example, we might see something like this as a way to make the relationships more obvious:

  ```
  Point(longitude=float(row[0]), latitude=float(row[1]))
  ```

It's helpful to have the flexibility of a variety of ways of created `namedtuple` instances. This allows us to more easily transform the structure of data. We can emphasize features of the data structure that are relevant for reading and understanding the application. Sometimes, the index number of 0 or 1 is an important thing to emphasize. Other times, the order of `start`, `end`, and `distance` is important.

Avoiding stateful classes by using families of tuples

In several previous examples, we've shown the idea of **Wrap-Unwrap** design patterns that allow us to work with immutable tuples and `namedtuples`. The point of this kind of designs is to use immutable objects that wrap other immutable objects instead of mutable instance variables.

A common statistical measure of correlation between two sets of data is the Spearman rank correlation. This compares the rankings of two variables. Rather than trying to compare values, which might have different scales, we'll compare the relative orders. For more information, visit http://en.wikipedia.org/wiki/Spearman%27s_rank_correlation_coefficient.

Computing the Spearman rank correlation requires assigning a rank value to each observation. It seems like we should be able to use enumerate(sorted()) to do this. Given two sets of possibly correlated data, we can transform each set into a sequence of rank values and compute a measure of correlation.

We'll apply the Wrap-Unwrap design pattern to do this. We'll wrap data items with their rank for the purposes of computing the correlation coefficient.

In *Chapter 3, Functions, Iterators, and Generators*, we showed how to parse a simple dataset. We'll extract the four samples from that dataset as follows:

```
from ch03_ex5 import series, head_map_filter, row_iter
with open("Anscombe.txt") as source:
    data = tuple(head_map_filter(row_iter(source)))
    series_I= tuple(series(0,data))
    series_II= tuple(series(1,data))
    series_III= tuple(series(2,data))
    series_IV= tuple(series(3,data))
```

Each of these series is a tuple of Pair objects. Each Pair object has x and y attributes. The data looks as follows:

```
(Pair(x=10.0, y=8.04), Pair(x=8.0, y=6.95), ..., Pair(x=5.0, y=5.68))
```

We can apply the enumerate() function to create sequences of values as follows:

```
y_rank= tuple(enumerate(sorted(series_I, key=lambda p: p.y)))
xy_rank= tuple(enumerate(sorted(y_rank, key=lambda rank: rank[1].x)))
```

The first step will create simple two-tuples with (0) a rank number and (1) the original Pair object. As the data was sorted by the y value in each pair, the rank value will reflect this ordering.

The sequence will look as follows:

```
((0, Pair(x=8.0, y=5.25)), (1, Pair(x=8.0, y=5.56)), ...,
(10, Pair(x=19.0, y=12.5)))
```

The second step will wrap these two-tuples into yet another layer of wrapping. We'll sort by the *x* value in the original raw data. The second enumeration will be by the *x* value in each pair.

We'll create more deeply nested objects that should look like the following:

```
((0, (0, Pair(x=4.0, y=4.26))), (1, (2, Pair(x=5.0, y=5.68))), ...,
(10, (9, Pair(x=14.0, y=9.96)))))
```

In principle, we can now compute rank-order correlations between the two variables by using the *x* and *y* rankings. The extraction expression, however, is rather awkward. For each ranked sample in the data set, r, we have to compare r[0] with r[1][0].

To overcome these awkward references, we can write selector functions as follows:

```
x_rank = lambda ranked: ranked[0]

y_rank= lambda ranked: ranked[1][0]

raw = lambda ranked: ranked[1][1]
```

This allows us to compute correlation using x_rank(r) and y_rank(r), making references to values less awkward.

We've wrapped the original Pair object twice, which created new tuples with the ranking value. We've avoided stateful class definitions to create complex data structures incrementally.

Why create deeply nested tuples? The answer is simple: laziness. The processing required to unpack a tuple and build a new, flat tuple is simply time consuming. There's less processing involved in wrapping an existing tuple. There are some compelling reasons for giving up the deeply nested structure.

There are two improvements we'd like to make; they are as follows:

We'd like a flatter data structure. The use of a nested tuple of (x rank, (y rank, Pair())) doesn't feel expressive or succinct:

- The enumerate() function doesn't deal properly with ties. If two observations have the same value, they should get the same rank. The general rule is to average the positions of equal observations. The sequence [0.8, 1.2, 1.2, 2.3, 18] should have rank values of 1, 2.5, 2.5, 4. The two ties in positions 2 and 3 have the midpoint value of 2.5 as their common rank.

Assigning statistical ranks

We'll break the rank ordering problem into two parts. First, we'll look at a generic, higher-order function that we can use to assign ranks to either the *x* or *y* value of a Pair object. Then, we'll use this to create a wrapper around the Pair object that includes both *x* and *y* rankings. This will avoid a deeply nested structure.

The following is a function that will create a rank order for each observation in a dataset:

```
from collections import defaultdict
def rank(data, key=lambda obj:obj):
    def rank_output(duplicates, key_iter, base=0):
        for k in key_iter:
            dups= len(duplicates[k])
            for value in duplicates[k]:
                yield (base+1+base+dups)/2, value
            base += dups
    def build_duplicates(duplicates, data_iter, key):
        for item in data_iter:
            duplicates[key(item)].append(item)
        return duplicates
    duplicates= build_duplicates(defaultdict(list), iter(data), key)
    return rank_output(duplicates, iter(sorted(duplicates)), 0)
```

Our function to create the rank ordering relies on creating an object that is like Counter to discover duplicate values. We can't use a simple Counter function, as it uses the entire object to create a collection. We only want to use a key function applied to each object. This allows us to pick either the *x* or *y* value of a Pair object.

The duplicates collection in this example is a stateful object. We could have written a properly recursive function. We'd then have to do tail-call optimization to allow working with large collections of data. We've shown the optimized version of that recursion here.

As a hint to how this recursion would look, we've provided the arguments to build_ duplicates() that expose the state as argument values. Clearly, the base case for the recursion is when data_iter is empty. When data_iter is not empty, a new collection is built from the old collection and the head next(data_iter). A recursive evaluation of build_duplicates() will handle all items in the tail of data_iter.

Similarly, we could have written two properly recursive functions to emit the collection with the assigned rank values. Again, we've optimized that recursion into nested `for` loops. To make it clear how we're computing the rank value, we've included the low end of the range (`base+1`) and the high end of the range (`base+dups`) and taken the midpoint of these two values. If there is only a single `duplicate`, we evaluate `(2*base+2)/2`, which has the advantage of being a general solution.

The following is how we can test this to be sure it works.

```
>>> list(rank([0.8, 1.2, 1.2, 2.3, 18]))
[(1.0, 0.8), (2.5, 1.2), (2.5, 1.2), (4.0, 2.3), (5.0, 18)]
>>> data= ((2, 0.8), (3, 1.2), (5, 1.2), (7, 2.3), (11, 18))
>>> list(rank(data, key=lambda x:x[1]))
[(1.0, (2, 0.8)), (2.5, (3, 1.2)), (2.5, (5, 1.2)), (4.0, (7, 2.3)),
(5.0, (11, 18))]
```

The sample data included two identical values. The resulting ranks split positions 2 and 3 to assign position 2.5 to both values. This is the common statistical practice for computing the Spearman rank-order correlation between two sets of values.

> The `rank()` function involves rearranging the input data as part of discovering duplicated values. If we want to rank on both the x and y values in each pair, we need to reorder the data twice.

Wrapping instead of state changing

We have two general strategies to do wrapping; they are as follows:

- **Parallelism**: We can create two copies of the data and rank each copy. We then need to reassemble the two copies into a final result that includes both rankings. This can be a bit awkward because we'll need to somehow merge two sequences that are likely to be in different orders.

- **Serialism**: We can compute ranks on one variable and save the results as a wrapper that includes the original raw data. We can then rank this wrapped data on the other variable. While this can create a complex structure, we can optimize it slightly to create a flatter wrapper for the final results.

The following is how we can create an object that wraps a pair with the rank order based on the y value:

```
Ranked_Y= namedtuple("Ranked_Y", ("r_y", "raw",))
def rank_y(pairs):
    return (Ranked_Y(*row)
    for row in rank(pairs, lambda pair: pair.y))
```

We've defined a `namedtuple` function that contains the y value rank plus the original (raw) value. Our `rank_y()` function will create instances of this tuple by applying the `rank()` function using a `lambda` that selects the y value of each `pairs` object. We then created instances of the resulting two tuples.

The idea is that we can provide the following input:

```
>>> data = (Pair(x=10.0, y=8.04), Pair(x=8.0, y=6.95), ...,
Pair(x=5.0, y=5.68))
```

We can get the following output:

```
>>> list(rank_y(data))
[Ranked_Y(r_y=1.0, raw=Pair(x=4.0, y=4.26)),
Ranked_Y(r_y=2.0, raw=Pair(x=7.0, y=4.82)), ...
Ranked_Y(r_y=11.0, raw=Pair(x=12.0, y=10.84))]
```

The raw `Pair` objects have been wrapped in a new object that includes the rank. This isn't all we need; we'll need to wrap this one more time to create an object that has both x and y rank information.

Rewrapping instead of state changing

We can use a `namedtuple` named `Ranked_X` that contains two attributes: `r_x` and `ranked_y`. The `ranked_y` attribute is an instance of `Ranked_Y` that has two attributes: `r_y` and `raw`. Although this looks simple, the resulting objects are annoying to work with because the `r_x` and `r_y` values aren't simple peers in a flat structure. We'll introduce a slightly more complex wrapping process that produces a slightly simpler result.

We want the output to look like this:

```
Ranked_XY= namedtuple("Ranked_XY", ("r_x", "r_y", "raw",))
```

We're going to create a flat `namedtuple` with multiple peer attributes. This kind of expansion is often easier to work with than deeply nested structures. In some applications, we might have a number of transformations. For this application, we have only two transformations: x-ranking and y-ranking. We'll break this into two steps. First, we'll look at a simplistic wrapping like the one shown previously and then a more general unwrap-rewrap.

The following is how the `x-y` ranking builds on the y-ranking:

```
def rank_xy(pairs):
    return (Ranked_XY(r_x=r_x, r_y=rank_y_raw[0],
    raw=rank_y_raw[1])
        for r_x, rank_y_raw in rank(rank_y(pairs),
        lambda r: r.raw.x))
```

We've used the `rank_y()` function to build `Rank_Y` objects. Then, we applied the `rank()` function to those objects to order them by the original x values. The result of the second rank function will be two tuples with `(0)` the x rank and `(1)` the `Rank_Y` object. We build a `Ranked_XY` object from the x ranking (`r_x`), the y ranking (`rank_y_raw[0]`), and the original object (`rank_y_raw[1]`).

What we've shown in this second function is a more general approach to adding data to a `tuple`. The construction of the `Ranked_XY` object shows how to unwrap the values from a data and rewrap to create a second, more complete structure. This approach can be used generally to introduce new variables to a `tuple`.

The following is some sample data:

```
>>> data = (Pair(x=10.0, y=8.04), Pair(x=8.0, y=6.95), ...,
Pair(x=5.0, y=5.68))
```

This allows us to create ranking objects as follows:

```
>>> list(rank_xy(data))
[Ranked_XY(r_x=1.0, r_y=1.0, raw=Pair(x=4.0, y=4.26)),
Ranked_XY(r_x=2.0, r_y=3.0, raw=Pair(x=5.0, y=5.68)), ...,

Ranked_XY(r_x=11.0, r_y=10.0, raw=Pair(x=14.0, y=9.96))]
```

Once we have this data with the appropriate *x* and *y* rankings, we can compute the Spearman rank-order correlation value. We can compute the Pearson correlation from the raw data.

Our multiranking approach involves decomposing a `tuple` and building a new, flat `tuple` with the additional attributes we need. We will often need this kind of design when computing multiple derived values from source data.

Computing the Spearman rank-order correlation

The Spearman rank-order correlation is a comparison between the rankings of two variables. It neatly bypasses the magnitude of the values, and it can often find a correlation even when the relationship is not linear. The formula is as follows:

$$\rho = 1 - \frac{6 \sum \left(r_x - r_y \right)^2}{n\left(n^2 - 1\right)}$$

This formula shows us that we'll be summing the differences in rank, x_i and y_i, for all of the pairs of observed values. The Python version of this depends on the `sum()` and `len()` functions, as follows:

```
def rank_corr(pairs):
    ranked= rank_xy(pairs)
    sum_d_2 = sum((r.r_x - r.r_y)**2 for r in ranked)
    n = len(pairs)
    return 1-6*sum_d_2/(n*(n**2-1))
```

We've created `Rank_XY` objects for each `pair`. Given this, we can then subtract the `r_x` and `r_y` values from those pairs to compare their difference. We can then square and sum the differences.

A good article on statistics will provide detailed guidance on what the coefficient means. A value around 0 means that there is no correlation between the data ranks of the two series of data points. A scatter plot shows a random scattering of points. A value around +1 or -1 indicates a strong relationship between the two values. A graph shows a clear line or curve.

The following is an example based on Anscombe's Quartet series I:

```
>>> data = (Pair(x=10.0, y=8.04), Pair(x=8.0, y=6.95), ...,
Pair(x=5.0, y=5.68))
>>> round(rank_corr( data ), 3)
0.818
```

For this particular data set, the correlation is strong.

In *Chapter 4, Working with Collections*, we showed how to compute the Pearson correlation coefficient. The function we showed, `corr()`, worked with two separate sequences of values. We can use it with our sequence of `Pair` objects as follows:

```
import ch04_ex4
def pearson_corr(pairs):
    X = tuple(p.x for p in pairs)
    Y = tuple(p.y for p in pairs)
    return ch04_ex4.corr(X, Y)
```

We've unwrapped the `Pair` objects to get the raw values that we can use with the existing `corr()` function. This provides a different correlation coefficient. The Pearson value is based on how well the standardized values compare between two sequences. For many data sets, the difference between the Pearson and Spearman correlations is relatively small. For some datasets, however, the differences can be quite large.

To see the importance of having multiple statistical tools for exploratory data analysis, compare the Spearman and Pearson correlations for the four sets of data in the Anscombe's Quartet.

Polymorphism and Pythonic pattern matching

Some functional programming languages offer clever approaches to working with statically typed function definitions. The issue is that many functions we'd like to write are entirely generic with respect to data type. For example, most of our statistical functions are identical for `integer` or `floating-point` numbers, as long as division returns a value that is a subclass of `numbers.Real` (for example, `Decimal`, `Fraction`, or `float`). In order to make a single generic definition work for multiple data types, sophisticated type or pattern-matching rules are used by the compiler.

Instead of the (possibly) complex features of statically typed functional languages, Python changes the issue using dynamic selection of the final implementation of an operator based on the data types being used. This means that a compiler doesn't certify that our functions are expecting and producing the proper data types. We generally rely on unit testing for this.

In Python, we're effectively writing generic definitions because the code isn't bound to any specific data type. The Python runtime will locate the appropriate operations using a simple set of matching rules. The *3.3.7 Coercion rules* section of the language reference manual and the `numbers` module in the library provide details on how this mapping from operation to special method name works.

In rare cases, we might need to have different behavior based on the types of the data elements. We have two ways to tackle this; they are as follows:

- We can use the `isinstance()` function to distinguish the different cases
- We can create our own subclass of `numbers.Number` or `tuple` and implement a proper polymorphic special method names

In some cases, we'll actually need to do both so that we can include appropriate data type conversions.

When we look back at the ranking example in the previous section, we're tightly bound to the idea of applying rank-ordering to simple pairs. While this is the way the Spearman correlation is defined, we might have a multivariate dataset and have a need to do rank-order correlation among all the variables.

The first thing we'll need to do is generalize our idea of rank-order information. The following is a `namedtuple` that handles a `tuple` of ranks and a `tuple` of raw data:

```
Rank_Data = namedtuple("Rank_Data", ("rank_seq", "raw"))
```

For any specific piece of `Rank_Data`, such as `r`, we can use `r.rank_seq[0]` to get a specific ranking and `r.raw` to get the original observation.

We'll add some syntactic sugar to our ranking function. In many previous examples, we've required either an iterable or a collection. The `for` statement is graceful about working with either one. However, we don't always use the `for` statement, and for some functions, we've had to explicitly use `iter()` to make an `iterable` out of a collection. We can handle this situation with a simple `isinstance()` check, as shown in the following code snippet:

```
def some_function(seq_or_iter):
    if not isinstance(seq_or_iter,collections.abc.Iterator):
        yield from some_function(iter(seq_or_iter), key)
        return
    # Do the real work of the function using the iterable
```

We've included a type check to handle the small difference between the two collections, which doesn't work with `next()` and an `iterable`, which supports `next()`.

In the context of our rank-ordering function, we will use this variation on the design pattern:

```
def rank_data(seq_or_iter, key=lambda obj:obj):
    # Not a sequence? Materialize a sequence object
    if isinstance(seq_or_iter, collections.abc.Iterator):
```

```
        yield from rank_data(tuple(seq_or_iter), key)
    data = seq_or_iter
    head= seq_or_iter[0]
    # Convert to Rank_Data and process.
    if not isinstance(head, Rank_Data):
        ranked= tuple(Rank_Data((),d) for d in data)
        for r, rd in rerank(ranked, key):
            yield Rank_Data(rd.rank_seq+(r,), rd.raw)
        return
    # Collection of Rank_Data is what we prefer.
    for r, rd in rerank(data, key):
        yield Rank_Data(rd.rank_seq+(r,), rd.raw)
```

We've decomposed the ranking into three cases for three different types of data. We're forced it to do this when the different kinds of data aren't polymorphic subclasses of a common superclass. The following are the three cases:

- Given an `iterable` (without a usable `__getitem__()` method), we'll materialize a `tuple` that we can work with

- Given a collection of some unknown type of data, we'll wrap the unknown objects into `Rank_Data` tuples

- Finally, given a collection of `Rank_Data` tuples, we'll add yet another ranking to the tuple of ranks inside the each `Rank_Data` container

This relies on a `rerank()` function that inserts and returns another ranking into the `Rank_Data` tuple. This will build up a collection of individual rankings from a complex record of raw data values. The `rerank()` function follows a slightly different design than the example of the `rank()` function shown previously.

This version of the algorithm uses sorting instead of creating a groups in a objects like `Counter` object:

```
def rerank(rank_data_collection, key):
    sorted_iter= iter(sorted( rank_data_collection, key=lambda
    obj: key(obj.raw)))
    head = next(sorted_iter)
    yield from ranker(sorted_iter, 0, [head], key)
```

We've started by reassembling a single, sortable collection from the head and the data iterator. In the context in which this is used, we can argue that this is a bad idea.

This function relies on two other functions. They can be declared within the body of `rerank()`. We'll show them separately. The following is the ranker, which accepts an iterable, a base rank number, a collection of values with the same rank, and a key:

```
def ranker(sorted_iter, base, same_rank_seq, key):
    """Rank values from a sorted_iter using a base rank value.
    If the next value's key matches same_rank_seq, accumulate those.
    If the next value's key is different, accumulate same rank values
    and start accumulating a new sequence.
    """
    try:
        value= next(sorted_iter)
    except StopIteration:
        dups= len(same_rank_seq)
        yield from yield_sequence((base+1+base+dups)/2,
        iter(same_rank_seq))
        return
    if key(value.raw) == key(same_rank_seq[0].raw):
        yield from ranker(sorted_iter, base, same_rank_seq+[value],
        key)
    else:
        dups= len(same_rank_seq)
        yield from yield_sequence( (base+1+base+dups)/2,
        iter(same_rank_seq))
        yield from ranker(sorted_iter, base+dups, [value], key)
```

We've extracted the next item from the `iterable` collection of sorted values. If this fails, there is no next item, and we need to emit the final collection of equal-valued items in the `same_rank_seq` sequence. If this works, then we need to use the `key()` function to see whether the next item, which is a value, has the same key as the collection of equal-ranked items. If the key is the same, the overall value is defined recursively; the reranking is the rest of the sorted items, the same base value for the rank, a larger collection of `same_rank` items, and the same `key()` function.

If the next item's key doesn't match the sequence of equal-valued items, the result is a sequence of equal-valued items. This will be followed by the reranking of the rest of the sorted items, a base value incremented by the number of equal-valued items, a fresh list of equal-rank items with just the new value, and the same `key` extraction function.

This depends on the `yield_sequence()` function, which looks as follows:

```
def yield_sequence(rank, same_rank_iter):
    head= next(same_rank_iter)
    yield rank, head
    yield from yield_sequence(rank, same_rank_iter)
```

We've written this in a way that emphasizes the recursive definition. We don't really need to extract the head, emit it, and then recursively emit the remaining items. While a single `for` statement might be shorter, it's sometimes more clear to emphasize the recursive structure that has been optimized into a `for` loop.

The following are some examples of using this function to rank (and rerank) data. We'll start with a simple collection of scalar values:

```
>>> scalars= [0.8, 1.2, 1.2, 2.3, 18]
>>> list(ranker(scalars))
[Rank_Data(rank_seq=(1.0,), raw=0.8), Rank_Data(rank_seq=(2.5,),
raw=1.2), Rank_Data(rank_seq=(2.5,), raw=1.2), Rank_Data(rank_seq=(4.0,),
raw=2.3), Rank_Data(rank_seq=(5.0,),
raw=18)]
```

Each value becomes the `raw` attribute of a `Rank_Data` object.

When we work with a slightly more complex object, we can also have multiple rankings. The following is a sequence of two tuples:

```
>>> pairs= ((2, 0.8), (3, 1.2), (5, 1.2), (7, 2.3), (11, 18))
>>> rank_x= tuple(ranker(pairs, key=lambda x:x[0] ))
>>> rank_x
(Rank_Data(rank_seq=(1.0,), raw=(2, 0.8)), Rank_Data(rank_seq=(2.0,),
raw=(3, 1.2)), Rank_Data(rank_seq=(3.0,), raw=(5, 1.2)),
Rank_Data(rank_seq=(4.0,), raw=(7, 2.3)), Rank_Data(rank_seq=(5.0,),
raw=(11, 18)))
>>> rank_xy= (ranker(rank_x, key=lambda x:x[1] ))
>>> tuple(rank_xy)
(Rank_Data(rank_seq=(1.0, 1.0), raw=(2, 0.8)),
 Rank_Data(rank_seq=(2.0, 2.5), raw=(3, 1.2)),
Rank_Data(rank_seq=(3.0, 2.5), raw=(5, 1.2)),
Rank_Data(rank_seq=(4.0, 4.0), raw=(7, 2.3)), Rank_Data(rank_seq=(5.0,
5.0), raw=(11, 18)))
```

Here, we defined a collection of pairs. Then, we ranked the two tuples, assigning the sequence of `Rank_Data` objects to the `rank_x` variable. We then ranked this collection of `Rank_Data` objects, creating a second rank value and assigning the result to the `rank_xy` variable.

The resulting sequence can be used to a slightly modified `rank_corr()` function to compute the rank correlations of any of the available values in the `rank_seq` attribute of the `Rank_Data` objects. We'll leave this modification as an exercise for the readers.

Summary

In this chapter, we looked at different ways to use `namedtuple` objects to implement more complex data structures. The essential features of a `namedtuple` are a good fit with functional design. They can be created with a creation function and accessed by position as well as name.

We looked at how to use immutable `namedtuples` instead of stateful object definitions. The core technique was to wrap an object in an immutable `tuple` to provide additional attribute values.

We also looked at ways to handle multiple data types in Python. For most arithmetic operations, Python's internal method dispatch locates proper implementations. To work with collections, however, we might want to handle iterators and sequences slightly differently.

In the next two chapters, we'll look at the `itertools` module. This `library` module provides a number of functions that help us work with iterators in sophisticated ways. Many of these tools are examples of higher-order functions. They can help make a functional design stay succinct and expressive.

8

The Itertools Module

Functional programming emphasizes stateless programming. In Python this leads us to work with generator expressions, generator functions, and iterables. In this chapter, we'll look at the itertools library with numerous functions to help us work with iterable collections.

We introduced iterator functions in *Chapter 3*, *Functions, Iterators, and Generators*. In this chapter, we'll expand on that superficial introduction. We used some related functions in *Chapter 5*, *Higher-order Functions*.

 Some of the functions merely behave like they are proper, lazy Python iterables. It's important to look at the implementation details for each of these functions. Some of them create intermediate objects, leading to the potential of consuming a large amount of memory. Since implementations might change with Python releases, we can't provide function-by-function advice here. If you have performance or memory issues, ensure that you check the implementation.

There are a large number of iterator functions in this module. We'll examine some of the functions in the next chapter. In this chapter, we'll look at three broad groupings of iterator functions. These are as follows:

- Functions that work with infinite iterators. These can be applied to any iterable or an iterator over any collection; they will consume the entire source.
- Functions that work with finite iterators. These can either accumulate a source multiple times, or they produce a reduction of the source.
- The tee iterator function which clones an iterator into several copies that can each be used independently. This provides a way to overcome the primary limitation of Python iterators: they can be used once only.

We need to emphasize an important limitation of iterables that we've touched upon in other places.

> Iterables can be used only once.
> This can be astonishing because there's no error. Once exhausted, they appear to have no elements and will raise the StopIteration exception every time they're used.

There are some other features of iterators that aren't such profound limitations. They are as follows:

- There's no len() function for an iterable. In almost every other respect, they appear to be a container.

- Iterables can do next() operations, unlike a container.

- The for statement makes the distinction between containers and iterables invisible; containers will produce an iterable via the iter() function. An iterable simply returns itself.

These points will provide some necessary background for this chapter. The idea of the itertools module is to leverage what iterables can do to create succinct, expressive applications without the complex-looking overheads associated with the details of managing the iterables.

Working with the infinite iterators

The itertools module provides a number of functions that we can use to enhance or enrich an iterable source of data. We'll look at the following three functions:

- count(): This is an unlimited version of the range() function

- cycle(): This will reiterate a cycle of values

- repeat(): This can repeat a single value an indefinite number of times

Our goal is to understand how these various iterator functions can be used in generator expressions and with generator functions.

Counting with count()

The built-in range() function is defined by an upper limit: the lower limit and step values are optional. The count() function, on the other hand, has a start and optional step, but no upper limit.

This function can be thought of as the primitive basis for a function like `enumerate()`. We can define the `enumerate()` function in terms of `zip()` and `count()` functions, as follows:

```
enumerate = lambda x, start=0: zip(count(start),x)
```

The `enumerate()` function behaves as if it's a `zip()` function that uses the `count()` function to generate the values associated with some iterator.

Consequently, the following two commands are equivalent to each other:

```
zip(count(), some_iterator)
```
```
enumerate(some_iterator)
```

Both will emit a sequence of numbers of two tuples paired with items from the iterator.

The `zip()` function is made slightly simpler with the use of the `count()` function, as shown in the following command:

```
zip(count(1,3), some_iterator)
```

This will provide values of 1, 4, 7, 10, and so on, as the identifiers for each value from the enumerator. This is a challenge because `enumerate` doesn't provide a way to change the step.

The following command describes the `enumerate()` function:

```
((1+3*e, x) for e,x in enumerate(a))
```

 The `count()` function permits non-integer values. We can use something like the `count(0.5, 0.1)` method to provide floating-point values. This will accumulate a substantial error if the increment value doesn't have an exact representation. It's generally better to use the `(0.5+x*.1 for x in count())` method to assure that representation errors don't accumulate.

Here's a way to examine the accumulating error. We'll define a function, which will evaluate items from an iterator until some condition is met. Here's how we can define the `until()` function:

```
def until(terminate, iterator):
    i = next(iterator)
    if terminate(*i): return i
    return until(terminate, iterator)
```

We'll get the next value from the iterator. If it passes the test, that's our value. Otherwise, we'll evaluate this function recursively to search for a value that passes the test.

We'll provide a source iterable and a comparison function as follows:

```
source = zip(count(0, .1), (.1*c for c in count()))
neq = lambda x, y: abs(x-y) > 1.0E-12
```

When we evaluate the `until(neq, source)` method, we find the result is as follows:

```
(92.799999999999, 92.80000000000001)
```

After 928 iterations, the sum of the error bits has accumulated to 10^{-12}. Neither value has an exact binary representation.

 The `count()` function is close to the Python recursion limit. We'd need to rewrite our `until()` function to use tail-call optimization to locate counts with larger accumulated errors.

The smallest detectible difference can be computed as follows:

```
>>> until(lambda x, y: x != y, source)
(0.6, 0.6000000000000001)
```

After just six steps, the `count(0, 0.1)` method has accumulated a measurable error of 10^{-16}. Not a large error, but within 1000 steps, it will be considerably larger.

Reiterating a cycle with cycle()

The `cycle()` function repeats a sequence of values. We can imagine using it to solve silly fizz-buzz problems.

Visit http://rosettacode.org/wiki/FizzBuzz for a comprehensive set of solutions to a fairly trivial programming problem. Also see https://projecteuler.net/problem=1 for an interesting variation on this theme.

We can use the `cycle()` function to emit sequences of `True` and `False` values as follows:

```
m3= (i == 0 for i in cycle(range(3)))

m5= (i == 0 for i in cycle(range(5)))
```

If we zip together a finite collection of numbers, we'll get a set of triples with a number, and two flags showing whether or not the number is a multiple of 3 or a multiple of 5. It's important to introduce a finite iterable to create a proper upper bound on the volume of data being generated. Here's a sequence of values and their multiplier flags:

```
multipliers = zip(range(10), m3, m5)
```

We can now decompose the triples and use a filter to pass numbers which are multiples and reject all others:

```
sum(i for i, *multipliers in multipliers if any(multipliers))
```

This function has another, more valuable use for exploratory data analysis.

We often need to work with samples of large sets of data. The initial phases of cleansing and model creation are best developed with small sets of data and tested with larger and larger sets of data. We can use the `cycle()` function to fairly select rows from within a larger set. The population size, N_P, and the desired sample size, N_S, denotes how long we can use a cycle:

$$c = \frac{N_P}{N_S}$$

We'll assume that the data can be parsed with the `csv` module. This leads to an elegant way to create subsets. We can create subsets using the following commands:

```
chooser = (x == 0 for x in cycle(range(c)))
rdr= csv.reader(source_file)
wtr= csv.writer(target_file)
wtr.writerows(row for pick, row in zip(chooser, rdr) if pick)
```

We created a `cycle()` function based on the selection factor, c. For example, we might have a population of 10 million records: a 1,000-record subset involves picking 1/10,000 of the records. We assumed that this snippet of code is nestled securely inside a `with` statement that opens the relevant files. We also avoided showing details of any dialect issues with the CSV format files.

We can use a simple generator expression to filter the data using the `cycle()` function and the source data that's available from the CSV reader. Since the `chooser` expression and the expression used to write the rows are both non-strict, there's little memory overhead from this kind of processing.

We can—with a small change—use the `random.randrange(c)` method instead of the `cycle(c)` method to achieve a randomized selection of a similar sized subset.

We can also rewrite this method to use `compress()`, `filter()`, and `islice()` functions, as we'll see later in this chapter.

This design will also reformat a file from any nonstandard CSV-like format into a standardized CSV format. As long as we define parser functions that return consistently defined tuples and write consumer functions that write tuples to the target files, we can do a great deal of cleansing and filtering with relatively short, clear scripts.

Repeating a single value with repeat()

The `repeat()` function seems like an odd feature: it returns a single value over and over again. It can serve as a replacement for the `cycle()` function. We can extend our data subset selection function using the `repeat(0)` method instead of the `cycle(range(100))` method in an expression line, for example, `(x==0 for x in some_function)`.

We can think of the following commands:

```
all = repeat(0)
subset= cycle(range(100))
chooser = (x == 0 for x in either_all_or_subset)
```

This allows us to make a simple parameter change, which will either pick all data or pick a subset of data.

We can embed this in nested loops to create more complex structures. Here's a simple example:

```
>>> list(tuple(repeat(i, times=i)) for i in range(10))
[(), (1,), (2, 2), (3, 3, 3), (4, 4, 4, 4), (5, 5, 5, 5, 5),
(6, 6, 6, 6, 6, 6), (7, 7, 7, 7, 7, 7, 7), (8, 8, 8, 8, 8, 8, 8, 8),
(9, 9, 9, 9, 9, 9, 9, 9, 9)]
>>> list(sum(repeat(i, times=i)) for i in range(10))
[0, 1, 4, 9, 16, 25, 36, 49, 64, 81]
```

We created repeating sequences of numbers using the `times` parameter on the `repeat()` function.

Using the finite iterators

The `itertools` module provides a number of functions that we can use to produce finite sequences of values. We'll look at ten functions in this module, plus some related built-in functions:

- `enumerate()`: This function is actually part of the `__builtins__` package, but it works with an iterator and is very similar to other functions in the `itertools` module.

- `accumulate()`: This function returns a sequence of reductions of the input iterable. It's a higher-order function and can do a variety of clever calculations.

- `chain()`: This function combines multiple iterables serially.

- `groupby()`: This function uses a function to decompose a single iterable into a sequence of iterables over subsets of the input data.

- `zip_longest()`: This function combines elements from multiple iterables. The built-in `zip()` function truncates the sequence at the length of the shortest iterable. The `zip_longest()` function pads the shorter iterables with the given fillvalue.

- `compress()`: This function filters one iterable based on a second iterable of `Boolean` values.

- `islice()`: This function is the equivalent of a slice of a sequence when applied to an iterable.

- `dropwhile()` and `takewhile()`: Both of these functions use a `Boolean` function to filter items from an iterable. Unlike `filter()` or `filterfalse()`, these functions rely on a single `True` or `False` value to change their filter behavior for all subsequent values.

- `filterfalse()`: This function applies a filter function to an iterable. This complements the built-in `filter()` function.

- `starmap()`: This function maps a function to an iterable sequence of tuples using each iterable as an `*args` argument to the given function. The `map()` function does a similar thing using multiple parallel iterables.

We've grouped these functions into approximate categories. The categories are roughly related to concepts of restructuring an iterable, filtering, and mapping.

Assigning numbers with enumerate()

In *Chapter 7, Additional Tuple Techniques*, we used the `enumerate()` function to make a naïve assignment of rank numbers to sorted data. We can do things like pairing up a value with its position in the original sequence, as follows:

```
pairs = tuple(enumerate(sorted(raw_values)))
```

This will sort the items in `raw_values` into order, create two tuples with an ascending sequence of numbers, and materialize an object we can use for further calculations. The command and the result are as follows:

```
>>> raw_values= [1.2, .8, 1.2, 2.3, 11, 18]
>>> tuple(enumerate( sorted(raw_values)))
((0, 0.8), (1, 1.2), (2, 1.2), (3, 2.3), (4, 11), (5, 18))
```

In *Chapter 7, Additional Tuple Techniques* we implemented an alternative form of enumerate, `rank()` function, which would handle ties in a more statistically useful way.

This is a common feature that is added to a parser to record the source data row numbers. In many cases, we'll create some kind of `row_iter()` function to extract the string values from a source file. This might iterate over the `string` values in tags of an XML file or in columns of a CSV file. In some cases, we might even be parsing data presented in an HTML file parsed with Beautiful Soup.

In *Chapter 4, Working with Collections*, we parsed an XML to create a simple sequence of position tuples. We then created legs with a start, end, and distance. We did not, however, assign an explicit leg number. If we ever sorted the trip collection, we'd be unable to determine the original ordering of the legs.

In *Chapter 7, Additional Tuple Techniques*, we expanded on the basic parser to create namedtuples for each leg of the trip. The output from this enhanced parser looks as follows:

```
(Leg(start=Point(latitude=37.54901619777347, longitude=
-76.33029518659048), end=Point(latitude=37.840832, longitude=
-76.273834), distance=17.7246),
Leg(start=Point(latitude=37.840832, longitude=-76.273834),
end=Point(latitude=38.331501, longitude=-76.459503),
distance=30.7382),
Leg(start=Point(latitude=38.331501, longitude=-76.459503),
end=Point(latitude=38.845501, longitude=-76.537331),
distance=31.0756),...,
Leg(start=Point(latitude=38.330166, longitude=-76.458504),
end=Point(latitude=38.976334, longitude=-76.473503),
distance=38.8019))
```

The first `Leg` function is a short trip between two points on the Chesapeake Bay.

We can add a function that will build a more complex tuple with the input order information as part of the tuple. First, we'll define a slightly more complex version of the `Leg` class:

```
Leg = namedtuple("Leg", ("order", "start", "end", "distance"))
```

This is similar to the `Leg` instance shown in *Chapter 7, Additional Tuple Techniques* but it includes the order as well as the other attributes. We'll define a function that decomposes pairs and creates `Leg` instances as follows:

```
def ordered_leg_iter(pair_iter):
    for order, pair in enumerate(pair_iter):
        start, end = pair
        yield Leg(order, start, end, round(haversine(start, end),4))
```

We can use this function to enumerate each pair of starting and ending points. We'll decompose the pair and then reassemble the `order`, `start`, and `end` parameters and the `haversine(start,end)` parameter's value as a single `Leg` instance. This `generator` function will work with an iterable sequence of pairs.

In the context of the preceding explanation, it is used as follows:

```
with urllib.request.urlopen("file:./Winter%202012-2013.kml") as
source:
    path_iter = float_lat_lon(row_iter_kml(source))
    pair_iter = legs(path_iter)
    trip_iter = ordered_leg_iter(pair_iter)
    trip= tuple(trip_iter)
```

We've parsed the original file into the path points, created start-end pairs, and then created a trip that was built of individual `Leg` objects. The `enumerate()` function assures that each item in the iterable sequence is given a unique number that increments from the default starting value of 0. A second argument value can be given to provide an alternate starting value.

Running totals with accumulate()

The `accumulate()` function folds a given function into an iterable, accumulating a series of reductions. This will iterate over the running totals from another iterator; the default function is `operator.add()`. We can provide alternative functions to change the essential behavior from sum to product. The Python library documentation shows a particularly clever use of the `max()` function to create a sequence of maximum values so far.

One application of running totals is quartiling data. We can compute the running total for each sample and divide them into quarters with an `int(4*value/total)` calculation.

In the *Assigning numbers with enumerate()* section, we introduced a sequence of latitude-longitude coordinates that describe a sequence of legs on a voyage. We can use the distances as a basis for quartiling the waypoints. This allows us to determine the midpoint in the trip.

The value of the `trip` variable looks as follows:

```
(Leg(start=Point(latitude=37.54901619777347, longitude=
-76.33029518659048), end=Point(latitude=37.840832, longitude=
-76.273834), distance=17.7246),
Leg(start=Point(latitude=37.840832, longitude=-76.273834),
end=Point(latitude=38.331501, longitude=-76.459503),
distance=30.7382), ...,
Leg(start=Point(latitude=38.330166, longitude=-76.458504),
end=Point(latitude=38.976334, longitude=-76.473503),
distance=38.8019))
```

Each `Leg` object has a start point, an end point, and a distance. The calculation of quartiles looks like the following example:

```
distances= (leg.distance for leg in trip)
distance_accum= tuple(accumulate(distances))
total= distance_accum[-1]+1.0
quartiles= tuple(int(4*d/total) for d in distance_accum)
```

We extracted the distance values and computed the accumulated distances for each leg. The last of the accumulated distances is the total. We've added `1.0` to the total to assure that `4*d/total` is 3.9983, which truncates to 3. Without the `+1.0`, the final item would have a value of `4`, which is an impossible fifth quartile. For some kinds of data (with extremely large values) we might have to add a larger value.

The value of the `quartiles` variable is as follows:

```
(0, 0, 0, 0, 0, 0, 0, 0, 0, 0, 0, 0, 0, 0, 0, 0, 0, 0, 0, 0, 0, 0,
1, 1, 1, 1, 1, 1, 1, 1, 1, 1, 1, 1, 1, 1, 2, 2, 2, 2, 2, 2, 2, 2, 2,
2, 2, 2, 2, 2, 2, 2, 2, 2, 3, 3, 3, 3, 3, 3, 3, 3, 3, 3, 3, 3, 3,
3, 3, 3, 3)
```

We can use the `zip()` function to merge this sequence of quartile numbers with the original data points. We can also use functions like `groupby()` to create distinct collections of the legs in each quartile.

Combining iterators with chain()

We can use the `chain()` function to combine a collection of iterators into a single, overall iterator. This can be helpful to combine data that was decomposed via the `groupby()` function. We can use this to process a number of collections as if they were a single collection.

In particular, we can combine the `chain()` function with the `contextlib.ExitStack()` method to process a collection of files as a single iterable sequence of values. We can do something like this:

```
from contextlib import ExitStack

import csv

def row_iter_csv_tab(*filenames):
    with ExitStack() as stack:
        files = [stack.enter_context(open(name, 'r', newline=''))
                    for name in filenames]
        readers = [csv.reader(f, delimiter='\t') for f in files]
        readers = map(lambda f: csv.reader(f, delimiter='\t'), files)
        yield from chain(*readers)
```

We've created an `ExitStack` object that can contain a number of individual contexts open. When the `with` statement finishes, all items in the `ExitStack` object will be closed properly. We created a simple sequence of open file objects; these objects were also entered into the `ExitStack` object.

Given the sequence of files in the `files` variable, we created a sequence of CSV readers in the `readers` variable. In this case, all of our files have a common tab-delimited format, which makes it very pleasant to open all of the files with a simple, consistent application of a function to the sequence of files.

We could also open the files using the following command:

```
readers = map(lambda f: csv.reader(f, delimiter='\t'), files)
```

Finally, we chained all of the readers into a single iterator with `chain(*readers)`. This was used to yield the sequence of rows from all of the files.

It's important to note that we can't return the `chain(*readers)` object. If we do, this would exit the `with` statement context, closing all the source files. Instead, we must yield individual rows so that the `with` statement context is kept active.

Partitioning an iterator with groupby()

We can use the `groupby()` function to partition an iterator into smaller iterators. This works by evaluating the given `key()` function for each item in the given iterable. If the key value matches the previous item's key, the two items are part of the same partition. If the key does not match the previous item's key, the previous partition is ended and a new partition is started.

The output from the `groupby()` function is a sequence of two tuples. Each tuple has the group's key value and an iterable over the items in the group. Each group's iterator can be preserved as a tuple or processed to reduce it to some summary value. Because of the way the group iterators are created, they can't be preserved.

In the *Running totals with accumulate()* section, earlier in the chapter, we showed how to compute quartile values for an input sequence.

Given the `trip` variable with the raw data and the quartile variable with the quartile assignments, we can group the data using the following commands:

```
group_iter= groupby(zip(quartile, trip), key=lambda q_raw:
    q_raw[0])
for group_key, group_iter in group_iter:
    print(group_key, tuple(group_iter))
```

This will start by zipping the quartile numbers with the raw trip data, iterating over two tuples. The `groupby()` function will use the given `lambda` variable to group by the quartile number. We used a `for` loop to examine the results of the `groupby()` function. This shows how we get a group key value and an iterator over members of the group.

The input to the `groupby()` function must be sorted by the key values. This will assure that all of the items in a group will be adjacent.

Note that we can also create groups using the `defaultdict(list)` method, as follows:

```
def groupby_2(iterable, key):
    groups = defaultdict(list)
    for item in iterable:
        groups[key(item)].append(item)
    for g in groups:
        yield iter(groups[g])
```

We created a `defaultdict` class with a `list` object as the value associated with each key. Each item will have the given `key()` function applied to create a key value. The item is appended to the list in the `defaultdict` class with the given key.

Once all of the items are partitioned, we can then return each partition as an iterator over the items that share a common key. This is similar to the `groupby()` function because the input iterator to this function isn't necessarily sorted in precisely the same order; it's possible that the groups might have the same members, but the order might differ.

Merging iterables with zip_longest() and zip()

We saw the `zip()` function in *Chapter 4, Working with Collections*. The `zip_longest()` function differs from the `zip()` function in an important way: where the `zip()` function stops at the end of the shortest iterable, the `zip_longest()` function pads short iterables and stops at the end of the longest iterable.

The `fillvalue` keyword parameter allows filling with a value other than the default value, `None`.

For most exploratory data analysis applications, padding with a default value is statistically difficult to justify. The **Python Standard Library** document shows a few clever things which can be done with the `zip_longest()` function. It's difficult to expand on these without drifting far from our focus on data analysis.

Filtering with compress()

The built-in `filter()` function uses a predicate to determine if an item is passed or rejected. Instead of a function that calculates a value, we can use a second, parallel iterable to determine which items to pass and which to reject.

We can think of the `filter()` function as having the following definition:

```
def filter(iterable, function):
    i1, i2 = tee(iterable, 2)
    return compress(i1, (function(x) for x in i2))
```

We cloned the iterable using the `tee()` function. (We'll look at this function in detail later.) We evaluated the filter predicate for each value. Then we provided the original iterable and the filter function iterable to compress, pass, and reject values. This builds the features of the `filter()` function from the more primitive features of the `compress()` function.

In the *Reiterating a cycle with cycle()* section of this chapter, we looked at data selection using a simple generator expression. Its essence was as follows:

```
chooser = (x == 0 for x in cycle(range(c)))
keep= (row for pick, row in zip(chooser, some_source) if pick)
```

We defined a function which would produce a value 1 followed by *c-1* zeroes. This cycle would be repeated, allowing to pick only *1/c* rows from the source.

We can replace the `cycle(range(c))` function with the `repeat(0)` function to select all rows. We can also replace it with the `random.randrange(c)` function to randomize the selection of rows.

The keep expression is really just a `compress(some_source, chooser)` method. If we make that change, the processing is simplified:

```
all = repeat(0)
subset = cycle(range(c))
randomized = random.randrange(c)
selection_rule = one of all, subset, or randomized
chooser = (x == 0 for x in selection_rule)
keep = compress(some_source, chooser)
```

We've defined three alternative selection rules: `all`, `subset`, and `randomized`. The subset and randomized versions will pick *1/c* rows from the source. The `chooser` expression will build an iterable over `True` and `False` values based on one of the selection rules. The rows to be kept are selected by applying the source iterable to the row selection iterable.

Since all of this is non-strict, rows are not read from the source until required. This allows us to process very large sets of data efficiently. Also, the relative simplicity of the Python code means that we don't really need a complex configuration file and an associated parser to make choices among the selection rules. We have the option to use this bit of Python code as the configuration for a larger data sampling application.

Picking subsets with islice()

In *Chapter 4, Working with Collections*, we looked at slice notation to select subsets from a collection. Our example was to pair up items sliced from a `list` object. The following is a simple list:

```
flat= ['2', '3', '5', '7', '11', '13', '17', '19', '23', '29', '31',
'37', '41', '43', '47', '53', '59', '61', '67', '71',... ]
```

We can create pairs using list slices as follows:

```
zip(flat[0::2], flat[1::2])
```

The `islice()` function gives us similar capabilities without the overhead of materializing a `list` object, and it looks like the following:

```
flat_iter_1= iter(flat)
flat_iter_2= iter(flat)
zip(islice(flat_iter_1, 0, None, 2), islice(flat_iter_2, 1, None, 2))
```

We created two independent iterators over a flat list of data points. These might be two separate iterators over an open file or a database result set. The two iterators need to be independent so that change in one `islice()` function doesn't interfere with the other `islice()` function.

The two sets of arguments to the `islice()` function are similar to the `flat[0::2]` and `flat[1::2]` methods. There's no slice-like shorthand, so the start and stop argument values are required. The step can be omitted and the default value is 1. This will produce a sequence of two tuples from the original sequence:

```
[(2, 3), (5, 7), (11, 13), (17, 19), (23, 29), ... (7883, 7901),
(7907, 7919)]
```

Since `islice()` works with an iterable, this kind of design will work with extremely large sets of data. We can use this to pick a subset out of a larger set of data. In addition to using the `filter()` or `compress()` functions, we can also use the `islice(source,0,None,c)` method to pick $1/c$ items from a larger set of data.

Stateful filtering with dropwhile() and takewhile()

The `dropwhile()` and `takewhile()` functions are stateful filter functions. They start in one mode; the given `predicate` function is a kind of flip-flop that switches the mode. The `dropwhile()` function starts in reject mode; when the function becomes `False`, it switches to pass mode. The `takewhile()` function starts in pass mode; when the given function becomes `False`, it switches into reject mode.

Since these are filters, both functions will consume the entire iterable. Given an infinite iterator like the `count()` function, it will continue indefinitely. Since there's no simple integer overflow in Python, an ill-considered use of `dropwhile()` or `takewhile()` functions won't crash after a few billion iterations with integer overflow. It really can run for a very, very long time.

We can use these with file parsing to skip headers or footers in the input. We use the `dropwhile()` function to reject header rows and pass the remaining data. We use the `takewhile()` function to pass data and reject trailer rows. We'll return to the simple GPL file format shown in *Chapter 3, Functions, Iterators, and Generators*. The file has a header that looks as follows:

```
GIMP Palette
Name: Crayola
Columns: 16
#
```

This is followed by rows that look like the following example:

```
255   73 108   Radical Red
```

We can easily locate the final line of the headers—the # line—using a parser based on the `dropwhile()` function, as follows:

```
with open("crayola.gpl") as source:
    rdr = csv.reader(source, delimiter='\t')
    rows = dropwhile(lambda row: row[0] != '#', rdr)
```

We created a CSV reader to parse the lines based on tab characters. This will neatly separate the `color` three tuple from the name. The three tuple will need further parsing. This will produce an iterator that starts with the # line and continues with the rest of the file.

We can use the `islice()` function to discard the first item of an iterable. We can then parse the color details as follows:

```
    color_rows = islice(rows, 1, None)
    colors = ((color.split(), name) for color, name in color_rows)
    print(list(colors))
```

The `islice(rows, 1, None)` expression is similar to asking for a `rows[1:]` slice: the first item is quietly discarded. Once the last of the heading rows have been discarded, we can parse the color tuples and return more useful color objects.

For this particular file, we can also use the number of columns located by the CSV reader function. We can use the `dropwhile(lambda row: len(row) == 1, rdr)` method to discard header rows. This doesn't always work out well in general. Locating the last line of the headers is often easier than trying to locate some general feature that distinguishes header (or trailer) lines from the meaningful file content.

Two approaches to filtering with filterfalse() and filter()

In *Chapter 5, Higher-order Functions* we looked at the built-in `filter()` function. The `filterfalse()` function from the `itertools` module could be defined from the `filter()` function, as follows:

```
filterfalse = lambda pred, iterable:
    filter(lambda x: not pred(x), iterable)
```

As with the `filter()` function, the predicate function can be of None value. The value of the `filter(None, iterable)` method is all the True values in the iterable. The value of the `filterfalse(None, iterable)` method is all of the False values from the iterable:

```
>>> filter(None, [0, False, 1, 2])
<filter object at 0x101b43a50>
>>> list(_)
[1, 2]
>>> filterfalse(None, [0, False, 1, 2])
<itertools.filterfalse object at 0x101b43a50>
>>> list(_)
[0, False]
```

The point of having the `filterfalse()` function is to promote reuse. If we have a succinct function that makes a filter decision, we should be able to use that function to partition input in to pass and reject groups without having to fiddle around with logical negation.

The idea is to execute the following commands:

```
iter_1, iter_2 = iter(some_source), iter(some_source)
good = filter(test, iter_1)
bad = filterfalse(test, iter_2)
```

This will obviously include all items from the source. The `test()` function is unchanged, and we can't introduce a subtle logic bug through improper use of `()`.

Applying a function to data via starmap() and map()

The built-in `map()` function is a higher-order function that applies a `map()` function to items from an iterable. We can think of the simple version of the `map()` function, as follows:

```
map(function, arg_iter) == (function(a) for a in arg_iter)
```

This works well when the `arg_iter` parameter is a list of individual values. The `starmap()` function in the `itertools` module is simply the `*a` version of the `map()` function, which is as follows:

```
starmap(function, arg_iter) == (function(*a) for a in arg_iter)
```

This reflects a small shift in the semantics of the `map()` function to properly handle a tuple-of-tuples structure.

The `map()` function can also accept multiple iterables; the values from these additional iterables are zipped and it behaves like the `starmap()` function. Each zipped item from the source iterables becomes multiple arguments to the given function.

We can think of the `map(function, iter1, iter2, ..., itern)` method being defined as the following two commands:

```
(function(*args) for args in zip(iter1, iter2, ..., itern))
```
```
starmap(function, zip(iter1, iter2, ..., itern))
```

Various iterator values are used to construct a tuple of arguments via the `*args` construct. In effect, `starmap()` function is like this more general case. We can build the simple `map()` function from the more general `starmap()` function.

When we look at the trip data, from the preceding commands, we can redefine the construction of a `Leg` object based on the `starmap()` function. Prior to creating `Leg` objects, we created pairs of points. Each pair looks as follows:

```
((Point(latitude=37.54901619777347, longitude=-76.33029518659048),
Point(latitude=37.840832, longitude=-76.273834)), ...,
(Point(latitude=38.330166, longitude=-76.458504),
Point(latitude=38.976334, longitude=-76.473503)))
```

We could use the `starmap()` function to assemble the `Leg` objects, as follows:

```
with urllib.request.urlopen(url) as source:
    path_iter = float_lat_lon(row_iter_kml(source))
    pair_iter = legs(path_iter)
```

```
make_leg = lambda start, end: Leg(start, end,
haversine(start,end))
trip = list(starmap(make_leg, pair_iter))
```

The `legs()` function creates pairs of point objects that reflect the start and end of a leg of the voyage. Given these pairs, we can create a simple function, `make_leg`, which accepts a pair of `Points` object, and returns a `Leg` object with the start point, end point, and distance between the two points.

The benefit of the `starmap(function, some_list)` method is to replace a potentially wordy `(function(*args) for args in some_list)` generator expression.

Cloning iterators with tee()

The `tee()` function gives us a way to circumvent one of the important Python rules for working with iterables. The rule is so important, we'll repeat it here.

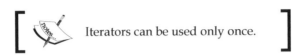 Iterators can be used only once.

The `tee()` function allows us to clone an iterator. This seems to free us from having to materialize a sequence so that we can make multiple passes over the data. For example, a simple average for an immense dataset could be written in the following way:

```
def mean(iterator):
    it0, it1= tee(iterator,2)
    s0= sum(1 for x in it0)
    s1= sum(x for x in it1)
    return s0/s1
```

This would compute an average without appearing to materialize the entire dataset in memory in any form.

While interesting in principle, the `tee()` function's implementation suffers from a severe limitation. In most Python implementations, the cloning is done by materializing a sequence. While this circumvents the "one time only" rule for small collections, it doesn't work out well for immense collections.

Also, the current implementation of the `tee()` function consumes the source iterator. It might be nice to create some syntactic sugar to allow unlimited use of an iterator. This is difficult to manage in practice. Instead, Python obliges us to optimize the `tee()` function carefully.

The itertools recipes

The *itertools* chapter of the Python library documentation, *Itertools Recipes*, is outstanding. The basic definitions are followed by a series of recipes that are extremely clear and helpful. Since there's no reason to reproduce these, we'll reference them here. They should be considered as required reading on functional programming in Python.

> 10.1.2 section, *Itertools Recipes* of *Python Standard Library*, is a wonderful resource. See
> `https://docs.python.org/3/library/itertools.html#itertools-recipes`.

It's important to note that these aren't importable functions in the `itertools` modules. A recipe needs to be read and understood and then, perhaps, copied or modified before inclusion in an application.

The following table summarizes some of the recipes that show functional programming algorithms built from the itertools basics:

Function Name	Arguments	Results
take	(n, iterable)	This returns the first n items of the iterable as a list. This wraps a use of `islice()` in a simple name.
tabulate	(function, start=0)	This returns `function(0)` and `function(1)`. This is based on a `map(function, count())`.
consume	(iterator, n)	This advances the iterator n steps ahead. If n is None, iterator consumes the steps entirely.
nth	(iterable, n, default=None)	This returns the nth item or a default value. This wraps the use of `islice()` in a simple name.
quantify	(iterable, pred=bool)	This counts how many times the predicate is true. This uses `sum()` and `map()`, and relies on the way a Boolean predicate is effectively 1 when converted to an integer value.
padnone	(iterable)	This returns the sequence elements and then returns None indefinitely. This can create functions that behave like `zip_longest()` or `map()`.
ncycles	(iterable, n)	This returns the sequence elements n times.

Function Name	Arguments	Results
`dotproduct`	`(vec1, vec2)`	This is the essential definition of a dot product. Multiply two vectors and find the sum of the result.
`flatten`	`(listOfLists)`	This flattens one level of nesting. This chains the various lists together into a single list.

`repeatfunc`	`(func,`
	`times=None,`
	`*args)`
		This calls to `func` repeatedly with specified arguments.

`pairwise`	`(iterable):`	`s -> (s0,s1), (s1,s2), (s2, s3).`
`grouper`	`(iterable, n,` `fillvalue=None)`	Collect data into fixed length chunks or blocks.

`roundrobin`	`(*iterables)`	`roundrobin('ABC', 'D', 'EF') -->`
		`A D`
		`E B F C`

`partition`	`(pred,` `iterable)`	This uses a predicate to partition entries into `False` entries and `True` entries.

`unique_`
`everseen`
	`(iterable,`
	`key=None)`
		This lists unique elements, preserving order. Remembers all elements ever seen. `unique_`
		`everseen('AAAABBBCCDAABBB') -`
		`-> A B C D.`

`unique_`
`justseen`
	`(iterable,`
	`key=None)`
		This lists unique elements, preserving order. Remembers only the element just seen. `unique_justseen('AAAABBBCCDAABBB')`
		`-`
		`-> A B C D A B.`

`iter_except`	`(func,`
	`exception,`
	`first=None)`
		Call a function repeatedly until an exception is raised. This can be used to iterate until `KeyError` or `IndexError`.

Summary

In this chapter, we've looked at a number of functions in the `itertools` module. This library module provides a number of functions that help us to work with iterators in sophisticated ways.

We've looked at the infinite iterators; these repeat without terminating. These include the `count()`, `cycle()`, and `repeat()` functions. Since they don't terminate, the consuming function must determine when to stop accepting values.

We've also looked at a number of finite iterators. Some of these are built-in and some of these are part of the `itertools` module. These work with a source iterable, so they terminate when that iterable is exhausted. These functions include `enumerate()`, `accumulate()`, `chain()`, `groupby()`, `zip_longest()`, `zip()`, `compress()`, `islice()`, `dropwhile()`, `takewhile()`, `filterfalse()`, `filter()`, `starmap()`, and `map()`. These functions allow us to replace possibly complex generator expressions with simpler-looking functions.

Additionally, we looked at the recipes from the documentation, which provide yet more functions we can study and copy for our own applications. The recipes list shows a wealth of common design patterns.

In *Chapter 9, More Itertools Techniques*, we'll continue our study of the `itertools` module. We'll look at the iterators focused on permutations and combinations. These don't apply to processing large sets of data. They're a different kind of iterator-based tool.

9
More Itertools Techniques

Functional programming emphasizes stateless programming. In Python, this leads us to work with generator expressions, generator functions, and iterables. In this chapter, we'll continue our study of the `itertools` library, with numerous functions to help us work with iterable collections.

In the previous chapter, we looked at three broad groupings of iterator functions. They are as follows:

- Functions that work with infinite iterators can be applied to any iterable or an iterator over any collection; they will consume the entire source

- Functions that work with finite iterators can either accumulate a source multiple times, or they produce a reduction of the source

- The `tee()` iterator function clones an iterator into several copies that can each be used independently

In this chapter, we'll look at the `itertools` functions that work with permutations and combinations. These include several functions and a few recipes built on these functions. The functions are as follows:

- `product()`: This function forms a Cartesian product equivalent to the nested `for` loops

- `permutations()`: This function emits tuples of length r from a universe p in all possible orderings; there are no repeated elements

- `combinations()`: This function emits tuples of length r from a universe p in sorted order; there are no repeated elements

- `combinations_with_replacement()`: This function emits tuples of length r from p in a sorted order, with repeated elements

These functions embody algorithms that iterate over potentially large result sets from small collections of input data. Some kinds of problems have exact solutions based on exhaustively enumerating a potentially gigantic universe of permutations. The functions make it simple to emit a large number of permutations; in some cases, the simplicity isn't actually optimal.

Enumerating the Cartesian product

The term Cartesian product refers to the idea of enumerating all the possible combinations of elements drawn from a number of sets.

Mathematically, we might say that the product of two sets, $\{1, 2, 3, ..., 13\} \times \{C, D, H, S\}$, has 52 pairs as follows:

```
{(1, C), (1, D), (1, H), (1, S), (2, C), (2, D), (2, H), (2, S), ...,
(13, C), (13, D), (13, H), (13, S)}
```

We can produce the preceding results by executing the following commands:

```
>>> list(product(range(1, 14), '♣♦♥♠'))
[(1, '♣'), (1, '♦'), (1, '♥'), (1, '♠'),(2, '♣'), (2, '♦'), (2, '♥'),
(2, '♠'),… (13, '♣'), (13, '♦'), (13, '♥'), (13, '♠')]
```

The calculation of a product can be extended to any number of iterable collections. Using a large number of collections can lead to a very large result set.

Reducing a product

In relational database theory, a join between tables can be thought of as a filtered product. A SQL SELECT statement that joins tables without a WHERE clause will produce a Cartesian product of rows in the tables. This can be thought of as the worst-case algorithm: a product without any filtering to pick the proper results.

We can use the join() function to join two tables, as shown in the following commands:

```
def join(t1, t2, where):):
    return filter(where, product(t1, t2)))))
```

All combinations of the two iterables, t1 and t2, are computed. The filter() function will apply the given where function to pass or reject items that didn't fit the given condition to match appropriate rows from each iterable. This will work when the where function returns a simple Boolean.

In some cases, we don't have a simple Boolean matching function. Instead, we're forced to search for a minimum or maximum of some distance between items.

Assume that we have a table of `Color` objects as follows:

```
[Color(rgb=(239, 222, 205), name='Almond'),
Color(rgb=(255, 255, 153), name='Canary'),
Color(rgb=(28, 172, 120), name='Green'),...
Color(rgb=(255, 174, 66), name='Yellow Orange')]
```

For more information, see *Chapter 6, Recursions and Reductions*, where we showed you how to parse a file of colors to create `namedtuple` objects. In this case, we've left the RGB as a triple, instead of decomposing each individual field.

An image will have a collection of pixels:

```
pixels= [(([(r, g, b), (r, g, b), (r, g, b), ...)
```

As a practical matter, the **Python Imaging Library** (PIL) package presents the pixels in a number of forms. One of these is the mapping from (x, y) coordinate to RGB triple. For more information, visit `https://pypi.python.org/pypi/Pillow` for the Pillow project documentation.

Given a `PIL.Image` object, we can iterate over the collection of pixels with something like the following commands:

```
def pixel_iter(image):
    w, h = img.size
    return ((c, img.getpixel(c)) for c in product(range(w),
range(h)))
```

We've determined the range of each coordinate based on the image size. The calculation of the `product(range(w), range(h))` method creates all the possible combinations of coordinates. It is, effectively, two nested `for` loops.

This has the advantage of providing each pixel with its coordinates. We can then process the pixels in no particular order and still reconstruct an image. This is particularly handy when using multiprocessing or multithreading to spread the workload among several cores or processors. The `concurrent.futures` module provides an easy way to distribute work among cores or processors.

Computing distances

A number of decision-making problems require that we find a close-enough match. We might not be able to use a simple equality test. Instead, we have to use a distance metric and locate items with the shortest distance to our target. For text, we might use the Levenshtein distance; this shows how many changes are required to get from a given block of text to our target.

We'll use a slightly simpler example. This will involve very simple math. However, even though it's simple, it doesn't work out well if we approach it naively.

When doing color matching, we won't have a simple equality test. We're rarely able to check for the exact equality of pixel colors. We're often forced to define a minimal distance function to determine whether two colors are close enough, without being the same three values of R, G, and B. There are several common approaches, including the Euclidean distance, Manhattan distance, and yet other complex weightings based on visual preferences.

Here are the Euclidean and Manhattan distance functions:

```
def euclidean(pixel, color):
    return math.sqrt(sum(map(lambda x, y: (x-y)**2, pixel,
    color.rgb)))))))
def manhattan(pixel, color):
    return sum(map(lambda x, y: abs(x-y), pixel, color.rgb)))))
```

The Euclidean distance measures the hypotenuse of a right-angled triangle among the three points in an RGB space. The Manhattan distance sums the edges of each leg of the right-angled triangle among the three points. The Euclidean distance offers precision where the Manhattan distance offers calculation speed.

Looking forward, we're aiming for a structure that looks like this. For each individual pixel, we can compute the distance from that pixel's color to the available colors in a limited color set. The results of this calculation for a single pixel might look like this:

```
(((0, 0), (92, 139, 195), Color(rgb=(239, 222, 205), name='Almond'),
169.10943202553784), ((0, 0), (92, 139, 195),
Color(rgb=(255, 255, 153), name='Canary'), 204.42357985320578),
((0, 0), (92, 139, 195), Color(rgb=(28, 172, 120), name='Green'),
103.97114984456024), ((0, 0), (92, 139, 195),
Color(rgb=(48, 186, 143), name='Mountain Meadow'),
82.75868534480233), ((0, 0), (92, 139, 195),
Color(rgb=(255, 73, 108), name='Radical Red'), 196.19887869200477),
((0, 0), (92, 139, 195), Color(rgb=(253, 94, 83),
name='Sunset Orange'), 201.2212712413874), ((0, 0), (92, 139, 195),
Color(rgb=(255, 174, 66), name='Yellow Orange'), 210.7961100210343))
```

We've shown an overall tuple that consists of a number of four tuples. Each of the four tuples contains the following contents:

- The pixel's coordinates, for example, (0,0)
- The pixel's original color, for example, (92, 139, 195)
- A `Color` object from our set of seven colors, for example, Color(rgb=(239, 222, 205),name='Almond')
- The Euclidean distance between the original color and the given `Color` object

We can see that the smallest Euclidean distance is the closest match color. This kind of reduction is done easily with the `min()` function. If the overall tuple is assigned to a variable name, `choices`, the pixel-level reduction would look like this:

```
min(choices, key=lambda xypcd: xypcd[3]))])
```

We've called each four tuple an xypcd, that is, an xy coordinate, pixel, color, and distance. The minimum distance calculation will then pick a single four tuple as the optimal match between pixel and color.

Getting all pixels and all colors

How do we get to the structure that contains all pixels and all colors? The answer is simple but, as we'll see, less than optimal.

One way to map pixels to colors is to enumerate all pixels and all colors using the `product()` function:

```
xy = lambda xyp_c: xyp_c[0][0]
p = lambda xyp_c: xyp_c[0][1]
c = lambda xyp_c: xyp_c[1]
distances= (( = ((xy(item), p(item), c(item), euclidean(p(item),
c(item)))
    for item in product(pixel_iter(img), colors)))))
```

The core of this is the `product(pixel_iter(img), colors)` method that creates all pixels combined with all colors. We will do a bit of restructuring of the data to flatten it out. We will apply the `euclidean()` function to compute distances between pixel colors and `Color` objects.

The final selection of colors uses the `groupby()` function and the `min(choices,...)` expression, as shown in the following command snippet:

```
for _, choices in groupby(distances, key=lambda xy_p_c_d:
    xy_p_c_d[0]):
        print(min(choices, key=lambda xypcd: xypcd[3])))]))
```

The overall product of pixels and colors is a long, flat iterable. We grouped the iterable into smaller collections where the coordinates match. This will break the big iterable into smaller iterables of just colors associated with a single pixel. We can then pick the minimal color distance for each color.

In a picture that's 3,648×2,736 with 133 Crayola colors, we have an iterable with 1,327,463,424 items to be evaluated. Yes. That's a billion combinations created by this `distances` expression. The number is not necessarily impractical. It's well within the limits of what Python can do. However, it reveals an important flaw in the naïve use of the `product()` function.

We can't trivially do this kind of large-scale processing without some analysis to see how large it is. Here are some `timeit` numbers for these that do each of these calculations only 1,000,000 times:

- Euclidean 2.8
- Manhattan 1.8

Scaling up from 1 million to 1 billion means 1,800 seconds, that is, about half an hour for the Manhattan distance and 46 minutes to calculate the Euclidean distance. It appears that the core arithmetic operations of Python are too slow for this kind of naïve bulk processing.

More importantly, we're doing it wrong. This kind of *width×height×color* processing is simply a bad design. In many cases, we can do much better.

Performance analysis

A key feature of any big data algorithm is locating a way to execute some kind of a divide-and-conquer strategy. This is true of functional programming design as well as imperative design.

We have three options to speed up this processing; they are as follows:

- We can try to use parallelism to do more of the calculations concurrently. On a four-core processor, the time can be cut to approximately ¼. This cuts the time to 8 minutes for Manhattan distances.

- We can see if caching intermediate results will reduce the amount of redundant calculation. The question arises of how many colors are the same and how many colors are unique.
- We can look for a radical change in the algorithm.

We'll combine the last two points by computing all the possible comparisons between source colors and target colors. In this case, as in many other contexts, we can easily enumerate the entire mapping and avoid redundant calculation when done on a pixel-by-pixel basis. We'll also change the algorithm from a series of comparisons to a series of simple lookups in a mapping object.

When looking at this idea of precomputing all transformations for source color to target color, we need some overall statistics for an arbitrary image. The code associated with this book includes IMG_2705.jpg. Here is a basic algorithm to collect some data from the specified image:

```
from collections import defaultdict, Counter
palette = defaultdict(list)
for xy_p in pixel_iter(img):
    xy, p = xy_p
    palette[p].append(xy)
w, h = img.size
print(""("Total pixels", w*h)
print(""("Total colors", len(palette)))))
```

We collected all pixels of a given color into a list organized by color. From this, we'll learn the first of the following facts:

- The total number of pixels is 9,980,928. This is not surprising for a 10 megapixel image.
- The total number of colors is 210,303. If we try to compute the Euclidean distance between actual colors and the 133 colors, we would merely do 27,970,299 calculations, which might take about 76 seconds.
- Using a 3-bit mask, 0b11100000, there are 214 colors used out of a possible 512.
- Using a 4-bit mask, 0b11110000, there are 1,150 colors used out of 4,096.
- Using a 5-bit mask, 0b11111000, there are 5,845 colors used out of 32,768.
- Using a 6-bit mask, 0b11111100, there are 27,726 colors out of 262,144.

This gives us some insight into how we can rearrange the data structure, calculate the matching colors quickly, and then rebuild the image without doing a billion comparisons.

We can apply mask values to the RGB bytes with the following piece of command:

```
masked_color= tuple(map(lambda x: x&0b11100000, c))
```

This will pick out the most significant 3 bits of red, green, and blue values. If we use this instead of the original color to create a `Counter` object, we'll see that we have 214 distinct values.

Rearranging the problem

The naïve use of the `product()` function to compare all pixels and all colors was a bad idea. There are 10 million pixels, but only 200,000 unique colors. When mapping the source colors to target colors, we only have to save 200,000 values in a simple map.

We'll approach it as follows:

- Compute the source to target color mapping. In this case, let's use 3-bit color values as output. Each R, G, and B value comes from the eight values in the `range(0, 256, 32)` method. We can use this expression to enumerate all the output colors:

  ```
  product(range(0,256,32), range(0,256,32), range(0,256,32))
  ```

- We can then compute the Euclidean distance to the nearest color in our source palette, doing just 68,096 calculations. This takes about 0.14 seconds. It's done one time only and computes the 200,000 mappings.

- In one pass through the image, build a new image using the revised color table. In some cases, we can exploit the truncation of integer values. We can use an expression such as (0b11100000&r, 0b11100000&g, 0b11100000&b) to remove the least significant bits of an image color. We'll look at this additional reduction in computation later.

This will replace a billion Euclidean distance calculations with 10 million dictionary lookups. This will replace 30 minutes of calculation with about 30 seconds of calculation.

Instead of doing color mapping for all pixels, we'll create a static mapping from input to output values. We can build the image building using simple lookup mapping from original color to new color.

Once we have the palette of all 200,000 colors, we can apply the fast Manhattan distance to locate the nearest color in an output, such as the Crayola colors. This will use the algorithm for color matching shown earlier to compute the mapping instead of a result image. The difference will center on using the `palette.keys()` function instead of the `pixel_iter()` function.

We'll fold in yet another optimization: truncation. This will give us an even faster algorithm.

Combining two transformations

When combining multiple transformations, we can build a more complex mapping from source through intermediate targets to the result. To illustrate this, we'll truncate the colors as well as apply a mapping.

In some problem contexts, truncation can be difficult. In other cases, it's often quite simple. For example, truncating US postal ZIP codes from 9 to 5 characters is common. Postal codes can be further truncated to three characters to determine a regional facility that represents a larger geography.

For colors, we can use the bit-masking shown previously to truncate colors form three 8-bit values (24 bits, 16 million colors) to three 3-bit values (9 bits, 512 colors).

Here is a way to build a color map that combines both distances to a given set of colors and truncation of the source colors:

```
bit3 = range(0, 256, 0b100000)
best = (min(((((euclidean(rgb, c), rgb, c) for c in colors)
    for rgb in product(bit3, bit3, bit3)))))
color_map = dict(((((b[1], b[2].rgb) for b in best)
```

We created a `range` object, `bit3`, that will iterate through all eight of the 3-bit color values.

 The `range` objects aren't like ordinary iterators; they can be used multiple times. As a result of this, the `product(bit3, bit3, bit3)` expression will produce all 512 color combinations that we'll use as the output colors.

For each truncated RGB color, we created a three tuple that has (0) the distance from all crayon colors, (1) the RGB color, and (2) the crayon `Color` object. When we ask for the minimum value of this collection, we'll get the closest crayon `Color` object to the truncated RGB color.

We built a dictionary that maps from the truncated RGB color to the closest crayon. In order to use this mapping, we'll truncate a source color before looking up the nearest crayon in the mapping. This use of truncation coupled with the precomputed mapping shows how we might need to combine mapping techniques.

The following are the commands for the image replacement:

```
clone = img.copy()
for xy, p in pixel_iter(img):
    r, g, b = p
    repl = color_map[((([(0b11100000&r, 0b11100000&g,
    0b11100000&b)]])])]
    clone.putpixel(xy, repl)
clone.show()
```

This simply uses a number of PIL features to replace all of the pixels in a picture with other pixels.

What we've seen is that the naïve use of some functional programming tools can lead to algorithms that are expressive and succinct, but also inefficient. The essential tools to compute the complexity of a calculation — sometimes called Big-O analysis — is just as important for functional programming as it is for imperative programming.

The problem is not that the `product()` function is inefficient. The problem is that we can use the `product()` function in an inefficient algorithm.

Permuting a collection of values

When we permute a collection of values, we'll elaborate all the possible orders for the items. There are n! ways to permute *n* items. We can use permutations as a kind of brute-force solution to a variety of optimization problems.

By visiting `http://en.wikipedia.org/wiki/Combinatorial_optimization`, we can see that the exhaustive enumeration of all permutations isn't appropriate for larger problems. The use of the `itertools.permutations()` function is a handy way to explore very small problems.

One popular example of these combinatorial optimization problems is the assignment problem. We have *n* agents and *n* tasks, but the cost of each agent performing a given task is not equal. Imagine that some agents have trouble with some details, while other agents excel at these details. If we can properly assign tasks to agents, we can minimize the costs.

We can create a simple grid that shows how well a given agent is able to perform a given task. For a small problem of a half-dozen agents and tasks, there will be a grid of 36 costs. Each cell in the grid shows agents 0 to 5 performing tasks A to F.

We can easily enumerate all the possible permutations. However, this approach doesn't scale well. 10! is 3,628,800. We can see this sequence of 3 million items with the `list(permutations(range(10)))` method.

We would expect to solve a problem of this size in a few seconds. If we double the size of the problem to 20!, we would have a bit of a scalability problem: there would be 2,432,902,008,176,640,000 permutations. If it takes about 0.56 seconds to generate 10! permutations, then to generate 20! permutations, it would take about 12,000 years.

Assume that we have a cost matrix with 36 values that show the costs of six agents and six tasks. We can formulate the problem as follows:

```
perms = permutations(range(6)))))
alt= [((([(sum(cost[x][y] for y, x in enumerate(perm)), perm) for perm
in perms]
m = min(alt)[0]
print([[(([ans for s, ans in alt if s == m]))])
```

We've created all permutations of tasks for our six agents. We've computed the sums of all the costs in our cost matrix for each task assigned to each agent. The minimum cost is the optimal solution. In many cases, there might be multiple optimal solutions; we'll locate all of them.

For small text-book examples, this is very fast. For larger examples, an approximation algorithm is more appropriate.

Generating all combinations

The `itertools` module also supports computing all combinations of a set of values. When looking at combinations, the order doesn't matter, so there are far fewer combinations than permutations. The number of combinations is often stated as $\binom{p}{r} = \frac{p!}{r!(p-r)!}$. This is the number of ways that we can take combinations of r things at a time from a universe of p items overall.

For example, there are 2,598,960 5-card poker hands. We can actually enumerate all 2 million hands by executing the following command:

```
hands = list(combinations(tuple(product(range(13), '♠♥♦♣')), 5))
```

More practically, we have a dataset with a number of variables. A common exploratory technique is to determine the correlation among all pairs of variables in a set of data. If there are v variables, then we will enumerate all variables that must be compared by executing the following command:

```
combinations(range(v), 2)
```

Let's get some sample data from http://www.tylervigen.com to show how this will work. We'll pick three datasets with the same time range: numbers 7, 43, and 3890. We'll simply laminate the data into a grid, repeating the year column.

This is how the first and the remaining rows of the yearly data will look:

```
[('year', 'Per capita consumption of cheese (US)Pounds (USDA)',
'Number of people who died by becoming tangled in their
bedsheetsDeaths (US) (CDC)',
'year', 'Per capita consumption of mozzarella cheese (US)Pounds
(USDA)', 'Civil engineering doctorates awarded (US)Degrees awarded
(National Science Foundation)',
'year', 'US crude oil imports from VenezuelaMillions of barrels
(Dept. of Energy)', 'Per capita consumption of high fructose corn
syrup (US)Pounds (USDA)'),
(2000, 29.8, 327, 2000, 9.3, 480, 2000, 446, 62.6),
(2001, 30.1, 456, 2001, 9.7, 501, 2001, 471, 62.5),
(2002, 30.5, 509, 2002, 9.7, 540, 2002, 438, 62.8),
(2003, 30.6, 497, 2003, 9.7, 552, 2003, 436, 60.9),
(2004, 31.3, 596, 2004, 9.9, 547, 2004, 473, 59.8),
(2005, 31.7, 573, 2005, 10.2, 622, 2005, 449, 59.1),
(2006, 32.6, 661, 2006, 10.5, 655, 2006, 416, 58.2),
(2007, 33.1, 741, 2007, 11, 701, 2007, 420, 56.1),
(2008, 32.7, 809, 2008, 10.6, 712, 2008, 381, 53),
(2009, 32.8, 717, 2009, 10.6, 708, 2009, 352, 50.1)]
```

This is how we can use the `combinations()` function to emit all the combinations of the nine variables in this dataset, taken two at a time:

```
combinations(range(9), 2)
```

There are 36 possible combinations. We'll have to reject the combinations that involve `year` and `year`. These will trivially correlate with a value of 1.00.

Here is a function that picks a column of data out of our dataset:

```
def column(source, x):
    for row in source:
        yield row[x]
```

This allows us to use the `corr()` function from *Chapter 4, Working with Collections,* to compare two columns of data.

This is how we can compute all combinations of correlations:

```
from itertools import *
from Chapter_4.ch04_ex4 import corr
for p, q in combinations(range(9), 2):
    header_p, *data_p = list(column(source, p))
    header_q, *data_q = list(column(source, q))
    if header_p == header_q: continue
    r_pq = corr(data_p, data_q)
    print("{"{("{2: 4.2f}: {0} vs {1}".
    format(header_p, header_q, r_pq)))))
```

For each combination of columns, we've extracted the two columns of data from our data set and used multiple assignments to separate the header from the remaining rows of data. If the headers match, we're comparing a variable to itself. This will be `True` for the three combinations of `year` and `year` that stem from the redundant year columns.

Given a combination of columns, we will compute the correlation function and then print the two headings along with the correlation of the columns. We've intentionally chosen some datasets that show spurious correlations with a dataset that doesn't follow the same pattern. In spite of this, the correlations are remarkably high.

The results look like this:

```
0.96: year vs Per capita consumption of cheese (US)Pounds (USDA)
0.95: year vs Number of people who died by becoming tangled in their
bedsheetsDeaths (US) (CDC)
0.92: year vs Per capita consumption of mozzarella cheese (US)Pounds
(USDA)
0.98: year vs Civil engineering doctorates awarded (US)Degrees
awarded (National Science Foundation)
-0.80: year vs US crude oil imports from VenezuelaMillions of barrels
(Dept. of Energy)
-0.95: year vs Per capita consumption of high fructose corn syrup
(US)Pounds (USDA)
0.95: Per capita consumption of cheese (US)Pounds (USDA) vs Number of
people who died by becoming tangled in their bedsheetsDeaths (US)
(CDC)
0.96: Per capita consumption of cheese (US)Pounds (USDA) vs year
```

```
0.98: Per capita consumption of cheese (US)Pounds (USDA) vs Per
capita consumption of mozzarella cheese (US)Pounds (USDA)

...

0.88: US crude oil imports from VenezuelaMillions of barrels
(Dept. of Energy) vs Per capita consumption of high fructose corn
syrup (US)Pounds (USDA)
```

It's not at all clear what this pattern means. We used a simple expression, `combinations(range(9), 2)`, to enumerate all the possible combinations of data. This kind of succinct, expressive technique makes it easier to focus on the data analysis issues instead of the Combinatoric algorithm considerations.

Recipes

The itertools chapter of the Python library documentation is outstanding. The basic definitions are followed by a series of recipes that are extremely clear and helpful. Since there's no reason to reproduce these, we'll reference them here. They are the required reading materials on functional programming in Python.

Section *10.1.2, Itertools Recipes*, of *Python Standard Library* is a wonderful resource. Visit `https://docs.python.org/3/library/itertools.html#itertools-recipes` more details.

These function definitions aren't importable functions in the `itertools` modules. These are ideas that need to be read and understood and then, perhaps, copied or modified before inclusion in an application.

The following table summarizes some recipes that show functional programming algorithms built from the itertools basics:

Function Name	Arguments	Results
powerset	(iterable)	This generates all the subsets of the iterable. Each subset is actually a `tuple` object, not a set instance.
random_product	(*args, repeat=1)	This randomly selects from `itertools.product(*args, **kwds)`.
random_permutation	(iterable, r=None)	This randomly selects from `itertools.permutations(iterable, r)`.
random_combination	(iterable, r)	This randomly selects from `itertools.combinations(iterable, r)`.

Summary

In this chapter, we looked at a number of functions in the `itertools` module. This library module provides a number of functions that help us work with iterators in sophisticated ways.

We looked at the `product()` function that will compute all the possible combinations of the elements chosen from two or more collections. The `permutations()` function gives us different ways to reorder a given set of values. The `combinations()` function returns all the possible subsets of the original set.

We also looked at ways in which the `product()` and `permutations()` functions can be used naïvely to create extremely large result sets. This is an important cautionary note. A succinct and expressive algorithm can also involve a vast amount of computation. We must perform basic complexity analysis to be sure that the code will finish in a reasonable amount of time.

In the next chapter, we'll look at the `functools` module. This module includes some tools to work with functions as first-class objects. This builds on some material shown in *Chapter 2, Introducing Some Functional Features*, and *Chapter 5, Higher-order Functions*.

10
The Functools Module

Functional programming emphasizes functions as first class objects. We have many high-order functions that accept functions as arguments or return functions as results. In this chapter, we'll look at the `functools` library with some functions to help us create and modify functions.

We'll look at some higher-order functions in this chapter. Earlier, we looked at higher-order functions in *Chapter 5, Higher-order Functions*. We'll continue to look at higher-order function techniques in *Chapter 11, Decorator Design Techniques*, as well.

We'll look at the following functions in this module:

- `@lru_cache`: This decorator can be a huge performance boost for certain types of applications.
- `@total_ordering`: This decorator can help create rich comparison operators. However, it lets us look at the more general question of object-oriented design mixed with functional programming.
- `partial()`: It creates a new function with some arguments applied to a given function.
- `reduce()`: It is a higher-order function which generalizes reductions like `sum()`.

We'll defer two additional members of this library to *Chapter 11, Decorator Design Techniques*: the `update_wrapper()` and `wraps()` functions. We'll look more closely at writing our own decorators in the next chapter also.

We'll ignore the `cmp_to_key()` function entirely. Its purpose is to help with converting Python 2 code—which uses a comparison—to run under Python 3 which uses key extraction. We're only interested in Python 3; we'll write proper key functions.

Function tools

We looked at a number of higher-order functions in *Chapter 5, Higher-order Functions*. These functions either accepted a function as an argument or returned a function (or generator expression) as a result. All these higher-order functions had an essential algorithm which was customized by injecting another function. Functions like `max()`, `min()`, and `sorted()` accepted a `key=` function that customized their behavior. Functions like `map()` and `filter()` accept a function and an iterable and apply this function to the arguments. In the case of the `map()` function, the results of the function are simply kept. In the case of the `filter()` function, the Boolean result of the function is used to pass or reject values from the iterable.

All the functions in *Chapter 5, Higher-order Functions* are part of the Python __builtins__ package: they're available without the need to do an `import`. They are ubiquitous because they are so universally useful. The functions in this chapter must be introduced with an `import` because they're not quite so universally usable.

The `reduce()` function straddles this fence. It was originally built-in. After much discussion, it was removed from the __builtins__ package because of the possibility of abuse. Some seemingly simple operations can perform remarkably poorly.

Memoizing previous results with lru_cache

The `lru_cache` decorator transforms a given function into a function that might perform more quickly. The **LRU** means **Least Recently Used**: a finite pool of recently used items is retained. Items not frequently used are discarded to keep the pool to a bounded size.

Since this is a decorator, we can apply it to any function that might benefit from caching previous results. We might use it as follows:

```
from functools import lru_cache
@lru_cache(128)
def fibc(n):
    """Fibonacci numbers with naive recursion and caching
    >>> fibc(20)
    6765
    >>> fibc(1)
    1
    """
```

```
if n == 0: return 0
if n == 1: return 1
return fibc(n-1) + fibc(n-2)
```

This is an example based on *Chapter 6, Recursions and Reductions*. We've applied the @lru_cache decorator to the naïve Fibonacci number calculation. Because of this decoration, each call to the fibc(n) function will now be checked against a cache maintained by the decorator. If the argument, n, is in the cache, the previously computed result is used instead of doing a potentially expensive re-calculation. Each return value is added to the cache. When the cache is full, the oldest value is ejected to make room for a new value.

We highlight this example because the naïve recursion is quite expensive in this case. The complexity of computing any given Fibonacci number, F_n, involves not merely computing F_{n-1} but F_{n-2} also. This tree of values leads to a complexity in the order of $O(2^n)$.

We can try to confirm the benefits empirically using the timeit module. We can execute the two implementations a thousand times each to see how the timing compares. Using the fib(20) and fibc(20) methods shows just how costly this calculation is without the benefit of caching. Because the naïve version is so slow, the timeit number of repetitions was reduced to only 1,000. Following are the results:

- Naive 3.23
- Cached 0.0779

Note that we can't trivially use the timeit module on the fibc() function. The cached values will remain in place: we'll only compute the fibc(20) function once, which populates this value in the cache. Each of the remaining 999 iterations will simply fetch the value from the cache. We need to actually clear the cache between uses of the fibc() function or the time drops to almost 0. This is done with a fibc.cache_clear() method built by the decorator.

The concept of memoization is powerful. There are many algorithms that can benefit from memoization of results. There are also some algorithms that might not benefit quite so much.

The number of combinations of p things taken in groups of r is often stated as follows:

$$\binom{p}{r} = \frac{p!}{r!(p-r)!}$$

This binomial function involves computing three factorial values. It might make sense to use an @lru_cache decorator on a factorial function. A program that calculates a number of binomial values will not need to re-compute all of those factorials. For cases where similar values are computed repeatedly, the speedup can be impressive. For situations where the cached values are rarely reused, the overheads of maintaining the cached values outweigh any speedups.

When computing similar values repeatedly, we see the following:

- Naive Factorial 0.174
- Cached Factorial 0.046
- Cleared Cache Factorial 1.335

If we re-calculate the same binomial with the timeit module, we'll only really do the computation once, and return the same value the rest of the time; the cleared cache factorial shows the impact of clearing the cache before each calculation. The cache clearing operation—the cache_clear() function—introduces some overheads, making it appear more costly than it actually is. The moral of the story is that an lru_cache decorator is trivial to add. It often has a profound impact; but it may also have no impact, depending on the distribution of the actual data.

It's important to note that the cache is a stateful object. This design pushes the edge of the envelope on purely functional programming. A possible ideal is to avoid assignment statements and the associated changes of state. This concept of avoiding stateful variables is exemplified by a recursive function: the current state is contained in the argument values, and not in the changing values of variables. We've seen how tail-call optimization is an essential performance improvement to assure that this idealized recursion actually works nicely with the available processor hardware and limited memory budgets. In Python, we do this tail-call optimization manually by replacing the tail recursions with a for loop. Caching is a similar kind of optimization: we'll implement it manually as needed.

In principle, each call to a function with an LRU cache has two results: the expected result and a new cache object which should be used for all future requests. Pragmatically, we encapsulate the new cache object inside the decorated version of the fibc() function.

Caching is not a panacea. Applications that work with float values might not benefit much from memoization because all floats differ by small amounts. The least-significant bits of a float value are sometimes just random noise which prevents the exact equality test in the lru_cache decorator from working.

We'll revisit this in *Chapter 16, Optimizations and Improvements*. We'll look at some additional ways to implement this.

Defining classes with total ordering

The `total_ordering` decorator is helpful for creating new class definitions that implement a rich set of comparison operators. This might apply to numeric classes that subclass `numbers.Number`. It may also apply to semi-numeric classes.

As an example of a semi-numeric class, consider a playing card. It has a numeric rank and a symbolic suit. The rank matters only when doing simulations of some games. This is particularly important when simulating casino Blackjack. Like numbers, cards have an ordering. We often sum the point values of each card, making them number-like. However, multiplication of *card × card* doesn't really make any sense.

We can almost emulate a playing card with a `namedtuple()` function as follows:

```
Card1 = namedtuple("Card1", ("rank", "suit"))
```

This suffers from a profound limitation: all comparisons include both a rank and a suit by default. This leads to the following awkward behavior:

```
>>> c2s= Card1(2, '\u2660')
>>> c2h= Card1(2, '\u2665')
>>> c2h == c2s
False
```

This doesn't work well for Blackjack. It's unsuitable for certain Poker simulations also.

We'd really prefer the cards to be compared only by their rank. Following is a much more useful class definition. We'll show this in two parts. The first part defines the essential attributes:

```
@total_ordering
class Card(tuple):
    __slots__ = ()
    def __new__( class_, rank, suit ):
        obj= tuple.__new__(Card, (rank, suit))
        return obj
    def __repr__(self):
        return "{0.rank}{0.suit}".format(self)
    @property
    def rank(self):
        return self[0]
    @property
    def suit(self):
        return self[1]
```

This class extends the `tuple` class; it has no additional slots, thereby making it immutable. We've overridden the __new__() method so that we can seed initial values of a rank and a suit. We've provided a __repr__() method to print a string representation of a `Card`. We've provided two properties to extract a rank and a suit using attribute names.

The rest of the class definition shows how we can define just two comparisons:

```
def __eq__(self, other):
    if isinstance(other,Card):
        return self.rank == other.rank
    elif isinstance(other,Number):
        return self.rank == other
def __lt__(self, other):
    if isinstance(other,Card):
        return self.rank < other.rank
    elif isinstance(other,Number):
        return self.rank < other
```

We've defined the __eq__() and __lt__() functions. The `@total_ordering` decorator handles the construction of all other comparisons. In both cases, we've allowed comparisons between cards and also between a card and a number.

First, we get proper comparison of only the ranks as follows:

```
>>> c2s= Card(2, '\u2660')
>>> c2h= Card(2, '\u2665')
>>> c2h == c2s
True
>>> c2h == 2
True
```

We can use this class for a number of simulations with simplified syntax to compare ranks of cards. Further, we also have a rich set of comparison operators as follows:

```
>>> c2s= Card(2, '\u2660')
>>> c3h= Card(3, '\u2665')
>>> c4c= Card(4, '\u2663')
>>> c2s <= c3h < c4c
True
>>> c3h >= c3h
```

```
True
>>> c3h > c2s
True
>>> c4c != c2s
True
```

We didn't need to write all of the comparison method functions; they were generated by the decorator. The decorator's creation of operators isn't perfect. In our case, we've asked for comparisons with integers as well as between `Card` instances. This reveals some problems.

Operations like the `c4c > 3` and `3 < c4c` commands would raise `TypeError` exceptions. This is a limitation in what the `total_ordering` decorator can do. The problem rarely shows up in practice, since this kind of mixed-class coercion is relatively uncommon.

Object-oriented programming is not antithetical to functional programming. There is a realm in which the two techniques are complementary. Python's ability to create immutable objects works particularly well with functional programming techniques. We can easily avoid the complexities of stateful objects, but still benefit from encapsulation to keep related method functions together. It's particularly helpful to define class properties that involve complex calculations; this binds the calculations to the class definition, making the application easier to understand.

Defining number classes

In some cases, we might want to extend the numeric tower available in Python. A subclass of `numbers.Number` may simplify a functional program. We can, for example, isolate parts of a complex algorithm to the `Number` subclass definition, making other parts of the application simpler or clearer.

Python already offers a rich variety of numeric types. The built-in types of the `int` and `float` variables cover a wide variety of problem domains. When working with currency, the `decimal.Decimal` package handles this elegantly. In some cases, we might find the `fractions.Fraction` class to be more appropriate than the `float` variable.

When working with geographic data, for example, we might consider creating a subclass of `float` variable that introduces additional attributes for conversion between degrees of latitude (or longitude) and radians. The arithmetic operations in this subclass could be done $mod\,(2\pi)$ to simplify calculations that move across the equator or the Greenwich meridian.

Since Python `Numbers` class is intended to be immutable, ordinary functional design can be applied to all of the various method functions. The exceptional Python in-place special methods (for example, `__iadd__()` function) can be simply ignored.

When working with subclasses of `Number`, we have a fairly extensive volume of design considerations as follows:

- Equality testing and hash value calculation. The core features of hash calculation for numbers is documented in the *9.1.2 Notes for type implementors* section of the *Python Standard Library*.

- The other comparison operators (often defined via `@total_ordering` decorator).

- The arithmetic operators: `+`, `-`, `*`, `/`, `//`, `%`, and `**`. There are special methods for the forward operations as well as additional methods for reverse type-matching. Given an expression like `a-b`, Python uses the type of a to attempt to locate an implementation of the `__sub__()` method function: effectively, the `a.__sub__(b)` method. If the class of the left-hand value, a in this case, doesn't have the method or returns the `NotImplemented` exception, then the right-hand value is examined to see if the `b.__rsub__(a)` method provides a result. There's an additional special case that applies when b's class is a subclass of a's class: this allows the subclass to override the left-hand side operation choice.

- The bit-fiddling operators: `&`, `|`, `^`, `>>`, `<<`, and `~`. These might not make sense for floating-point values; omitting these special methods might be the best design.

- Some additional functions like `round()`, `pow()`, and `divmod()` are implemented by numeric special method names. These might be meaningful for this class of numbers.

Chapter 7, Mastering Object-Oriented Python provides a detailed example of creating a new type of number. Visit the link for more details:

```
https://www.packtpub.com/application-development/mastering-object-
oriented-python.
```

As we noted previously, functional programming and object-oriented programming can be complementary. We can easily define classes that follow functional programming design patterns. Adding new kinds of numbers is one example of leveraging Python's object-oriented features to create more readable functional programs.

Applying partial arguments with partial()

The `partial()` function leads to something called partial application. A partially applied function is a new function built from an old function and a subset of the required arguments. It is closely related to the concept of currying. Much of the theoretical background is not relevant here, since currying doesn't apply to the way Python functions are implemented. The concept, however, can lead us to some handy simplifications.

We can look at trivial examples as follows:

```
>>> exp2= partial(pow, 2)
>>> exp2(12)
4096
>>> exp2(17)-1
131071
```

We've created a function, `exp2(y)`, which is the `pow(2,y)` function. The `partial()` function bounds the first positional parameter to the `pow()` function. When we evaluate the newly created `exp2()` function, we get values computed from the argument bound by the `partial()` function, plus the additional argument provided to the `exp2()` function.

The bindings of positional parameters are handed in a strict left-to-right order. For functions that accept keyword parameters, these can also be provided when building the partially applied function.

We can also create this kind of partially applied function with a lambda form as follows:

```
exp2= lambda y: pow(2,y)
```

Neither is clearly superior. Measuring performance shows that the `partial()` function is a hair faster than a lambda form in the following manner:

- partial 0.37
- lambda 0.42

This is 0.05 seconds over 1,000,000 iterations: not a remarkable savings.

Since lambda forms have all of the capabilities of the `partial()` function, it seems that we can safely set this function aside as not being profoundly useful. We'll return to it in *Chapter 14, The PyMonad Library*, and look at how we can accomplish this with currying also.

Reducing sets of data with reduce()

The `sum()`, `len()`, `max()`, and `min()` functions are — in a way — all specializations of a more general algorithm expressed by the `reduce()` function. The `reduce()` function is a higher-order function that folds a function into each pair of items in an iterable.

A sequence object is given as follows:

```
d = [2, 4, 4, 4, 5, 5, 7, 9]
```

The function, `reduce(lambda x,y: x+y, d)`, will fold in + operators to the list as follows:

```
2+4+4+4+5+5+7+9
```

Including `()` can show the effective grouping as follows:

```
((((((2+4)+4)+4)+5)+5)+7)+9
```

Python's standard interpretation of expressions involves a left-to-right evaluation of operators. The fold left isn't a big change in meaning.

We can also provide an initial value as follows:

```
reduce(lambda x,y: x+y**2, iterable, 0)
```

If we don't, the initial value from the sequence is used as the initialization. Providing an initial value is essential when there's a `map()` function as well as a `reduce()` function. Following is how the right answer is computed with an explicit 0 initializer:

```
0+ 2**2+ 4**2+ 4**2+ 4**2+ 5**2+ 5**2+ 7**2+ 9**2
```

If we omit the initialization of 0, and the `reduce()` function uses the first item as an initial value, we get the following wrong answer:

```
2+ 4**2+ 4**2+ 4**2+ 5**2+ 5**2+ 7**2+ 9**2
```

We can define a number of built-in reductions using the `reduce()` higher-order function as follows:

```
sum2= lambda iterable: reduce(lambda x,y: x+y**2, iterable, 0)
sum= lambda iterable: reduce(lambda x, y: x+y, iterable)
count= lambda iterable: reduce(lambda x, y: x+1, iterable, 0)
min= lambda iterable: reduce(lambda x, y: x if x < y else y,
iterable)
```

```
max= lambda iterable: reduce(lambda x, y: x if x > y else y,
iterable)
```

The `sum2()` reduction function is the sum of squares, useful for computing standard deviation of a set of samples. This `sum()` reduction function mimics the built-in `sum()` function. The `count()` reduction function is similar to the `len()` function, but it can work on an iterable, where the `len()` function can only work on a materialized `collection` object.

The `min()` and `max()` functions mimic the built-in reductions. Because the first item of the iterable is used for initialization, these two functions will work properly. If we provided any initial value to these `reduce()` functions, we might incorrectly use a value that never occurred in the original iterable.

Combining map() and reduce()

We can see how to build higher-order functions around these simple definitions. We'll show a simplistic map-reduce function that combines the `map()` and `reduce()` functions as follows:

```
def map_reduce(map_fun, reduce_fun, iterable):
    return reduce(reduce_fun, map(map_fun, iterable))
```

We've created a composite function from the `map()` and `reduce()` functions that take three arguments: the mapping, the reduction operation, and the iterable or sequence to process.

We can build a sum-squared reduction using the `map()` and `reduce()` functions separately as follows:

```
def sum2_mr(iterable):
    return map_reduce(lambda y: y**2, lambda x,y: x+y, iterable)
```

In this case, we've used the `lambda y: y**2` parameter as a mapping to square each value. The reduction is simply `lambda x,y: x+y` parameter. We don't need to explicitly provide an initial value because the initial value will be the first item in the iterable after the `map()` function has squared it.

The `lambda x,y: x+y` parameter is merely the + operator. Python offers all of the arithmetic operators as short functions in the `operator` module. Following is how we can slightly simplify our map-reduce operation:

```
import operator
def sum2_mr2(iterable):
    return map_reduce(lambda y: y**2, operator.add, iterable)
```

We've used the `operator.add` method to sum our values instead of the longer lambda form.

Following is how we can count values in an iterable:

```
def count_mr(iterable):

    return map_reduce(lambda y: 1, operator.add, iterable)
```

We've used the `lambda y: 1` parameter to map each value to a simple 1. The count is then a `reduce()` function using the `operator.add` method.

The general-purpose `reduce()` function allows us to create any species of reduction from a large dataset to a single value. There are some limitations, however, on what we should do with the `reduce()` function.

We should avoid executing commands such as the following:

```
reduce(operator.add, ["1", ",", "2", ",", "3"], "")
```

Yes, it works. However, the `"".join(["1", ",", "2", ",", "3"])` method is considerably more efficient. We measured 0.23 seconds per million to do the `"".join()` function versus 0.69 seconds to do the `reduce()` function.

Using reduce() and partial()

The `sum()` function can be seen as the `partial(reduce, operator.add)` method. This, too, gives us a hint as to how we can create other mappings and other reductions. We can, indeed, define all of the commonly used reductions as partials instead of lambdas.

Following are two examples:

```
sum2= partial(reduce, lambda x,y: x+y**2)
count= partial(reduce, lambda x,y: x+1)
```

We can now use these functions via the `sum2(some_data)` or the `count(some_iter)` method. As we noted previously, it's not clear how much benefit this has. It's possible that a particularly complex calculation can be explained simply with functions like this.

Using map() and reduce() to sanitize raw data

When doing data cleansing, we'll often introduce filters of various degrees of complexity to exclude invalid values. We may also include a mapping to sanitize values in the cases where a valid but improperly formatted value can be replaced with a valid but proper value.

We might produce the following output:

```
def comma_fix(data):
    try:
        return float(data)
    except ValueError:
        return float(data.replace(",", ""))
def clean_sum(cleaner, data):
    return reduce(operator.add, map(cleaner, data))
```

We've defined a simple mapping, the `comma_fix()` class, that will convert data from a nearly correct format into a usable floating-point value.

We've also defined a map-reduce that applies a given cleaner function, the `comma_fix()` class, in this case, to the data before doing a `reduce()` function using the `operator.add` method.

We can apply the previously described function as follows:

```
>>> d = ('1,196', '1,176', '1,269', '1,240', '1,307',
... '1,435', '1,601', '1,654', '1,803', '1,734')
>>> clean_sum(comma_fix, d)
14415.0
```

We've cleaned the data, by fixing the commas, as well as computed a sum. The syntax is very convenient for combining these two operations.

We have to be careful, however, of using the cleaning function more than once. If we're also going to compute a sum of squares, we really should not execute the following command:

```
comma_fix_squared = lambda x: comma_fix(x)**2
```

If we use the `clean_sum(comma_fix_squared, d)` method as part of computing a standard deviation, we'll do the comma-fixing operation twice on the data: once to compute the sum and once to compute the sum of squares. This is a poor design; caching the results with an `lru_cache` decorator can help. Materializing the sanitized intermediate values as a temporary `tuple` object is probably better.

Using groupby() and reduce()

A common requirement is to summarize data after partitioning it into groups. We can use a `defaultdict(list)` method to partition data. We can then analyze each partition separately. In *Chapter 4, Working with Collections*, we looked at some ways to group and partition. In *Chapter 8, The Itertools Module*, we looked at others.

Following is some sample data that we need to analyze:

```
>>> data = [('4', 6.1), ('1', 4.0), ('2', 8.3), ('2', 6.5),
... ('1', 4.6), ('2', 6.8), ('3', 9.3), ('2', 7.8), ('2', 9.2),
... ('4', 5.6), ('3', 10.5), ('1', 5.8), ('4', 3.8), ('3', 8.1),
... ('3', 8.0), ('1', 6.9), ('3', 6.9), ('4', 6.2), ('1', 5.4),
... ('4', 5.8)]
```

We've got a sequence of raw data values with a key and a measurement for each key.

One way to produce usable groups from this data is to build a dictionary that maps a key to a list of members in this group as follows:

```
from collections import defaultdict
def partition(iterable, key=lambda x:x):
    """Sort not required."""
    pd = defaultdict(list)
    for row in iterable:
        pd[key(row)].append(row)
    for k in sorted(pd):
        yield k, iter(pd[k])
```

This will separate each item in the iterable into individual groups. The `key()` function is used to extract a key value from each item. This key is used to append each item to a list in the `pd` dictionary. The resulting value of this function matches the results of the `itertools.groupby()` function: it's an iterable sequence of the (group key, iterator) pairs.

Following is the same feature done with the `itertools.groupby()` function:

```
def partition_s(iterable, key= lambda x:x):
    """Sort required"""
    return groupby(iterable, key)
```

The important difference in the inputs to each function is that the `groupby()` function version requires data already sorted by the key whereas the `defaultdict` version doesn't require sorting. For very large sets of data, the sort can be expensive measured in both time and storage. The final sort of the keys does create an intermediate list object, but this object might not be as large as the original set of data, depending on the cardinality of the keys.

We can summarize the grouped data as follows:

```
mean= lambda seq: sum(seq)/len(seq)
var= lambda mean, seq: sum( (x-mean)**2/mean for x in seq)
def summarize( key_iter ):
    key, item_iter= key_iter
    values= tuple((v for k,v in item_iter))
    μ= mean(values)
    return key, μ, var(μ, values)
```

The results of the `partition()` functions will be a sequence of `(key, iterator)` two tuples. We'll separate the key from the item iterator. Each item in the item iterator is one of the original objects in the source data; these are `(key, value)` pairs; we only want the values, and so we've used a simple generator expression to separate the source keys from the values.

We can also execute the following command to pick the second item from each of the two tuples:

```
map(snd, item_iter)
```

This requires the `snd= lambda x: x[1]` method.

We can use the following command to apply the `summarize()` function to each partition:

```
>>> partition1= partition(list(data), key=lambda x:x[0])
>>> groups= map(summarize, partition1)
```

The alternative commands are as follows:

```
>>> partition2= partition_s(sorted(data), key=lambda x:x[0])
>>> groups= map(summarize, partition2)
```

Both will provide us summary values for each group. The resulting group statistics look as follows:

```
1 5.34 0.93
2 7.72 0.63
3 8.56 0.89
4 5.5 0.7
```

The variance can be used as part of a x^2 test to determine if the null hypothesis holds for this data. The null hypothesis asserts that there's nothing to see; the variance in the data is essentially random. We can also compare the data between the four groups to see if the various means are consistent with the null hypothesis or there is some statistically significant variation.

Summary

In this chapter, we've looked at a number of functions in the `functools` module. This library module provides a number of functions that help us create sophisticated functions and classes.

We've looked at the `@lru_cache` function as a way to boost certain types of applications with frequent re-calculations of the same values. This decorator is of tremendous value for certain kinds of functions that take the `integer` or the `string` argument values. It can reduce processing by simply implementing memoization.

We looked at the `@total_ordering` function as a decorator to help us build objects that support rich ordering comparisons. This is at the fringe of functional programming, but is very helpful when creating new kinds of numbers.

The `partial()` function creates a new function with the partial application of argument values. As an alternative, we can build a `lambda` with similar features. The use case for this is ambiguous.

We also looked at the `reduce()` function as a higher-order function. This generalizes reductions like the `sum()` function. We'll use this function in several examples in the later chapters. This fits logically with the `filter()` and `map()` functions as an important higher-order function.

In the next chapters, we'll look at how we can build higher-order functions using decorators. These higher-order functions can lead to slightly simpler and clearer syntax. We can use decorators to define an isolated aspect that we need to incorporate into a number of other functions or classes.

11
Decorator Design Techniques

Python offers us many ways to create higher-order functions. In *Chapter 5,
Higher-order Functions*, we looked at two techniques: defining a function which
accepts a function as an argument and defining a subclass of `Callable` which is
either initialized with a function or called with a function as an argument.

In this chapter, we'll look at using a decorator to build a function based on
another function. We'll also look at two functions from the `functools` module,
the `update_wrapper()` and `wraps()` functions, that can help us build decorators.

One of the benefits of decorated functions is that we can create composite
functions. These are single functions that embody functionality from several
sources. A composite function, $f \circ g(x)$, can be somewhat more expressive of
a complex algorithm than $f(g(x))$. It's often helpful to have a number of syntax
alternatives for expressing complex processing.

Decorators as higher-order functions

The core idea of a decorator is to transform some original function into another form.
A decorator creates a kind of composite function based on the decorator and the
original function being decorated.

A decorator function can be used in one of the two following ways:

- As a prefix that creates a new function with the same name as the base
  function as follows:

```
@decorator
def original_function():
    pass
```

- As an explicit operation that returns a new function, possibly with a new name:

```
def original_function():
    pass
original_function= decorator(original_function)
```

These are two different syntaxes for the same operation. The prefix notation has the advantages of being tidy and succinct. The prefix location is more visible to some readers. The suffix notation is explicit and slightly more flexible. While the prefix notation is common, there is one reason for using the suffix notation: we might not want the resulting function to replace the original function. We might want to execute the following command that allows us to use both the decorated and the undecorated functions:

```
new_function = decorator(original_function)
```

Python functions are first-class objects. A function that accepts a function as an argument and returns a function as the result is clearly a built-in feature of the language. The open question then is how do we update or adjust the internal code structure of a function?

The answer is we don't.

Rather than messing about on the inside of the code, it's much cleaner to define a new function that wraps the original function. We have two tiers of higher-order functions involved in defining a decorator as follows:

- The decorator function applies a wrapper to a base function and returns the new wrapper. This function can do some one-time only evaluation as part of building the decorated function.
- The wrapper function can (and usually does) evaluate the base function. This function will be evaluated every time the decorated function is evaluated.

Here's an example of a simple decorator:

```
from functools import wraps
def nullable(function):
    @wraps(function)
    def null_wrapper(arg):
        return None if arg is None else function(arg)
    return null_wrapper
```

We almost always want to use the `functools.wraps()` function to assure that the decorated function retains the attributes of the original function. Copying the __ name__ , and __doc__ attributes, for example, assures that the resulting decorated function has the name and docstring of the original function.

The resulting composite function, called `null_wrapper()` function in the definition of the decorator, is also a kind of higher-order function that combines the original function, the `function()` function, in an expression that preserves the None values. The original function is not an explicit argument; it is a free variable that will get its value from the context in which the `wrapper()` function is defined.

The decorator function's return value will return the newly minted function. It's important that decorators only return functions, and not attempt any processing of data. Decorators are meta-programming: a code that creates a code. The `wrapper()` function, however, will be used to process the real data.

We can apply our `@nullable` decorator to create a composite function as follows:

```
nlog = nullable(math.log)
```

We now have a function, `nlog()`, which is a null-aware version of the `math.log()` function. We can use our composite, `nlog()` function, as follows:

```
>>> some_data = [10, 100, None, 50, 60]
>>> scaled = map(nlog, some_data)
>>> list(scaled)
[2.302585092994046, 4.605170185988092, None, 3.912023005428146,
4.0943445622221]
```

We've applied the function to a collection of data values. The None value politely leads to a None result. There was no exception processing involved.

 This example isn't really suitable for unit testing. We'll need to round the values for testing purposes. For this, we'll need a null-aware `round()` function too.

Here's how we can create a null-aware rounding function using decorator notation:

```
@nullable
def nround4(x):
    return round(x,4)
```

This function is a partial application of the `round()` function, wrapped to be null-aware. In some respects, this is a relatively sophisticated bit of functional programming that's readily available to Python programmers.

We could also create the null-aware rounding function using the following:

```
nround4= nullable(lambda x: round(x,4))
```

This has the same effect, at some cost in clarity.

We can use this round4() function to create a better test case for our nlog() function as follows:

```
>>> some_data = [10, 100, None, 50, 60]
>>> scaled = map(nlog, some_data)
>>> [nround4(v) for v in scaled]
[2.3026, 4.6052, None, 3.912, 4.0943]
```

This result will be independent of any platform considerations.

This decorator makes an assumption that the decorated function is unary. We would need to revisit this design to create a more general-purpose null-aware decorator that works with arbitrary collections of arguments.

In *Chapter 14, The PyMonad Library*, we'll look at an alternative approach to this problem of tolerating the None values. The PyMonad library defines a Maybe class of objects which may have a proper value or may be the None value.

Using functool's update_wrapper() functions

The @wraps decorator applies the update_wrapper() function to preserve a few attributes of a wrapped function. In general, this does everything we need by default. This function copies a specific list of attributes from the original function to the resulting function created by a decorator. What's the specific list of attributes? It's defined by a module global.

The update_wrapper() function relies on a module global variable to determine what attributes to preserve. The WRAPPER_ASSIGNMENTS variable defines the attributes that are copied by default. The default value is this list of attributes to copy:

```
('__module__', '__name__', '__qualname__', '__doc__',
'__annotations__')
```

It's difficult to make meaningful modifications to this list. In order to copy additional attributes, we have to assure that our functions are defined with these additional attributes. This is challenging, since the internals of the def statement aren't open to simple modification or change.

Because we can't easily fold in new attributes, it's difficult to locate reasons to modify or extend the way the wrapping works on a function. It's mostly interesting to use this variable as a piece of reference information.

If we're going to use the `callable` objects, then we might have a class that provides some additional attributes as part of the definition. We could then have a situation where a decorator might need to copy these additional attributes from the original wrapped `callable` object to the wrapping function being created. However, it seems simpler to make these kinds of changes in the class definition itself, rather than exploit tricky decorator techniques.

While there's a lot of flexibility available, much of it isn't helpful for ordinary application development.

Cross-cutting concerns

One general principle behind decorators is to allow us to build a composite function from the decorator and the original function to which the decorator is applied. The idea is to have a library of common decorators that can provide implementations for common concerns.

We often call these cross-cutting concerns because they apply across several functions. These are the sorts of things that we would like to design once via a decorator and have them applied in relevant classes throughout an application or a framework.

Concerns that are often centralized as described previously include the following:

- Logging
- Auditing
- Security
- Handling incomplete data

A `logging` decorator, for example, might write standardized messages to the application's logfile. An audit decorator might write details surrounding a database update. A security decorator might check some runtime context to be sure that the login user has the necessary permissions.

Our example of a *null-aware* wrapper for a function is a cross-cutting concern. In this case, we'd like to have a number of functions handle the `None` values by returning the `None` values instead of raising an exception. In applications where data is incomplete, we may have a need to process rows in a simple, uniform way without having to write lots of distracting `if` statements to handle missing values.

Composite design

The common mathematical notation for a composite function looks as follows:

$$f \circ g(x) = f\big(g(x)\big)$$

The idea is that we can define a new function, $f \circ g(x)$, that combines two other functions, $f(y)$ and $g(x)$.

Python's multiple-line definition of the form is as follows:

```
@f
def g(x):
    something
```

This is vaguely equivalent to $f \circ g(x)$. The equivalence isn't very precise because the @f decorator isn't the same as the mathematical abstraction of composing $f(y)$ and $g(x)$. For the purposes of discussing function composition, we'll ignore the implementation disconnect between the abstraction of $f(y)$ and the @f decorator.

Because decorators wrap another function, Python offers a slightly more generalized composition. We can think of Python design as follows:

$$w_\beta \bullet g \bullet w_\alpha (x) = w_\beta \big(g\big(w_\alpha(x)\big)\big)$$

A decorator applied to some application function, $g(x)$, will include a wrapper function. One portion of the wrapper, $w_\alpha(x)$, applies before the wrapped function and the other portion, $w_\beta(x)$, applies after the wrapped function.

The Wrapper() function often looks as follows:

```
@wraps(argument_function)
def something_wrapper(*args, **kw):
    # The "before" part, w_α, applied to *args or **kw
    result= argument_function(*args, **kw)
    # the "after" part, w_Ø, applied to the result
```

Details will vary, and vary widely. There are many clever things that can be done within this general framework.

A great deal of functional programming amounts to $f(g(x))$ kinds of constructs. We often spell these functions out because there's no real benefit from summarizing the function into a composite, $f \circ g(x)$. In some cases, however, we might want to use a composite function with a higher-order function like map(), filter(), or reduce().

We can always resort to the map(f, map(g, x)) method. It might be more clear, however, to use the map(f_g, x) method to apply a composite to a collection. It's important to note that there's no inherent performance advantage to either technique. The map() function is lazy: with two map() functions, one item will be taken from x, processed by the g() function, and then processed by the f() function. With a single map() function, an item will be taken from x and then processed by the f_g() composite function.

In *Chapter 14*, *The PyMonad Library*, we'll look at an alternative approach to this problem of creating composite functions from individual curried functions.

Preprocessing bad data

One cross-cutting concern in some exploratory data analysis applications is how to handle numeric values that are missing or cannot be parsed. We often have a mixture of float, int, and Decimal currency values that we'd like to process with some consistency.

In other contexts, we have *not applicable* or *not available* data values that shouldn't interfere with the main thread of the calculation. It's often handy to allow the Not Applicable values to pass through an expression without raising an exception. We'll focus on three bad-data conversion functions: bd_int(), bd_float(), and bd_decimal(). The composite feature we're adding will be defined before the built-in conversion function.

Here's a simple bad-data decorator:

```
import decimal
def bad_data(function):
    @wraps(function)
    def wrap_bad_data(text, *args, **kw):
        try:
            return function(text, *args, **kw)
        except (ValueError, decimal.InvalidOperation):
            cleaned= text.replace(",", "")
            return function(cleaned, *args, **kw)
    return wrap_bad_data
```

This function wraps a given conversion function to try a second conversion in the event the first conversion involved bad data. In the case of preserving the None values as a Not Applicable code, the exception handling would simply return the None value.

In this case, we've provided Python *args and **kw parameters. This assures that the wrapped functions can have additional argument values provided.

We can use this wrapper as follows:

```
bd_int= bad_data(int)
bd_float= bad_data(float)
bd_decimal= bad_data(Decimal)
```

This will create a suite of functions that can do conversions of good data as well as a limited amount of data cleansing to handle specific kinds of bad data.

Following are some examples of using the bd_int() function:

```
>>> bd_int("13")
13
>>> bd_int("1,371")
1371
>>> bd_int("1,371", base=16)
4977
```

We've applied the bd_int() function to a string that converted neatly and a string with the specific type of punctuation that we'll tolerate. We've also shown that we can provide additional parameters to each of these conversion functions.

We might like to have a more flexible decorator. One feature that we might like to add is the ability to handle a variety of data scrubbing alternatives. Simple, removal isn't always what we need. We may also need to remove $, or ° symbols, too. We'll look at more sophisticated, parameterized decorators in the next section.

Adding a parameter to a decorator

A common requirement is to customize a decorator with additional parameters. Rather than simply creating a composite $f \circ g(x)$, we're doing something a bit more complex. We're creating $\left(f(c) \bullet g \right)(x)$. We've applied a parameter, c, as part of creating the wrapper. This parameterized composite, $f(c) \circ g$, can then be used with the actual data, x.

In Python syntax, we can write it as follows:

```
@deco(arg)
def func( ):
    something
```

This will provide a parameterized `deco(arg)` function to the base function definition.

The effect is as follows:

```
def func( ):
    something

func= deco(arg)(func)
```

We've done three things and they are as follows:

1. Define a function, `func`.
2. Apply the abstract decorator, `deco()`, to its arguments to create a concrete decorator, `deco(arg)`.
3. Apply the concrete decorator, `deco(arg)`, to the base function to create the decorated version of the function, `deco(arg)(func)`.

A decorator with arguments involves indirect construction of the final function. We seem to have moved beyond merely higher-order functions into something even more abstract: higher-order functions that create higher-order functions.

We can expand our *bad-data* aware decorator to create a slightly more flexible conversion. We'll define a decorator that can accept parameters of characters to remove. Following is a parameterized decorator:

```
import decimal
def bad_char_remove(*char_list):
    def cr_decorator(function):
        @wraps(function)
        def wrap_char_remove(text, *args, **kw):
            try:
                return function(text, *args, **kw)
            except (ValueError, decimal.InvalidOperation):
                cleaned= clean_list(text, char_list)
                return function(cleaned, *args, **kw)
        return wrap_char_remove
    return cr_decorator
```

A parameterized decorator has three parts and they are as follows:

- The overall decorator. This defines and returns the abstract decorator. In this case, the `cr_decorator` is an abstract decorator. This has a free variable, `char_list`, that comes from the initial decorator.

- The abstract decorator. In this case, the `cr_decorator` decorator will have its free variable, `char_list`, bound so that it can be applied to a function.

- The decorating wrapper. In this example, the `wrap_char_remove` function will replace the wrapped function. Because of the `@wraps` decorator, the `__name__` (and other attributes) will be replaced with the name of the function being wrapped.

We can use this decorator to create conversion functions as follows:

```
@bad_char_remove("$", ",")
def currency(text, **kw):
    return Decimal(text, **kw)
```

We've used our decorator to wrap a `currency()` function. The essential feature of the `currency()` function is a reference to the `decimal.Decimal` constructor.

This `currency()` function will now handle some variant data formats:

```
>>> currency("13")
Decimal('13')
>>> currency("$3.14")
Decimal('3.14')
>>> currency("$1,701.00")
Decimal('1701.00')
```

We can now process input data using a relatively simple `map(currency, row)` method to convert source data from strings to usable `Decimal` values. The `try:`/`except:` error-handling has been isolated to a function that we've used to build a composite conversion function.

We can use a similar design to create Null-tolerant functions. These functions would use a similar `try:`/`except:` wrapper, but would simply return the `None` values.

Implementing more complex descriptors

We can easily write the following commands:

```
@f_wrap
```

```
@g_wrap
```

```
def h(x):
    something
```

There's nothing in Python to stop us. This has a meaning somewhat like $f \circ g \circ h(x)$. However, the name is merely $h(x)$. Because of this potential confusion, we need to be cautious when creating functions that involve deeply nested descriptors. If our intent is simply to handle some cross-cutting concerns, then each decorator can handle a concern without creating much confusion.

If, on the other hand, we're using a decoration to create a composite function, it might also be better to use the following command:

```
f_g_h= f_wrap(g_wrap(h))
```

This clarifies as to what precisely is going on. Decorator functions don't correspond precisely with the mathematical abstraction of functions being composed. The decorator function actually contains a wrapper function that will contain the function being composed. This distinction between a function and a decorator that creates a composite from the function can become a problem when trying to understand an application.

As with other aspects of functional programming, a succinct and expressive program is the goal. Decorators who are expressive are welcome. Writing an über-meta-super-callable that can do everything in the application with only minor customizations may be succinct, but it's rarely expressive.

Recognizing design limitations

In the case of our data cleanup, the simplistic removal of stray characters may not be sufficient. When working with the geolocation data, we may have a wide variety of input formats that include simple degrees (`37.549016197`), degrees and minutes (`37° 32.94097⊠`), and degrees-minutes-seconds (`37° 32⊠ 56.46⊠`). Of course, there can be even more subtle cleaning problems: some devices will create an output with the Unicode U+00BA character, º, instead of the similar-looking degree character, °, which is U+00B0.

For this reason, it is often necessary to provide a separate cleansing function that's bundled in with the conversion function. This function will handle the more sophisticated conversions required by inputs that are as wildly inconsistent in format as latitudes and longitudes.

How can we implement this? We have a number of choices. Simple higher-order functions are a good choice. A decorator, on the other hand, doesn't work out terribly well. We'll look at a decorator-based design to see that there are limitations to what makes sense in a decorator.

The requirements have two orthogonal design considerations and they are as follows:

1.   The output conversion (`int`, `float`, `Decimal`)
2.   The input cleaning (clean stray characters, reformat coordinates)

Ideally, one of these aspects is an essential function that gets wrapped and the other aspect is something that's included via a wrapper. The choice of essence versus wrap isn't clear. One of the reasons it isn't clear is that our previous examples are a bit more complex than a simple two-part composite.

In the previous examples, we were actually creating a three-part composite:

*   The output conversion (`int`, `float`, `Decimal`)
*   The input cleansing—either a simple replace or a more complex multiple-character replacement
*   The function which attempted the conversion, did the cleansing as a response to an exception, and attempted the conversion again

The third part – attempting the conversion and retrying – is the actual wrapper that also forms a part of the composite function. As we noted previously, a wrapper contains a before phase and an after phase, which we've called $w_\alpha(x)$ and $w_\beta(x)$, respectively.

We want to use this wrapper to create a composite of two additional functions. We have two choices for the syntax. We could include the cleansing function as an argument to the decorator on the conversion as follows:

```
@cleanse_before(cleanser)
def convert(text):
    something
```

Or, we could include the conversion function as an argument to the decorator for a
cleansing function as follows:

```
@then_convert(converter)
def clean(text):
    something
```

In this case, we can choose the `@then_convert(converter)` style decorator because
we're relying—for the most part—on the built-in conversions. Our point is to show
that the choice is not crystal clear.

The decorator looks as follows:

```
def then_convert(convert_function):
    def clean_convert_decorator(clean_function):
        @wraps(clean_function)
        def cc_wrapper(text, *args, **kw):
            try:
                return convert_function(text, *args, **kw)
            except (ValueError, decimal.InvalidOperation):
                cleaned= clean_function(text)
                return convert_function(cleaned, *args, **kw)
        return cc_wrapper
    return clean_convert_decorator
```

We've defined a three-layer decorator. At the heart is the `cc_wrapper()` function that
applies the `convert_function` function. If this fails, then it uses a `clean_function`
function and then tries the `convert_function` function again. This function is
wrapped around the `clean_function` function by the `then_convert_decorator()`
concrete decorator function. The concrete decorator has the `convert_function`
function as a free variable. The concrete decorator is created by the decorator
interface, `then_convert()`, which is customized by a conversion function.

We can now build a slightly more flexible cleanse and convert function as follows:

```
@then_convert(int)
def drop_punct(text):
    return text.replace(",", "").replace("$", "")
```

The integer conversion is a decorator applied to the given cleansing function. In this
case, the cleansing function removes $ and , characters. The integer conversion is
wrapped around this cleansing.

We can use the integer conversion as follows:

```
>>> drop_punct("1,701")
1701
>>> drop_punct("97")
97
```

While this can encapsulate some sophisticated cleansing and converting into a very tidy package, the results are potentially confusing. The name of the function is the name of the core cleansing algorithm; the other function's contribution to the composite is lost.

As an alternative, we can use the integer conversion as follows:

```
def drop_punct(text):
    return text.replace(",", "").replace("$", "")
drop_punct_int = then_convert(int)(drop_punct)
```

This will allow us to provide a new name to the decorated cleaning function. This solves the naming problem, but the construction of the final function via the `then_convert(int)(drop_punct)` method is rather opaque.

It seems like we've reached the edge of the envelope here. The decorator model isn't ideal for this kind of design. Generally, decorators work well when we have a number of relatively simple and fixed aspects that we want to include with a given function (or a class). Decorators are also important when these additional aspects can be looked at as an infrastructure or a support, and not something essential to the meaning of the application code.

For something that involves multiple orthogonal dimensions, we might want to result to the `Callables` function with various kinds of plugin strategy objects. This might provide something more palatable. We might want to look closely at creating higher-order functions. We can then create partial functions with various combinations of parameters for the higher-order functions.

The typical examples of logging or security testing can be considered as the kind of background processing that isn't specific to the problem domain. When we have processing that is as ubiquitous as the air that surrounds us, then a decorator might be more appropriate.

Summary

In this chapter, we've looked at two kinds of decorators: the simple decorator with no arguments and parameterized decorators. We've seen how decorators involve an indirect composition between functions: the decorator wraps a function (defined inside the decorator) around another function.

Using the `functools.wraps()` decorator assures that our decorators will properly copy attributes from the function being wrapped. This should be a piece of every decorator we write.

In the next chapter, we'll look at the multiprocessing and multithreading techniques that are available to us. These packages become particularly helpful in a functional programming context. When we eliminate a complex shared state and design around nonstrict processing, we can leverage parallelism to improve the performance.

12
The Multiprocessing and Threading Modules

When we eliminate complex, shared state and design around non-strict processing, we can leverage parallelism to improve performance. In this chapter, we'll look at the multiprocessing and multithreading techniques that are available to us. Python library packages become particularly helpful when applied to algorithms that permit lazy evaluation.

The central idea here is to distribute a functional program across several threads within a process or across several processes. If we've created a sensible functional design, we don't have complex interactions among application components; we have functions that accept argument values and produce results. This is an ideal structure for a process or a thread.

We'll focus on the `multiprocessing` and `concurrent.futures` modules. These modules allow a number of parallel execution techniques.

We'll also focus on process-level parallelism instead of multithreading. The idea behind process parallelism allows us to ignore Python's **Global Interpreter Lock (GIL)** and achieve outstanding performance.

For more information on Python's GIL, see `https://docs.python.org/3.3/c-api/init.html#thread-state-and-the-global-interpreter-lock`.

We won't emphasize features of the `threading` module. This is often used for parallel processing. If we have done our functional programming design well, any issues that stem from multithreaded write access should be minimized. However, the presence of the GIL means that multithreaded applications in **CPython** suffer from some small limitations. As waiting for I/O doesn't involve the GIL, it's possible that some I/O bound programs might have unusually good performance.

The most effective parallel processing occurs where there are no dependencies among the tasks being performed. With some careful design, we can approach parallel programming as an ideal processing technique. The biggest difficulty in developing parallel programs is coordinating updates to shared resources.

When following functional design patterns and avoiding stateful programs, we can also minimize concurrent updates to shared objects. If we can design software where lazy, non-strict evaluation is central, we can also design software where concurrent evaluation is possible.

Programs will always have some strict dependencies where ordering of operations matters. In the 2*(3+a) expression, the (3+a) subexpression must be evaluated first. However, when working with a collection, we often have situations where the processing order among items in the collection doesn't matter.

Consider the following two examples:

```
x = list(func(item) for item in y)
x = list(reversed([func(item) for item in y[::-1]]))
```

Both of these commands have the same result even though the items are evaluated in the reverse order.

Indeed, even this following command snippet has the same result:

```
import random
indices= list(range(len(y)))
random.shuffle(indices)
x = [None]*len(y)
for k in indices:
    x[k] = func(y[k])
```

The evaluation order is random. As the evaluation of each item is independent, the order of evaluation doesn't matter. This is the case with many algorithms that permit non-strict evaluation.

What concurrency really means

In a small computer, with a single processor and a single core, all evaluations are serialized only through the core of the processor. The operating system will interleave multiple processes and multiple threads through clever time-slicing arrangements.

On a computer with multiple CPUs or multiple cores in a single CPU, there can be some actual concurrent processing of CPU instructions. All other concurrency is simulated through time slicing at the OS level. A Mac OS X laptop can have 200 concurrent processes that share the CPU; this is far more processes than the number of available cores. From this, we can see that the OS time slicing is responsible for most of the apparently concurrent behavior.

The boundary conditions

Let's consider a hypothetical algorithm which has $O(n^2)$. Assume that there is an inner loop that involves 1,000 bytes of Python code. When processing 10,000 objects, we're executing 100 billion Python operations. This is the essential processing budget. We can try to allocate as many processes and threads as we feel might be helpful, but the processing budget can't change.

The individual CPython bytecode doesn't have a simple execution timing. However, a long-term average on a Mac OS X laptop shows that we can expect about 60 MB of code to be executed per second. This means that our 100 billion bytecode operation will take about 1,666 seconds, or 28 minutes.

If we have a dual processor, four-core computer, then we might cut the elapsed time to 25 percent of the original total: 7 minutes. This presumes that we can partition the work into four (or more) independent OS processes.

The important consideration here is that our budget of 100 billion bytecodes can't be changed. Parallelism won't magically reduce the workload. It can only change the schedule to, perhaps, reduce the elapsed time.

Switching to a better algorithm which is $O(n \log n)$ can reduce the workload to 132 MB of operations. At 60 MBps, this workload is considerably smaller. Parallelism won't have the kind of dramatic improvements that algorithm change will have.

Sharing resources with process or threads

The OS assures that there is little or no interaction between processes. For two processes to interact, some common OS resource must be explicitly shared. This can be a common file, a specific shared memory object, or a semaphore with a shared state between the processes. Processes are inherently independent, interaction is exceptional.

Multiple threads, on the other hand, are part of a single process; all threads of a process share OS resources. We can make an exception to get some thread-local memory that can be freely written without interference from other threads. Outside thread-local memory, operations that write to memory can set the internal state of the process in a potentially unpredictable order. Explicit locking must be used to avoid problems with these stateful updates. As noted previously, the overall sequence of instruction executions is rarely, strictly speaking, concurrent. The instructions from concurrent threads and processes are generally interleaved in an unpredictable order. With threading comes the possibility of destructive updates to shared variables and the need for careful locking. With parallel processing come the overheads of OS-level process scheduling.

Indeed, even at the hardware level, there are some complex memory write situations. For more information on issues in memory writes, visit `http://en.wikipedia.org/wiki/Memory_disambiguation`.

The existence of concurrent object updates is what raises havoc with trying to design multithreaded applications. Locking is one way to avoid concurrent writes to shared objects. Avoiding shared objects is another viable design technique. This is more applicable to functional programming.

In CPython, the GIL is used to assure that OS thread scheduling will not interfere with updates to Python data structures. In effect, the GIL changes the granularity of scheduling from machine instructions to Python virtual machine operations. Without the GIL, it's possible that an internal data structure might be corrupted by the interleaved interaction of competing threads.

Where benefits will accrue

A program that does a great deal of calculation and relatively little I/O will not see much benefit from concurrent processing. If a calculation has a budget of 28 minutes of computation, then interleaving the operations in different ways won't have very much impact. Switching from strict to non-strict evaluation of 100 billion bytecodes won't shrink the elapsed execution time.

However, if a calculation involves a great deal of I/O, then interleaving CPU processing and I/O requests can have an impact on performance. Ideally, we'd like to do our computations on some pieces of data while waiting for the OS to complete input of the next pieces of data.

We have two approaches to interleaving computation and I/O. They are as follows:

- We can try to interleave I/O and calculation for the entire problem as a whole. We might create a pipeline of processing with read, compute, and write as operations. The idea is to have individual data objects flowing through the pipe from one stage to the next. Each stage can operate in parallel.

- We can decompose the problem into separate, independent pieces that can be processed from the beginning to the end in parallel.

The differences between these approaches aren't crisp; there is a blurry middle region that's not clearly one or the other. For example, multiple parallel pipelines are a hybrid mixture of both designs. There are some formalisms that make it somewhat easier to design concurrent programs. The **Communicating Sequential Processes (CSP)** paradigm can help design message-passing applications. Packages such as `pycsp` can be used to add CSP formalisms to Python.

I/O-intensive programs often benefit from concurrent processing. The idea is to interleave I/O and processing. CPU-intensive programs rarely benefit from attempting concurrent processing.

Using multiprocessing pools and tasks

To make non-strict evaluation available in a larger context, the `multiprocessing` package introduces the concept of a `Pool` object. We can create a `Pool` object of concurrent worker processes, assign tasks to them, and expect the tasks to be executed concurrently. As noted previously, this creation does not actually mean simultaneous creation of `Pool` objects. It means that the order is difficult to predict because we've allowed OS scheduling to interleave execution of multiple processes. For some applications, this permits more work to be done in less elapsed time.

To make the most use of this capability, we need to decompose our application into components for which non-strict concurrent execution is beneficial. We'd like to define discrete tasks that can be processed in an indefinite order.

An application that gathers data from the Internet via web scraping is often optimized through parallel processing. We can create a `Pool` object of several identical website scrapers. The tasks are URLs to be analyzed by the pooled processes.

An application that analyzes multiple logfiles is also a good candidate for parallelization. We can create a `Pool` object of analytical processes. We can assign each logfile to an analyzer; this allows reading and analysis to proceed in parallel among the various workers in the `Pool` object. Each individual worker will involve serialized I/O and computation. However, one worker can be analyzing the computation while other workers are waiting for I/O to complete.

Processing many large files

Here is an example of a multiprocessing application. We'll scrape **Common Log Format** (CLF) lines in web logfiles. This is the generally used format for an access log. The lines tend to be long, but look like the following when wrapped to the book's margins:

```
99.49.32.197 - - [01/Jun/2012:22:17:54 -0400] "GET /favicon.ico
HTTP/1.1" 200 894 "-" "Mozilla/5.0 (Windows NT 6.0)
AppleWebKit/536.5 (KHTML, like Gecko) Chrome/19.0.1084.52
Safari/536.5"
```

We often have large numbers of large files that we'd like to analyze. The presence of many independent files means that concurrency will have some benefit for our scraping process.

We'll decompose the analysis into two broad areas of functionality. The first phase of any processing is the essential parsing of the logfiles to gather the relevant pieces of information. We'll decompose this into four stages. They are as follows:

1. All the lines from multiple source logfiles are read.
2. Then, create simple namedtuples from the lines of log entries in a collection of files.
3. The details of more complex fields such as dates and URLs are parsed.
4. Uninteresting paths from the logs are rejected; we can also think of this as passing only the interesting paths.

Once past the parsing phase, we can perform a large number of analyses. For our purposes in demonstrating the `multiprocessing` module, we'll look at a simple analysis to count occurrences of specific paths.

The first portion, reading from source files, involves the most input processing. The Python use of file iterators will translate into lower-level OS requests for buffering of data. Each OS request means that the process must wait for the data to become available.

Clearly, we want to interleave the other operations so that they are not waiting for I/O to complete. We can interleave operations along a spectrum from individual rows to whole files. We'll look at interleaving whole files first, as this is relatively simple to implement.

The functional design for parsing Apache CLF files can look as follows:

```
data = path_filter(access_detail_iter(access_iter(local_gzip
(filename))))
```

We've decomposed the larger parsing problem into a number of functions that will handle each portion of the parsing problem. The `local_gzip()` function reads rows from locally-cached GZIP files. The `access_iter()` function creates a simple `namedtuple` object for each row in the access log. The `access_detail_iter()` function will expand on some of the more difficult to parse fields. Finally, the `path_filter()` function will discard some paths and file extensions that aren't of much analytical value.

Parsing log files – gathering the rows

Here is the first stage in parsing a large number of files: reading each file and producing a simple sequence of lines. As the logfiles are saved in the `.gzip` format, we need to open each file with the `gzip.open()` function instead of the `io.open()` function or the `__builtins__.open()` function.

The `local_gzip()` function reads lines from locally cached files, as shown in the following command snippet:

```
def local_gzip(pattern):
    zip_logs= glob.glob(pattern)
    for zip_file in zip_logs:
        with gzip.open(zip_file, "rb") as log:
            yield (line.decode('us-ascii').rstrip() for line in log)
```

The preceding function iterates through all files. For each file, the yielded value is a generator function that will iterate through all lines within that file. We've encapsulated several things, including wildcard file matching, the details of opening a logfile compressed with the `.gzip` format, and breaking a file into a sequence of lines without any trailing \n characters.

The essential design pattern here is to yield values that are generator expressions for each file. The preceding function can be restated as a function and a mapping that applies that function to each file.

There are several other ways to produce similar output. For example, here is an alternative version of the inner `for` loop in the preceding example. The `line_iter()` function will also emit lines of a given file:

```
def line_iter(zip_file):
    log= gzip.open(zip_file, "rb")
    return (line.decode('us-ascii').rstrip() for line in log)
```

The `line_iter()` function applies the `gzip.open()` function and some line cleanup. We can use a mapping to apply the `line_iter()` function to all files that match a pattern as follows:

```
map(line_iter, glob.glob(pattern))
```

While this alternative mapping is succinct, it has the disadvantage of leaving open file objects lying around waiting to be properly garbage-collected when there are no more references. When processing a large number of files, this seems like a needless bit of overhead. For this reason, we'll focus on the `local_gzip()` function shown previously.

The previous alternative mapping has the distinct advantage of fitting well with the way the `multiprocessing` module works. We can create a worker pool and map tasks (such as file reading) to the pool of processes. If we do this, we can read these files in parallel; the open file objects will be part of separate processes.

An extension to this design will include a second function to transfer files from the web host using FTP. As the files are collected from the web server, they can be analyzed using the `local_gzip()` function.

The results of the `local_gzip()` function are used by the `access_iter()` function to create namedtuples for each row in the source file that describes a file access.

Parsing log lines into namedtuples

Once we have access to all of the lines of each logfile, we can extract details of the access that's described. We'll use a regular expression to decompose the line. From there, we can build a `namedtuple` object.

Here is a regular expression to parse lines in a CLF file:

```
format_pat= re.compile(
    r"(?P<host>[\d\.]+)\s+"
    r"(?P<identity>\S+)\s+"
    r"(?P<user>\S+)\s+"
    r"\[(?P<time>.+?)\]\s+"
    r'"(?P<request>.+?)"\s+'
```

```
    r"(?P<status>\d+)\s+"
    r"(?P<bytes>\S+)\s+"
    r'"(?P<referer>.*?)"\s+' # [SIC]
    r'"(?P<user_agent>.+?)"\s*'
)
```

We can use this regular expression to break each row into a dictionary of nine individual data elements. The use of [] and " to delimit complex fields such as the time, request, referrer, and user_agent parameters are handled gracefully by the namedtuple pattern.

Each individual access can be summarized as a namedtuple() function as follows:

```
Access = namedtuple('Access', ['host', 'identity', 'user', 'time',
'request', 'status', 'bytes', 'referer', 'user_agent'])
```

> We've taken pains to assure that the namedtuple function's fields match the regular expression group names in the (?P<name>) constructs for each portion of the record. By making sure the names match, we can very easily transform the parsed dictionary into a tuple for further processing.

Here is the access_iter() function that requires each file to be represented as an iterator over the lines of the file:

```
def access_iter(source_iter):
    for log in source_iter:
        for line in log:
            match= format_pat.match(line)
            if match:
                yield Access(**match.groupdict())
```

The output from the local_gzip() function is a sequence of sequences. The outer sequence consists of individual logfiles. For each file, there is an iterable sequence of lines. If the line matches the given pattern, it's a file access of some kind. We can create an Access namedtuple from the match dictionary.

The essential design pattern here is to build a static object from the results of a parsing function. In this case, the parsing function is a regular expression matcher.

There are some alternative ways to do this. For example, we can revise the use of the map() function as follows:

```
def access_builder(line):
    match= format_pat.match(line)
    if match:
        return Access(**match.groupdict())
```

The preceding alternative function embodies just the essential parse and builds an Access object processing. It will either return an Access or a None object. This differs from the version above that also filters items that don't match the regular expression.

Here is how we can use this function to flatten logfiles into a single stream of the Access objects:

```
map(access_builder, (line for log in source_iter for line in
log))
```

This shows how we can transform the output from the local_gzip() function into a sequence of the Access instances. In this case, we apply the access_builder() function to the nested iterator of iterable structure that results from reading a collection of files.

Our point here is to show that we have a number of functional styles for parsing files. In *Chapter 4, Working with Collections* we showed very simple parsing. Here, we're performing more complex parsing, using a variety of techniques.

Parsing additional fields of an Access object

The initial Access object created previously doesn't decompose some inner elements in the nine fields that comprise an access log line. We'll parse those items separately from the overall decomposition into high-level fields. It keeps the regular expressions for parsing somewhat simpler if we break this down into separate parsing operations.

The resulting object is a namedtuple object that will wrap the original Access tuple. It will have some additional fields for the details parsed separately:

```
AccessDetails = namedtuple('AccessDetails', ['access', 'time',
'method', 'url', 'protocol', 'referrer', 'agent'])
```

The `access` attribute is the original `Access` object. The `time` attribute is the parsed `access.time` string. The `method`, `url`, and `protocol` attributes come from decomposing the `access.request` field. The `referrer` attribute is a parsed URL. The `agent` attribute can also be broken down into fine-grained fields. Here are the fields that comprise agent details:

```
AgentDetails= namedtuple('AgentDetails', ['product', 'system',
'platform_details_extensions'])
```

These fields reflect the most common syntax for agent descriptions. There is considerable variation in this area, but this particular subset of values seems to be reasonably common.

We'll combine three detailed parser functions into a single overall parsing function. Here is the first part with the various detail parsers:

```
def access_detail_iter(iterable):
    def parse_request(request):
        words = request.split()
        return words[0], ' '.join(words[1:-1]), words[-1]
    def parse_time(ts):
        return datetime.datetime.strptime(ts, "%d/%b/%Y:%H:%M:%S %z")
    agent_pat= re.compile(r"(?P<product>\S*?)\s+"
        r"\((?P<system>.*?)\)\s*"
        r"(?P<platform_details_extensions>.*)")
    def parse_agent(user_agent):
        agent_match= agent_pat.match(user_agent)
        if agent_match:
            return AgentDetails(**agent_match.groupdict())
```

We've written three parsers for the HTTP request, the time stamp, and the user agent information. The request is usually a three-word string such as GET /some/path HTTP/1.1. The `parse_request()` function extracts these three space-separated values. In the unlikely event that the path has spaces in it, we'll extract the first word and the last word as the method and protocol; all the remaining words are part of the path.

Time parsing is delegated to the `datetime` module. We've simply provided the proper format in the `parse_time()` function.

Parsing the user agent is challenging. There are many variations; we've chosen a common one for the `parse_agent()` function. If the user agent matches the given regular expression, we'll have the attributes of an `AgentDetails` namedtuple. If the user agent information doesn't match the regular expression, we'll simply use the `None` value instead.

We'll use these three parsers to build `AccessDetails` instances from the given `Access` objects. The main body of the `access_detail_iter()` function looks as follows:

```
for access in iterable:
    try:
        meth, uri, protocol = parse_request(access.request)
        yield AccessDetails(
            access= access,
            time= parse_time(access.time),
            method= meth,
            url= urllib.parse.urlparse(uri),
            protocol= protocol,
            referrer = urllib.parse.urlparse(access.referer),
            agent= parse_agent(access.user_agent)
        )
    except ValueError as e:
        print(e, repr(access))
```

We've used a similar design pattern to the previous `access_iter()` function. A new object is built from the results of parsing some input object. The new `AccessDetails` object will wrap the previous `Access` object. This technique allows us to use immutable objects, yet still contain more refined information.

This function is essentially a mapping from an `Access` object to an `AccessDetails` object. We can imagine changing the design to use `map()` as follows:

```
def access_detail_iter2(iterable):
    def access_detail_builder(access):
        try:
            meth, uri, protocol = parse_request(access.request)
            return AccessDetails(
                access= access,
                time= parse_time(access.time),
                method= meth,
                url= urllib.parse.urlparse(uri),
                protocol= protocol,
                referrer = urllib.parse.urlparse(access.referer),
                agent= parse_agent(access.user_agent)
            )
```

```
    except ValueError as e:
        print(e, repr(access))
return filter(None, map(access_detail_builder, iterable))
```

We've changed the construction of the `AccessDetails` object to be a function that returns a single value. We can map that function to the iterable input stream of the `Access` objects. This also fits nicely with the way the `multiprocessing` module works.

In an object-oriented programming environment, these additional parsers might be method functions or properties of a class definition. The advantage of this design is that items aren't parsed unless they're needed. This particular functional design parses everything, assuming that it's going to be used.

A different function design might rely on the three parser functions to extract and parse the various elements from a given `Access` object as needed. Rather than using the `details.time` attribute, we'd use the `parse_time(access.time)` parameter. The syntax is longer, but the attribute is only parsed as needed.

Filtering the access details

We'll look at several filters for the `AccessDetails` objects. The first is a collection of filters that reject a lot of overhead files that are rarely interesting. The second filter will be part of the analysis functions, which we'll look at later.

The `path_filter()` function is a combination of three functions:

1. Exclude empty paths.
2. Exclude some specific filenames.
3. Exclude files that have a given extension.

An optimized version of the `path_filter()` function looks as follows:

```
def path_filter(access_details_iter):
    name_exclude = {
        'favicon.ico', 'robots.txt', 'humans.txt',
        'crossdomain.xml' ,
        '_images', 'search.html', 'genindex.html',
        'searchindex.js', 'modindex.html', 'py-modindex.html',
    }
    ext_exclude = {
        '.png', '.js', '.css',
    }
    for detail in access_details_iter:
        path = detail.url.path.split('/')
```

```
        if not any(path):
            continue
        if any(p in name_exclude for p in path):
            continue
        final= path[-1]
        if any(final.endswith(ext) for ext in ext_exclude):
            continue
        yield detail
```

For each individual `AccessDetails` object, we'll apply three filter tests. If the path is essentially empty or the part includes one of the excluded names or the path's final name has an excluded extension, the item is quietly ignored. If the path doesn't match any of these criteria, it's potentially interesting and is part of the results yielded by the `path_filter()` function.

This is an optimization because all of the tests are applied using an imperative style `for` loop body.

The design started with each test as a separate first-class filter-style function. For example, we might have a function like the following to handle empty paths:

```
def non_empty_path(detail):
    path = detail.url.path.split('/')
    return any(path)
```

This function simply assures that the path contains a name. We can use the `filter()` function as follows:

```
filter(non_empty_path, access_details_iter)
```

We can write similar tests for the `non_excluded_names()` and `non_excluded_ext()` functions. The entire sequence of `filter()` functions will look as follows:

```
filter(non_excluded_ext,
    filter(non_excluded_names,
        filter(non_empty_path, access_details_iter)))
```

This applies each `filter()` function to the results of the previous `filter()` function. The empty paths are rejected; from this subset, the excluded names and the excluded extensions are rejected. We can also state the preceding example as a series of assignment statements as follows:

```
    ne= filter(non_empty_path, access_details_iter)
    nx_name= filter(non_excluded_names, ne)
    nx_ext= filter(non_excluded_ext, nx_name)
    return nx_ext
```

This version has the advantage of being slightly easier to expand when we add new filter criteria.

 The use of generator functions (such as the `filter()` function) means that we aren't creating large intermediate objects. Each of the intermediate variables, `ne, nx_name,` and `nx_ext`, are proper lazy generator functions; no processing is done until the data is consumed by a client process.

While elegant, this suffers from a small inefficiency because each function will need to parse the path in the `AccessDetails` object. In order to make this more efficient, we will need to wrap a `path.split('/')` function with the `lru_cache` attribute.

Analyzing the access details

We'll look at two analysis functions we can use to filter and analyze the individual `AccessDetails` objects. The first function, a `filter()` function, will pass only specific paths. The second function will summarize the occurrences of each distinct path.

We'll define the `filter()` function as a small function and combine this with the built-in `filter()` function to apply the function to the details. Here is the composite `filter()` function:

```
def book_filter(access_details_iter):
    def book_in_path(detail):
        path = tuple(l for l in detail.url.path.split('/') if l)
        return path[0] == 'book' and len(path) > 1
    return filter(book_in_path, access_details_iter)
```

We've defined a rule, the `book_in_path()` attribute, that we'll apply to each `AccessDetails` object. If the path is not empty and the first-level attribute of the path is `book`, then we're interested in these objects. All other `AccessDetails` objects can be quietly rejected.

Here is the final reduction that we're interested in:

```
from collections import Counter
def reduce_book_total(access_details_iter):
    counts= Counter()
    for detail in access_details_iter:
        counts[detail.url.path] += 1
    return counts
```

This function will produce a `Counter()` object that shows the frequency of each path in an `AccessDetails` object. In order to focus on a particular set of paths, we'll use the `reduce_total(book_filter(details))` method. This provides a summary of only items that are passed by the given filter.

The complete analysis process

Here is the composite `analysis()` function that digests a collection of logfiles:

```
def analysis(filename):
    details= path_filter(access_detail_iter(access_iter(local_gzip
    (filename))))
    books= book_filter(details)
    totals= reduce_book_total(books)
    return totals
```

The preceding command snippet will work with a single filename or file pattern. It applies a standard set of parsing functions, `path_filter()`, `access_detail_iter()`, `access_iter()`, and `local_gzip()`, to a filename or file pattern and returns an iterable sequence of the `AccessDetails` objects. It then applies our analytical filter and reduction to that sequence of the `AccessDetails` objects. The result is a `Counter` object that shows the frequency of access for certain paths.

A specific collection of saved `.gzip` format logfiles totals about 51 MB. Processing the files serially with this function takes over 140 seconds. Can we do better using concurrent processing?

Using a multiprocessing pool for concurrent processing

One elegant way to make use of the `multiprocessing` module is to create a processing `Pool` object and assign work to the various processes in that pool. We will use the OS to interleave execution among the various processes. If each of the processes has a mixture of I/O and computation, we should be able to assure that our processor is very busy. When processes are waiting for I/O to complete, other processes can do their computation. When an I/O completes, a process will be ready to run and can compete with others for processing time.

The recipe for mapping work to a separate process looks as follows:

```
import multiprocessing
with multiprocessing.Pool(4) as workers:
    workers.map(analysis, glob.glob(pattern))
```

We've created a `Pool` object with four separate processes and assigned this `Pool` object to the `workers` variable. We've then mapped a function, `analysis`, to an iterable queue of work to be done, using the pool of processes. Each process in the `workers` pool will be assigned items from the iterable queue. In this case, the queue is the result of the `glob.glob(pattern)` attribute, which is a sequence of file names.

As the `analysis()` function returns a result, the parent process that created the `Pool` object can collect those results. This allows us to create several concurrently-built `Counter` objects and merge them into a single, composite result.

If we start *p* processes in the pool, our overall application will include *p+1* processes. There will be one parent process and *p* children. This often works out well because the parent process will have little to do after the subprocess pools are started. Generally, the workers will be assigned to separate CPUs (or cores) and the parent will share a CPU with one of the children in the `Pool` object.

The ordinary Linux parent/child process rules apply to the subprocesses created by this module. If the parent crashes without properly collecting final status from the child processes, then "zombie" processes can be left running. For this reason, a process `Pool` object is a context manager. When we use a pool via the `with` statement, at the end of the context, the children are properly terminated.

By default, a `Pool` object will have a number of workers based on the value of the `multiprocessing.cpu_count()` function. This number is often optimal, and simply using the `with multiprocessing.Pool() as workers:` attribute might be sufficient.

In some cases, it can help to have more workers than CPUs. This might be true when each worker has I/O-intensive processing. Having many worker processes waiting for I/O to complete can improve the elapsed running time of an application.

If a given `Pool` object has *p* workers, this mapping can cut the processing time to almost $\frac{1}{p}$ of the time required to process all of the logs serially. Pragmatically, there is some overhead involved with communication between the parent and child processes in the `Pool` object. Therefore, a four-core processor might only cut the processing time in half.

The multiprocessing `Pool` object has four map-like methods to allocate work to a pool: `map()`, `imap()`, `imap_unordered()`, and `starmap()`. Each of these is a variation on the common theme of mapping a function to a pool of processes. They differ in the details of allocating work and collecting results.

The `map(function, iterable)` method allocates items from the iterable to each worker in the pool. The finished results are collected in the order they were allocated to the `Pool` object so that order is preserved.

The `imap(function, iterable)` method is described as "lazier" than map. By default, it sends each individual item from the iterable to the next available worker. This might involve more communication overhead. For this reason, a chunk size larger than 1 is suggested.

The `imap_unordered(function, iterable)` method is similar to the `imap()` method, but the order of the results is not preserved. Allowing the mapping to be processed out of order means that, as each process finishes, the results are collected. Otherwise, the results must be collected in order.

The `starmap(function, iterable)` method is similar to the `itertools. starmap()` function. Each item in the iterable must be a tuple; the tuple is passed to the function using the * modifier so that each value of the tuple becomes a positional argument value. In effect, it's performing `function(*iterable[0])`, `function(*iterable[1])`, and so on.

Here is one of the variations on the preceding mapping theme:

```
import multiprocessing
pattern = "*.gz"
combined= Counter()
with multiprocessing.Pool() as workers:
    for result in workers.imap_unordered(analysis,
    glob.glob(pattern)):
        combined.update(result)
```

We've created a `Counter()` function that we'll use to consolidate the results from each worker in the pool. We created a pool of subprocesses based on the number of available CPUs and used the `Pool` object as a context manager. We then mapped our `analysis()` function to each file in our file-matching pattern. The resulting `Counter` objects from the `analysis()` function are combined into a single resulting counter.

This takes about 68 seconds. The time to analyze the logs was cut in half using several concurrent processes.

We've created a two-tiered map-reduce process with the `multiprocessing` module's `Pool.map()` function. The first tier was the `analysis()` function, which performed a map-reduce on a single logfile. We then consolidated these reductions in a higher-level reduce operation.

Using apply() to make a single request

In addition to the `map()` function's variants, a pool also has an `apply(function, *args, **kw)` method that we can use to pass one value to the worker pool. We can see that the `map()` method is really just a `for` loop wrapped around the `apply()` method, we can, for example, use the following command:

```
list(workers.apply(analysis, f) for f in glob.glob(pattern))
```

It's not clear, for our purposes, that this is a significant improvement. Almost everything we need to do can be expressed as a `map()` function.

Using map_async(), starmap_async(), and apply_async()

The behavior of the `map()`, `starmap()`, and `apply()` functions is to allocate work to a subprocess in the `Pool` object and then collect the response from the subprocess when that response is ready. This can cause the child to wait for the parent to gather the results. The `_async()` function's variations do not wait for the child to finish. These functions return an object that can be queried to get the individual results from the child processes.

The following is a variation using the `map_async()` method:

```
import multiprocessing
pattern = "*.gz"
combined= Counter()
with multiprocessing.Pool() as workers:
    results = workers.map_async(analysis, glob.glob(pattern))
    data= results.get()
    for c in data:
        combined.update(c)
```

We've created a `Counter()` function that we'll use to consolidate the results from each worker in the pool. We created a pool of subprocesses based on the number of available CPUs and used this `Pool` object as a context manager. We then mapped our `analysis()` function to each file in our file-matching pattern. The response from the `map_async()` function is a `MapResult` object; we can query this for results and overall status of the pool of workers. In this case, we used the `get()` method to get the sequence of the `Counter` objects.

The resulting Counter objects from the analysis() function are combined into a single resulting Counter object. This aggregate gives us an overall summary of a number of logfiles. This processing is not any faster than the previous example. The use of the map_async() function allows the parent process to do additional work while waiting for the children to finish.

More complex multiprocessing architectures

The multiprocessing package supports a wide variety of architectures. We can easily create multiprocessing structures that span multiple servers and provide formal authentication techniques to create a necessary level of security. We can pass objects from process to process using queues and pipes. We can share memory between processes. We can also share lower-level locks between processes as a way to synchronize access to shared resources such as files.

Most of these architectures involve explicitly managing state among several working processes. Using locks and shared memory, in particular, are imperative in nature and don't fit well with a functional programming approach.

We can, with some care, treat queues and pipes in a functional manner. Our objective is to decompose a design into producer and consumer functions. A producer can create objects and insert them into a queue. A consumer will take objects out of a queue and process them, perhaps putting intermediate results into another queue. This creates a network of concurrent processors and the workload is distributed among these various processes. Using the pycsp package can simplify the queue-based exchange of messages among processes. For more information, visit https://pypi.python.org/pypi/pycsp.

This design technique has some advantages when designing a complex application server. The various subprocesses can exist for the entire life of the server, handling individual requests concurrently.

Using the concurrent.futures module

In addition to the multiprocessing package, we can also make use of the concurrent.futures module. This also provides a way to map data to a concurrent pool of threads or processes. The module API is relatively simple and similar in many ways to the multiprocessing.Pool() function's interface.

Here is an example to show just how similar they are:

```
import concurrent.futures
pool_size= 4
pattern = "*.gz"
combined= Counter()
with concurrent.futures.ProcessPoolExecutor
(max_workers=pool_size) as workers:
    for result in workers.map(analysis, glob.glob(pattern)):
        combined.update(result)
```

The most significant change between the preceding example and previous examples is that we're using an instance of the `concurrent.futures.ProcessPoolExecutor` object instead of the `multiprocessing.Pool` method. The essential design pattern is to map the `analysis()` function to the list of filenames using the pool of available workers. The resulting `Counter` objects are consolidated to create a final result.

The performance of the `concurrent.futures` module is nearly identical to the `multiprocessing` module.

Using concurrent.futures thread pools

The `concurrent.futures` module offers a second kind of executor that we can use in our applications. Instead of creating a `concurrent.futures.ProcessPoolExecutor` object, we can use the `ThreadPoolExecutor` object. This will create a pool of threads within a single process.

The syntax is otherwise identical to using a `ProcessPoolExecutor` object. The performance, however, is remarkably different. The logfile processing is dominated by I/O. All of the threads in a process share the same OS scheduling constraints. Due to this, the overall performance of multithreaded logfile analysis is about the same as processing the logfiles serially.

Using sample logfiles and a small four-core laptop running Mac OS X, these are the kinds of results that indicate the difference between threads that share I/O resources and processes:

- Using the `concurrent.futures` thread pool, the elapsed time was 168 seconds

- Using a process pool, the elapsed time was 68 seconds

In both cases, the `Pool` object's size was 4. It's not clear which kind of applications benefit from a multithreading approach. In general, multiprocessing seems to be best for Python applications.

Using the threading and queue modules

The Python `threading` package involves a number of constructs helpful for building imperative applications. This module is not focused on writing functional applications. We can make use of thread-safe queues in the `queue` module to pass objects from thread to thread.

The `threading` module doesn't have a simple way to distribute work to various threads. The API isn't ideally suited to functional programming.

As with the more primitive features of the `multiprocessing` module, we can try to conceal the stateful and imperative nature of locks and queues. It seems easier, however, to make use of the `ThreadPoolExecutor` method in the `concurrent.futures` module. The `ProcessPoolExecutor.map()` method provides us with a very pleasant interface to concurrent processing of the elements of a collection.

The use of the `map()` function primitive to allocate work seems to fit nicely with our functional programming expectations. For this reason, it's best to focus on the `concurrent.futures` module as the most accessible way to write concurrent functional programs.

Designing concurrent processing

From a functional programming perspective, we've seen three ways to use the `map()` function concept applied to data items concurrently. We can use any one of the following:

- `multiprocessing.Pool`
- `concurrent.futures.ProcessPoolExecutor`
- `concurrent.futures.ThreadPoolExecutor`

These are almost identical in the way we interact with them; all three have a `map()` method that applies a function to items of an iterable collection. This fits elegantly with other functional programming techniques. The performance is different because of the nature of concurrent threads versus concurrent processes.

As we stepped through the design, our log analysis application decomposed into two overall areas:

- The lower-level parsing: This is generic parsing that will be used by almost any log analysis application
- The higher-level analysis application: This is more specific filtering and reduction focused on our application needs

The lower-level parsing can be decomposed into four stages:

- Reading all the lines from multiple source logfiles. This was the `local_gzip()` mapping from file name to a sequence of lines.

- Creating simple namedtuples from the lines of log entries in a collection of files. This was the `access_iter()` mapping from text lines to Access objects.

- Parsing the details of more complex fields such as dates and URLs. This was the `access_detail_iter()` mapping from `Access` objects to `AccessDetails` objects.

- Rejecting uninteresting paths from the logs. We can also think of this as passing only the interesting paths. This was more of a filter than a map operation. This was a collection of filters bundled into the `path_filter()` function.

We defined an overall `analysis()` function that parsed and analyzed a given logfile. It applied the higher-level filter and reduction to the results of the lower-level parsing. It can also work with a wild-card collection of files.

Given the number of mappings involved, we can see several ways to decompose this problem into work that can be mapped to into a pool of threads or processes. Here are some of the mappings we can consider as design alternatives:

- Map the `analysis()` function to individual files. We use this as a consistent example throughout this chapter.

- Refactor the `local_gzip()` function out of the overall `analysis()` function. We can now map the revised `analysis()` function to the results of the `local_gzip()` function.

- Refactor the `access_iter(local_gzip(pattern))` function out of the overall `analysis()` function. We can map this revised `analysis()` function against the iterable sequence of the `Access` objects.

- Refactor the `access_detail_iter(access-iter(local_gzip(pattern)))` function into a separate iterable. We will then map the `path_filter()` function and the higher-level filter and reduction against the iterable sequence of the `AccessDetail` objects.

- We can also refactor the lower-level parsing into a function that is separate from the higher-level analysis. We can map the analysis filter and reduction against the output from the lower-level parsing.

All of these are relatively simple restructurings of the example application. The benefit of using functional programming techniques is that each part of the overall process can be defined as a mapping. This makes it practical to consider different architectures to locate an optimal design.

In this case, however, we need to distribute the I/O processing to as many CPUs or cores as we have available. Most of these potential refactorings will perform all of the I/O in the parent process; these will only distribute the computations to multiple concurrent processes with little resulting benefit. Then, we want to focus on the mappings, as these distribute the I/O to as many cores as possible.

It's often important to minimize the amount of data being passed from process to process. In this example, we provided just short filename strings to each worker process. The resulting `Counter` object was considerably smaller than the 10 MB of compressed detail data in each logfile. We can further reduce the size of each `Counter` object by eliminating items that occur only once; or we can limit our application to only the 20 most popular items.

The fact that we can reorganize the design of this application freely doesn't mean we should reorganize the design. We can run a few benchmarking experiments to confirm our suspicion that logfile parsing is dominated by the time required to read the files.

Summary

In this chapter, we've looked at two ways to support concurrent processing of multiple pieces of data:

- The `multiprocessing` module: Specifically, the `Pool` class and the various kinds of mappings available to a pool of workers.

- The `concurrent.futures` module: Specifically the `ProcessPoolExecutor` and `ThreadPoolExecutor` class. These classes also support a mapping that will distribute work among workers that are threads or processes.

We've also noted some alternatives that don't seem to fit well with functional programming. There are numerous other features of the `multiprocessing` module, but they're not a good fit with functional design. Similarly, the `threading` and `queue` modules can be used to build multithreaded applications, but the features aren't a good fit with functional programs.

In the next chapter, we'll look at the `operator` module. This can be used to simplify some kinds of algorithms. We can use a built-in operator function instead of defining a lambda form. We'll also look at some techniques to design flexible decision making and allow expressions to be evaluated in a non-strict order.

13

Conditional Expressions and the Operator Module

Functional programming emphasizes lazy or non-strict ordering of operations. The idea is to allow the compiler or runtime to do as little work as possible to compute the answer. Python tends to impose strict ordering on evaluations.

For example, we used the Python `if`, `elif`, and `else` statements. They're clear and readable, but they imply a strict ordering on the evaluation of the conditions. We can, to an extent, free ourselves from the strict ordering here, and develop a limited kind of non-strict conditional statement. It's not clear if this is helpful but it shows some alternative ways to express an algorithm in a functional style.

The first part of this chapter will look at ways we can implement non-strict evaluation. This is a tool that's interesting because it can lead to performance optimizations.

In the previous chapters, we looked at a number of higher-order functions. In some cases, we used these higher-order functions to apply fairly sophisticated functions to collections of data. In other cases, we applied simple functions to collections of data.

Indeed, in many cases, we wrote tiny `lambda` objects to apply a single Python operator to a function. For example, we can use the following to define a `prod()` function:

```
>>> prod= lambda iterable: functools.reduce(lambda x, y: x*y,
iterable, 1)
>>> prod((1,2,3))
```

6

The use of the `lambda x,y: x*y` parameter seems a bit wordy for multiplication. After all, we just want to use the multiplication operator, `*`. Can we simplify the syntax? The answer is yes; the `operator` module provides us with definitions of the built-in operators.

There are a number of features of the `operator` module that lead to some simplification and potential clarification to create higher-order functions. While important conceptually, the `operator` module isn't as interesting as it initially appears.

Evaluating conditional expressions

Python imposes relatively strict ordering on expressions; the notable exceptions are the short-circuit operators, `and` and `or`. It imposes very strict ordering on statement evaluation. This makes it challenging to find different ways to avoid this strict evaluation.

It turns out that evaluating condition expressions is one way in which we can experiment with non-strict ordering of statements. We'll examine some ways to refactor the `if` and `else` statements to explore this aspect of non-strict evaluation in Python.

The Python `if`, `elif`, and `else` statements are evaluated in a strict order from first to last. Ideally, a language might relax this rule so that an optimizing compiler can find a faster order for evaluating the conditional expressions. The idea is for us to write the expressions in an order that makes sense to a reader, even if the actual evaluation order is non-strict.

Lacking an optimizing compiler, this concept is a bit of a stretch for Python. Nonetheless, we do have alternative ways to express conditions that involve the evaluation of functions instead of the execution of imperative statements. This can allow you to make some rearrangement at runtime.

Python does have a conditional `if` and `else` expression. This expression form can be used when there's a single condition. When we have multiple conditions, however, it can get awkwardly complex: we'd have to carefully nest the subexpressions. We might wind up with a command, as follows, which is rather difficult to comprehend:

```
(x if n==1 else (y if n==2 else z))
```

We can use dictionary keys and the `lambda` objects to create a very complex set of conditions. Here's a way to express the factorial function as expressions:

```
def fact(n):
    f= { n == 0: lambda n: 1,
    n == 1: lambda n: 1,
    n == 2: lambda n: 2,
    n > 2: lambda n: fact(n-1)*n }[True]
    return f(n)
```

This rewrites the conventional `if`, `elif`, `elif`, and `else` sequence of statements into a single expression. We've decomposed it into two steps to make what's happening slightly clearer.

In the first step, we'll evaluate the various conditions. One of the given conditions will evaluate to `True`, the others should all evaluate to `False`. The resulting dictionary will have two items in it: a `True` key with a `lambda` object and a `False` key with a `lambda` object. We'll select the `True` item and assign it to the `f` variable.

We used lambdas as the values in this mapping so that the value expressions aren't evaluated when the dictionary is built. We want to evaluate just one of the value expressions. The `return` statement evaluates the one expression associated with the `True` condition.

Exploiting non-strict dictionary rules

A dictionary's keys have no order. If we try to create a dictionary with multiple items that share a common key value, we'll only have one item in the resulting `dict` object. It's not clear which of the duplicated key values will be preserved, and it shouldn't matter.

Here's a situation where we explicitly don't care which of the duplicated keys is preserved. We'll look at a degenerate case of the `max()` function, it simply picks the largest of two values:

```
def max(a, b):
    f = {a >= b: lambda: a, b >= a: lambda: b}[True]
    return f()
```

In the case where `a == b`, both items in the dictionary will have a key of the `True` condition. Only one of the two will actually be preserved. Since the answer is the same, it doesn't matter which is kept and which is treated as a duplicate and overwritten.

Filtering true conditional expressions

We have a number of ways of determining which expression is `True`. In the previous example, we loaded the keys into a dictionary. Because of the way the dictionary is loaded, only one value will be preserved with a key of `True`.

Here's another variation to this theme, written using the `filter()` function:

```
def semifact(n):
    alternatives= [(n == 0, lambda n: 1),
    (n == 1, lambda n: 1),
    (n == 2, lambda n: 2),
    (n > 2, lambda n: semifact(n-2)*n)]
    c, f= next(filter(itemgetter(0), alternatives))
    return f(n)
```

We defined the alternatives as a sequence of `condition` and `function` pairs. When we apply the `filter()` function using the `itemgetter(0)` parameter, we'll select those pairs with a `True` condition. Of those which are `True`, we'll select the first item in the iterable created by the `filter()` function. The selected condition is assigned to the `c` variable, the selected function is assigned to the `f` variable. We can ignore the condition (it will be `True`), and we can evaluate the `filter()` function.

As with the previous example, we used lambdas to defer evaluation of the functions until after the conditions have been evaluated.

This `semifact()` function is also called **double factorial**. The definition of the semifactorial is similar to the definition of factorial. The important difference is that it is the product of alternate numbers instead of all numbers. For example, take a look at the following formulas:

$5!! = 5 \times 3 \times 1$, and $7!! = 7 \times 5 \times 3 \times 1$

Using the operator module instead of lambdas

When using the `max()`, `min()`, and `sorted()` functions, we have an optional `key=` parameter. The function provided as an argument value modifies the behavior of the higher-order function. In many cases, we used simple lambda forms to pick items from a tuple. Here are two examples we heavily relied on:

```
fst = lambda x: x[0]
snd = lambda x: x[1]
```

These match built-in functions in other functional programming languages.

We don't really need to write these functions. There's a version available in the `operator` module which describes these functions.

Here's some sample data we can work with:

```
>>> year_cheese = [(2000, 29.87), (2001, 30.12), (2002, 30.6),
(2003, 30.66), (2004, 31.33), (2005, 32.62), (2006, 32.73),
(2007, 33.5), (2008, 32.84), (2009, 33.02), (2010, 32.92)]
```

This is the annual cheese consumption. We used this example in *Chapter 2, Introducing Some Functional Features* and *Chapter 9, More Itertools Techniques*.

We can locate the data point with minimal cheese using the following commands:

```
>>> min(year_cheese, key=snd)
(2000, 29.87)
```

The `operator` module gives us an alternative to pick particular elements from a tuple. This saves us from using a `lambda` variable to pick the second item.

Instead of defining our own `fst()` and `snd()` functions, we can use the `itemgetter(0)` and the `itemgetter(1)` parameters, as shown in the following command:

```
>>> from operator import *
>>> max( year_cheese, key=itemgetter(1))
(2007, 33.5)
```

The `itemgetter()` function relies on the special method, `__getitem__()`, to pick items out of a tuple (or list) based on their index position.

Getting named attributes when using higher-order functions

Let's look at a slightly different collection of data. Let's say we were working with namedtuples instead of anonymous tuples. We have two ways to locate the range of cheese consumption shown as follows:

```
>>> from collections import namedtuple
>>> YearCheese = namedtuple("YearCheese", ("year", "cheese"))
>>> year_cheese_2 = list(YearCheese(*yc) for yc in year_cheese)
>>> year_cheese_2
```

```
[YearCheese(year=2000, cheese=29.87), YearCheese(year=2001,
cheese=30.12), YearCheese(year=2002, cheese=30.6),
YearCheese(year=2003, cheese=30.66), YearCheese(year=2004,
cheese=31.33), YearCheese(year=2005, cheese=32.62),
YearCheese(year=2006, cheese=32.73), YearCheese(year=2007,
cheese=33.5), YearCheese(year=2008, cheese=32.84),
YearCheese(year=2009, cheese=33.02), YearCheese(year=2010,
cheese=32.92)]
```

We can use lambda forms or we can use the `attrgetter()` function, as follows:

```
>>> min(year_cheese_2, key=attrgetter('cheese'))
YearCheese(year=2000, cheese=29.87)
>>> max(year_cheese_2, key=lambda x: x.cheese)
YearCheese(year=2007, cheese=33.5)
```

What's important here is that with a `lambda` object, the attribute name is expressed as a token in the code. With the `attrgetter()` function, the attribute name is a character string. This could be a parameter, which allows us to be considerably flexible.

Starmapping with operators

The `itertools.starmap()` function can be applied to an operator and a sequence of pairs of values. Here's an example:

```
>>> d= starmap(pow, zip_longest([], range(4), fillvalue=60))
```

The `itertools.zip_longest()` function will create a sequence of pairs such as the following:

```
[(60, 0), (60, 1), (60, 2), (60, 3)]
```

It does this because we provided two sequences: the `[]` brackets and the `range(4)` parameter. The `fillvalue` parameter will be used when the shorter sequence runs out of data.

When we use the `starmap()` function, each pair becomes the argument to the given function. In this case, we provided the `operator.pow()` function, which is the `**` operator. We've calculated values for `[60**0, 60**1, 60**2, 60**3]`. The value of the d variable is `[1, 60, 3600, 216000]`.

The `starmap()` function is useful when we have a sequence of tuples. We have a tidy equivalence between the `map(f, x, y)` and `starmap(f, zip(x,y))` functions.

Here's a continuation of the preceding example of the `itertools.starmap()` function:

```
>>> p = (3, 8, 29, 44)
>>> pi = sum(starmap(truediv, zip(p, d)))
```

We've zipped together two sequences of four values. We used the `starmap()` function with the `operator.truediv()` function, which is the / operator. This will compute a sequence of fractions that we sum. The sum is really an approximation of π

Here's a simpler version that uses the `map(f, x, y)` function instead of the `starmap(f, zip(x,y))` function:

```
>>> pi = sum(map(truediv, p, d))
>>> pi
3.1415925925925925
```

In this example, we effectively converted a base 60 fractional value to base 10. The sequence of values in the d variable are the appropriate denominators. A technique similar to the one explained earlier in this section can be used to convert other bases.

Some approximations involve potentially infinite sums (or products). These can be evaluated using similar techniques explained previously in this section. We can leverage the `count()` function in the `itertools` module to generate an arbitrary number of terms in an approximation. We can then use the `takewhile()` function to only use values that contribute a useful level of precision to the answer.

Here's an example of a potentially infinite sequence:

```
>>> num= map(fact, count())
>>> den= map(semifact, (2*n+1 for n in count()))
>>> terms= takewhile(lambda t: t > 1E-10, map(truediv, num, den))
>>> 2*sum(terms)
3.1415926533011587
```

The num variable is a potentially infinite sequence of numerators, based on a factorial function. The den variable is a potentially infinite sequence of denominators, based on the semifactorial (sometimes called the double factorial) function.

To create terms, we used the `map()` function to apply the `operators.truediv()` function, the / operator, to each pair of values. We wrapped this in a `takewhile()` function so that we only take values while the fraction is greater than some relatively small value; in this case, 1×10^{-10}.

This is a series expansion based on 4 arctan(1)=π. The expansion is $\pi = 2\sum_{n=0}^{\infty} \frac{n!}{(2n+1)!!}$

An interesting variation to the series expansion theme is to replace the `operator.truediv()` function with the `fractions.Fraction()` function. This will create exact rational values that don't suffer from the limitations of floating-point approximations.

All of the Python operators are available in the `operators` module. This includes all of the bit-fiddling operators as well as the comparison operators. In some cases, a generator expression may be more succinct or expressive than a rather complex-looking `starmap()` function with a function that represents an operator.

The issue is that the `operator` module provides only a single operator, essentially a shorthand for `lambda`. We can use the `operator.add` method instead of the `add=lambda a,b: a+b` method. If we have more complex expressions, then the `lambda` object is the only way to write them.

Reducing with operators

We'll look at one more way that we might try to use the operator definitions. We can use them with the built-in `functools.reduce()` function. The `sum()` function, for example, can be defined as follows:

```
sum= functools.partial(functools.reduce, operator.add)
```

We created a partially evaluated version of the `reduce()` function with the first argument supplied. In this case, it's the + operator, implemented via the `operator.add()` function.

If we have a requirement for a similar function that computes a product, we can define it like this:

```
prod= functools.partial(functools.reduce, operator.mul)
```

This follows the pattern shown in the preceding example. We have a partially evaluated `reduce()` function with the first argument of * operator, as implemented by the `operator.mul()` function.

It's not clear whether we can do similar things with too many of the other operators. We might be able to find a use for the `operator.concat()` function as well as the `operator.and()` and `operator.or()` functions.

> The `and()` and `or()` functions are the bit-wise & and / operators. If we want the proper Boolean operators, we have to use the `all()` and `any()` functions instead of the `reduce()` function.

Once we have a `prod()` function, this means that the factorial can be defined as follows:

```
fact= lambda n: 1 if n < 2 else n*prod(range(1,n))
```

This has the advantage of being succinct: it provides a single line definition of factorial. It also has the advantage of not relying on recursion but has the potential of running afoul Python's stack limit.

It's not clear that this has any dramatic advantages over the many alternatives we have in Python. The concept of building a complex function from primitive pieces like the `partial()` and `reduce()` functions, and the `operator` module is very elegant. In most cases, though, the simple functions in the `operator` module aren't very helpful; we'll almost always want to use more complex lambdas.

Summary

In this chapter, we looked at alternatives to the `if`, `elif`, and `else` statement sequence. Ideally, using a conditional expression allows some optimization to be done. Pragmatically, Python doesn't optimize, so there's little tangible benefit to the more exotic ways to handle conditions.

We also looked at how we can use the `operator` module with higher order functions like `max()`, `min()`, `sorted()`, and `reduce()`. Using operators can save us from having to create a number of small lambdas.

In the next chapter, we'll look at the `PyMonad` library to express a functional programming concept directly in Python. We don't require monads generally because Python is an imperative programming language under the hood.

Some algorithms might be expressed more clearly with monads than with stateful variable assignments. We'll look at an example where monads lead to a succinct expression of a rather complex set of rules. Most importantly, the `operator` module shows off many functional programming techniques.

14
The PyMonad Library

A monad allows us to impose an order on expression evaluation in an otherwise lenient language. We can use a monad to insist that an expression such as $a + b + c$ is evaluated in left-to-right order. Generally, there seems to be no point to a monad. When we want files to have their content read or written in a specific order, however, a monad is a handy way to assure that the `read()` and `write()` functions are evaluated in a particular order.

Languages that are lenient and have optimizing compilers benefit from monads to impose order on evaluation of expressions. Python, for the most part, is strict and does not optimize. We have little practical use for monads.

However, the PyMonad module is more than just monads. There are a number of functional programming features that have a distinctive implementation. In some cases, the PyMonad module can lead to programs which are more succinct and expressive than those written using only the standard library modules.

Downloading and installing

The PyMonad module is available on **Python Package Index (PyPi)**. In order to add PyMonad to your environment, you'll need to use pip or Easy Install. Here are some typical situations:

- If you have Python 3.4 or higher, you have both of these installation package tools
- If you have Python 3.x, you may already have either one of the necessary installers because you've added packages already
- If you have Python 2.x, you should consider an upgrade to Python 3.4
- If you don't have pip or Easy Install, you'll need to install them first; consider upgrading to Python 3.4 to get these installation tools

Visit `https://pypi.python.org/pypi/PyMonad/` for more information.

For Mac OS and Linux developers, the command `pip install PyMonad` or `easy_install-3.3 pymonad` must be run using the `sudo` command. When running a command such as `sudo easy_install-3.3 pymonad`, you'll be prompted for your password to assure that you have the administrative permissions necessary to do the installation. For Windows developers, the `sudo` command is not relevant, but you do need to have administrative rights.

Once the `pymonad` package is installed, you can confirm it using the following commands:

```
>>> import pymonad
>>> help(pymonad)
```

This will display the `docstring` module and confirm that things really are properly installed.

Functional composition and currying

Some functional languages work by transforming a multiargument function syntax into a collection of single argument functions. This process is called **currying**—it's named after logician Haskell Curry, who developed the theory from earlier concepts.

Currying is a technique for transforming a multiargument function into higher order single argument functions. In the simple case, we have a function $f(x,y) \rightarrow z$; given two arguments x and y, this will return some resulting value, z. We can curry this into two functions: $f_{c1}(x) \rightarrow f_{c2}(y)$ and $f_{c2}(y) \rightarrow z$. Given the first argument value, x, the function returns a new one-argument function, $f_{c1}(x)$ returns a new one-argument function, $f_{c2}(y)$. This second function can be given an argument, y, and will return the resulting value, z.

We can evaluate a curried function in Python as follows: `f_c(2)(3)`. We apply the curried function to the first argument value of 2, creating a new function. Then, we apply that new function to the second argument value of 3.

This applies recursively to functions of any complexity. If we start with a function $g(a,b,c) \rightarrow z$, we curry this into a function $g_{c1}(a) \rightarrow g_{c2}(b) \rightarrow g_{c3}(c) \rightarrow z$. This is done recursively. First, the $g_{c1}(a)$ function returns a new function with the b and c arguments, $g_{c2}(b,c) \rightarrow z$. Then we can curry the returned two-argument function to create $g_{c2}(b) \rightarrow g_{c3}(c)$.

We can evaluate this curried function with `g_c(1)(2)(3)`. When we apply g_{c1} to an argument of 1, we get a function; when we apply this returned function to 2, we get another function. When we apply the final function to 3, we get the expected result. Clearly, formal syntax is bulky, so we use some syntactic sugar to reduce `g_c(1)(2)(3)` to something more palatable like `g(1,2,3)`.

Let's look at a concrete example in Python, for example, we have a function like the following one:

```
from pymonad import curry

@curry

def systolic_bp(bmi, age, gender_male, treatment):

    return 68.15+0.58*bmi+0.65*age+0.94*gender_male+6.44*treatment
```

This is a simple, multiple-regression-based model for systolic blood pressure. This predicts blood pressure from **body mass index (BMI)**, age, gender (1 means male), and history of previous treatment (1 means previously treated). For more information on the model and how it's derived, visit http://sphweb.bumc.bu.edu/otlt/MPH-Modules/BS/BS704_Multivariable/BS704_Multivariable7.html.

We can use the systolic_bp() function with all four arguments, as follows:

```
>>> systolic_bp(25, 50, 1, 0)
116.09
>>> systolic_bp(25, 50, 0, 1)
121.59
```

A male person with a BMI of 25, age 50, and no previous treatment will likely have a blood pressure of 116. The second example shows a similar woman with a history of treatment who will likely have a blood pressure of 121.

Because we've used the @curry decorator, we can create intermediate results that are similar to partially applied functions. Take a look at the following command snippet:

```
>>> treated= systolic_bp(25, 50, 0)
>>> treated(0)
115.15
>>> treated(1)
121.59
```

In the preceding case, we evaluated the systolic_bp(25, 50, 0) method to create a curried function and assigned this to the variable treatment. The BMI, age, and gender values don't typically change for a given patient. We can now apply the new function, treatment, to the remaining argument to get different blood pressure expectations based on patient history.

This is similar in some respects to the `functools.partial()` function. The important difference is that currying creates a function that can work in a variety of ways. The `functools.partial()` function creates a more specialized function that can only be used with the given set of bound values.

Here's an example of creating some additional curried functions:

```
>>> g_t= systolic_bp(25, 50)
>>> g_t(1, 0)
116.09
>>> g_t(0, 1)
121.59
```

This is a gender-based treatment function based on our initial model. We must provide gender and treatment values to get a final value from the model.

Using curried higher-order functions

While currying is simple to visualize using ordinary functions, the real value shows up when we apply currying to higher-order functions. In the ideal situation, the `functools.reduce()` function would be "curryable" so that we can do this:

```
sum= reduce(operator.add)
prod= reduce(operator.mul)
```

The `reduce()` function, however, isn't curryable by the pymonad library, so this doesn't actually work. If we define our own `reduce()` function, however, we can then curry it as shown previously. Here's an example of a home-brewed `reduce()` function that can be used as shown earlier:

```
import collections.abc
from pymonad import curry
@curry
def myreduce(function, iterable_or_sequence):
    if isinstance(iterable_or_sequence, collections.abc.Sequence):
        iterator= iter(iterable_or_sequence)
    else:
        iterator= iterable_or_sequence
    s = next(iterator)
    for v in iterator:
        s = function(s,v)
    return s
```

The `myreduce()` function will behave like the built-in `reduce()` function. The `myreduce()` function works with an iterable or a sequence object. Given a sequence, we'll create an iterator; given an iterable object, we'll simply use it. We initialize the result with the first item in the iterator. We apply the function to the ongoing sum (or product) and each subsequent item.

 It's also possible to wrap the built-in `reduce()` function to create a curryable version. That's only two lines of code; an exercise left for you.

Since the `myreduce()` function is a curried function, we can now use it to create functions based on our higher-order function, `myreduce()`:

```
>>> from operator import *
>>> sum= myreduce(add)
>>> sum([1,2,3])
6
>>> max= myreduce(lambda x,y: x if x > y else y)
>>> max([2,5,3])
5
```

We defined our own version of the `sum()` function using the curried reduce applied to the `add` operator. We also defined our own version of the default `max()` function using a `lambda` object that picks the larger of two values.

We can't easily create the more general form of the `max()` function this way, because currying is focused on positional parameters. Trying to use the `key=` keyword parameter adds too much complexity to make the technique work toward our overall goals of succinct and expressive functional programs.

To create a more generalized version of the `max()` function, we need to step outside the `key=` keyword parameter paradigm that functions such as `max()`, `min()`, and `sorted()` rely on. We would have to accept the higher-order function as the first argument in the same way as `filter()`, `map()`, and `reduce()` functions do. We could also create our own library of more consistent higher-order curried functions. These functions would rely exclusively on positional parameters. The higher-order function would be provided first so that our own curried `max(function, iterable)` method would follow the pattern set by the `map()`, `filter()`, and `functools.reduce()` functions.

Currying the hard way

We can create curried functions manually, without using the decorator from the pymonad library; one way of doing this is to execute the following commands:

```
def f(x, *args):
    def f1(y, *args):
        def f2(z):
            return (x+y)*z
        if args:
            return f2(*args)
        return f2
    if args:
        return f1(*args)
    return f1
```

This curries a function, $F(x,y,z) \rightarrow (x+y) \times z$, into a function, f(x), which returns a function. Conceptually, $f(x) \rightarrow F'(y,z)$. We then curried the intermediate function to create the f1(y) and f2(z) function.

When we evaluate the f(x) function, we'll get a new function, f1, as a result. If additional arguments are provided, those arguments are passed to the f1 function for evaluation, either resulting in a final value or another function.

Clearly, this is potentially error-prone. It does, however, serve to define what currying really means and how it's implemented in Python.

Functional composition and the PyMonad multiplication operator

One of the significant values of curried functions is the ability to combine them via functional composition. We looked at functional composition in *Chapter 5*, *Higher-order Functions*, and *Chapter 11*, *Decorator Design Techniques*.

When we've created a curried function, we can easily perform function composition to create a new, more complex curried function. In this case, the PyMonad package defines the * operator for composing two functions. To show how this works, we'll define two curried functions that we can compose. First, we'll define a function that computes the product, and then we'll define a function that computes a specialized range of values.

Here's our first function that computes the product:

```
import  operator
prod = myreduce(operator.mul)
```

This is based on our curried myreduce() function that was defined previously. It uses the operator.mul() function to compute a "times-reduction" of an iterable: we can call a product a times-reduce of a sequence.

Here's our second curried function that will produce a range of values:

```
@curry
def alt_range(n):
    if n == 0: return range(1,2) # Only 1
    if n % 2 == 0:
        return range(2,n+1,2)
    else:
        return range(1,n+1,2)
```

The result of the alt_range() function will be even values or odd values. It will have only values up to (and including) n, if n is odd. If n is even, it will have only even values up to n. The sequences are important for implementing the semifactorial or double factorial function, *n!!*.

Here's how we can combine the prod() and alt_range() functions into a new curried function:

```
>>> semi_fact= prod * alt_range
>>> semi_fact(9)
945
```

The PyMonad * operator here combines two functions into a composite function, named semi_fact. The alt_range() function is applied to the arguments. Then, the prod() function is applied to the results of the alt_range function.

By doing this manually in Python, we're effectively creating a new lambda object:

```
semi_fact= lambda x: prod(alt_range(x))
```

The composition of curried functions involves somewhat less syntax than creating a new lambda object.

Ideally, we would like to use functional composition and curried functions like this:

```
sumwhile= sum * takewhile(lambda x: x > 1E-7)
```

This will define a version of the `sum()` function that works with infinite sequences, stopping the generation of values when the threshold had been met. This doesn't seem to work because the `pymonad` library doesn't seem to handle infinite iterables as well as it handles the internal `List` objects.

Functors and applicative functors

The idea of a functor is a functional representation of a piece of simple data. A functor version of the number 3.14 is a function of zero arguments that returns this value. Consider the following example:

```
pi= lambda : 3.14
```

We created a zero-argument `lambda` object that has a simple value.

When we apply a curried function to a functor, we're creating a new curried functor. This generalizes the idea of "apply a function to an argument to get value" by using functions to represent the arguments, the values, and the functions themselves.

Once everything in our program is a function, then all processing is simply a variation on the theme of functional composition. The arguments and results of curried functions can be functors. At some point, we'll apply a `getValue()` method to a `functor` object to get a Python-friendly, simple type that we can use in uncurried code.

Since all we've done is functional composition, no calculation needs to be done until we actually demand a value using the `getValue()` method. Instead of performing a lot of calculations, our program defines a complex object that can produce a value when requested. In principle, this composition can be optimized by a clever compiler or runtime system.

When we apply a function to a `functor` object, we're going to use a method similar to `map()` that is implemented as the * operator. We can think of the `function *  functor` or `map(function, functor)` methods as a way to understand the role a functor plays in an expression.

In order to work politely with functions that have multiple arguments, we'll use the & operator to build composite functors. We'll often see `functor & functor` method to build a `functor` object from a pair of functors.

We can wrap Python simple types with a subclass of the `Maybe` functor. The `Maybe` functor is interesting, because it gives us a way to deal gracefully with missing data. The approach we used in *Chapter 11, Decorator Design Techniques*, was to decorate built-in functions to make them `None` aware. The approach taken by the PyMonad library is to decorate the data so that it gracefully declines being operated on.

There are two subclasses of the `Maybe` functor:

- `Nothing`
- `Just(some simple value)`

We use `Nothing` as a stand-in for the simple Python value of `None`. This is how we represent missing data. We use `Just(some simple value)` to wrap all other Python objects. These functors are function-like representations of constant values.

We can use a curried function with these `Maybe` objects to tolerate missing data gracefully. Here's a short example:

```
>>> x1= systolic_bp * Just(25) & Just(50) & Just(1) & Just(0)
>>> x1.getValue()
116.09
>>> x2= systolic_bp * Just(25) & Just(50) & Just(1) & Nothing
>>> x2.getValue() is None
True
```

The `*` operator is functional composition: we're composing the `systolic_bp()` function with an argument composite. The `&` operator builds a composite functor that can be passed as an argument to a curried function of multiple arguments.

This shows us that we get an answer instead of a `TypeError` exception. This can be very handy when working with large, complex datasets in which data could be missing or invalid. It's much nicer than having to decorate all of our functions to make them `None` aware.

This works nicely for curried functions. We can't operate on the `Maybe` functors in uncurried Python code as functors have very few methods.

 We must use the `getValue()` method to extract the simple Python value for uncurried Python code.

Using the lazy List() functor

The `List()` functor can be confusing at first. It's extremely lazy, unlike Python's built-in `list` type. When we evaluate the built-in `list(range(10))` method, the `list()` function will evaluate the `range()` object to create a list with 10 items. The PyMonad `List()` functor, however, is too lazy to even do this evaluation.

Here's the comparison:

```
>>> list(range(10))
[0, 1, 2, 3, 4, 5, 6, 7, 8, 9]
>>> List(range(10))
[range(0, 10)]
```

The `List()` functor did not evaluate the `range()` object, it just preserved it without being evaluated. The `PyMonad.List()` function is useful to collect functions without evaluating them. We can evaluate them later as required:

```
>>> x= List(range(10))
>>> x
[range(0, 10)]
>>> list(x[0])
[0, 1, 2, 3, 4, 5, 6, 7, 8, 9]
```

We created a lazy `List` object with a `range()` object. Then we extracted and evaluated a `range()` object at position `0` in that list.

A `List` object won't evaluate a generator function or `range()` object; it treats any iterable argument as a single iterator object. We can, however, use the `*` operator to expand the values of a generator or the `range()` object.

> Note that there are several meanings for `*` operator: it is the built-in mathematical times operator, the function composition operator defined by PyMonad, and the built-in modifier used when calling a function to bind a single sequence object as all of the positional parameters of a function. We're going to use the third meaning of the `*` operator to assign a sequence to multiple positional parameters.

Here's a curried version of the `range()` function. This has a lower bound of 1 instead of 0. It's handy for some mathematical work because it allows us to avoid the complexity of the positional arguments in the built-in `range()` function.

```
@curry
def range1n(n):
    if n == 0: return range(1,2) # Only 1
    return range(1,n+1)
```

We simply wrapped the built-in `range()` function to make it curryable by the PyMonad package.

Since a `List` object is a functor, we can map functions to the `List` object. The function is applied to each item in the `List` object. Here's an example:

```
>>> fact= prod * range1n
>>> seq1 = List(*range(20))
>>> f1 = fact * seq1
>>> f1[:10]
[1, 1, 2, 6, 24, 120, 720, 5040, 40320, 362880]
```

We defined a composite function, `fact()`, which was built from the `prod()` and `range1n()` functions shown previously. This is the factorial function, *n*!. We created a `List()` functor, `seq1`, which is a sequence of 20 values. We mapped the `fact()` function to the `seq1` functor, which created a sequence of factorial values, `f1`. We showed the first 10 of these values earlier.

> There is a similarity between the composition of functions and the composition of a function and a functor. Both `prod*range1n` and `fact*seq1` use functional composition: one combines things that are obviously functions, and the other combines a function and a functor.

Here's another little function that we'll use to extend this example:

```
@curry
def n21(n):
    return 2*n+1
```

This little `n21()` function does a simple computation. It's curried, however, so we can apply it to a functor like a `List()` function. Here's the next part of the preceding example:

```
>>> semi_fact= prod * alt_range
>>> f2 = semi_fact * n21 * seq1
>>> f2[:10]
[1, 3, 15, 105, 945, 10395, 135135, 2027025, 34459425, 654729075]
```

We've defined a composite function from the `prod()` and `alt_range()` functions shown previously. The function `f2` is semifactorial or double factorial, *n*!!. The value of the function `f2` is built by mapping our small `n21()` function applied to the `seq1` sequence. This creates a new sequence. We then applied the `semi_fact` function to this new sequence to create a sequence of $2n+1!!$ values that parallels the sequence of *n*! values.

We can now map the / operator to the `map()` and `operator.truediv` parallel functors:

```
>>> 2*sum(map(operator.truediv, f1, f2))
3.1415919276751456
```

The `map()` function will apply the given operator to both functors, yielding a sequence of fractions that we can add.

> The `f1 & f2` method will create all combinations of values from the two `List` objects. This is an important feature of `List` objects: they readily enumerate all combinations allowing a simple algorithm to compute all alternatives and filter the alternatives for the proper subset. This is something we don't want; that's why we used the `map()` function instead of the `operator.truediv * f1 & f2` method.

We defined a fairly complex calculation using a few functional composition techniques and a functor class definition. Here's the full definition for this calculation:

$$\pi = 2\sum_{n=0}^{\infty} \frac{n!}{(2n+1)!!}$$

Ideally, we prefer not to use a fixed sized `List` object. We'd prefer to have a lazy and potentially infinite sequence of integer values. We could then use a curried version of `sum()` and `takewhile()` functions to find the sum of values in the sequence until the values are too small to contribute to the result. This would require an even lazier version of the `List()` object that could work with the `itertools.counter()` function. We don't have this potentially infinite list in PyMonad 1.3; we're limited to a fixed sized `List()` object.

Monad concepts, the bind() function and the Binary Right Shift operator

The name of the PyMonad library comes from the functional programming concept of a **monad**, a function that has a strict order. The underlying assumption behind much functional programming is that functional evaluation is liberal: it can be optimized or rearranged as necessary. A monad provides an exception that imposes a strict left-to-right ordering.

Python, as we have seen, is strict. It doesn't require monads. We can, however, still apply the concept in places where it can help clarify a complex algorithm.

The technology for imposing strict evaluation is a binding between a monad and a function that will return a monad. A *flat* expression will become nested bindings that can't be reordered by an optimizing compiler. The `bind()` function is mapped to the `>>` operator, allowing us to write expressions like this:

```
Just(some file) >> read header >> read next >> read next
```

The preceding expression would be converted to the following:

```
bind(bind(bind(Just(some file), read header), read next), read next)
```

The `bind()` functions assure that a strict left-to-right evaluation is imposed on this expression when it's evaluated. Also, note that the preceding expression is an example of functional composition. When we create a monad with the `>>` operator, we're creating a complex object that will be evaluated when we finally use the `getValue()` method.

The `Just()` subclass is required to create a simple monad compatible object that wraps a simple Python object.

The monad concept is central to expressing a strict evaluation order — in a language that's heavily optimized and lenient. Python doesn't require a monad because it uses left-to-right strict evaluation. This makes the monad difficult to demonstrate because it doesn't really do something completely novel in a Python context. Indeed, the monad redundantly states the typical strict rules that Python follows.

In other languages, such as Haskell, a monad is crucial for file input and output where strict ordering is required. Python's imperative mode is much like a Haskell `do` block, which has an implicit Haskell `>>=` operator to force the statements to be evaluated in order. (PyMonad uses the `bind()` function and the `>>` operator for Haskell's `>>=` operation.)

Implementing simulation with monads

Monads are expected to pass through a kind of "pipeline": a monad will be passed as an argument to a function and a similar monad will be returned as the value of the function. The functions must be designed to accept and return similar structures.

We'll look at a simple pipeline that can be used for simulation of a process. This kind of simulation may be a formal part of some Monte Carlo simulation. We'll take the Monte Carlo simulation literally and simulate a casino dice game, Craps. This involves what might be thought of as stateful rules for a fairly complex simulation.

There's a lot of very strange gambling terminology involved. We can't provide much background about the various buzzwords involved. In some cases, the origins are lost in history.

Craps involves someone rolling the dice (a shooter) and additional bettors. The game works like this:

The first roll is called a *come out* roll. There are three conditions:

1. If the dice total is 7 or 11, the shooter wins. Anyone betting on the *pass* line will be paid off as a winner, and all other bets lose. The game is over, and the shooter can play again.
2. If the dice total is 2, 3, or 12, the shooter loses. Anyone betting on the *don't pass* line will win, and all other bets lose. The game is over, and the shooter must pass the dice to another shooter.
3. Any other total (that is, 4, 5, 6, 8, 9, or 10) establishes a *point*. The game changes state from the *come out* roll to the *point* roll. The game continues.

If a point was established, each *point* roll is evaluated with three conditions:

*   If the dice total is 7, the shooter loses. Indeed, almost all bets are losers except for don't pass bets and a special proposition bet. Since the shooter lost, the dice are passed to another shooter.
*   If the dice totals the original point, the shooter wins. Anyone betting on the pass line will be paid off as a winner, and all other bets lose. The game is over, and the shooter can play again.
*   Any other total continues the game with no resolution.

The rules involve a kind of state change. We can look at this as a sequence of operations rather than a state change. There's one function that must be used first. Another recursive function is used after that. In this way, it fits the monad design pattern nicely.

As a practical matter, a casino allows numerous fairly complex side bets during the game. We can evaluate those separately from the essential rules of the game. Many of those bets (the propositions, field bets, and buying a number) are bets a player simply makes during the *point roll* phase of the game. There's an additional *come* and *don't come* pair of bets that establishes a point-within-a-point nested game. We'll stick the the basic outline of the game for the following example.

We'll need a source of random numbers:

```
import random
def rng():
    return (random.randint(1,6), random.randint(1,6))
```

The preceding function will generate a pair of dice for us.

Here's our expectation from the overall game:

```
def craps():
    outcome= Just(("",0, []) ) >> come_out_roll(rng) >> point_roll
    (rng)
    print(outcome.getValue())
```

We create an initial monad, Just(("",0, [])), to define the essential type we're going to work with. A game will produce a three tuple with an outcome, a point, and a sequence of rolls. Initially, it's a default three tuple to define the type we're working with.

We pass this monad to two other functions. This will create a resulting monad, outcome, with the results of the game. We used the >> operator to connect the functions in the specific order they must be executed. In an optimizing language, this will prevent the expression from being rearranged.

We get the value of the monad at the end using the getValue() method. Since the monad objects are lazy, this request is what triggers the evaluation of the various monads to create the required output.

The come_out_roll() function has the rng() function curried as the first argument. The monad will become the second argument to this function. The come_out_roll() function can roll the dice and apply the come out rules to determine if we have a win, a loss, or a point.

The point_roll() function also has the rng() function curried as the first argument. The monad will become the second argument. The point_roll() function can then roll the dice to see if the bet is resolved. If the bet is unresolved, this function will operate recursively to continue looking for resolution.

The come_out_roll() function looks like this:

```
@curry
def come_out_roll(dice, status):
    d= dice()
    if sum(d) in (7, 11):
        return Just(("win", sum(d), [d]))
    elif sum(d) in (2, 3, 12):
        return Just(("lose", sum(d), [d]))
    else:
        return Just(("point", sum(d), [d]))
```

We rolled the dice once to determine if we have a first-roll win, loss, or point. We return an appropriate monad value that includes the outcome, a point value, and the roll of the dice. The point values for an immediate win and immediate loss aren't really meaningful. We could sensibly return a 0 here, since no point was really established.

The point_roll() function looks like this:

```
@curry
def point_roll(dice, status):
    prev, point, so_far = status
    if prev != "point":
        return Just(status)
    d = dice()
    if sum(d) == 7:
        return Just(("craps", point, so_far+[d]))
    elif sum(d) == point:
        return Just(("win", point, so_far+[d]))
    else:
        return Just(("point", point, so_far+[d])) >> point_roll(dice)
```

We decomposed the status monad into the three individual values of the tuple. We could have used small lambda objects to extract the first, second, and third values. We could also have used the operator.itemgetter() function to extract the tuples' items. Instead, we used multiple assignment.

If a point was not established, the previous state will be "win" or "lose". The game was resolved in a single throw, and this function simply returns the status monad.

If a point was established, the dice are rolled and rules applied to the new roll. If roll is 7, the game is a loser and a final monad is returned. If the roll is the point, the game is a winner and the appropriate monad is returned. Otherwise, a slightly revised monad is passed to the point_roll() function. The revised status monad includes this roll in the history of rolls.

A typical output looks like this:

```
>>> craps()
('craps', 5, [(2, 3), (1, 3), (1, 5), (1, 6)])
```

The final monad has a string that shows the outcome. It has the point that was established and the sequence of dice rolls. Each outcome has a specific payout that we can use to determine the overall fluctuation in the bettor's stake.

We can use simulation to examine different betting strategies. We might be searching for a way to defeat any house edge built into the game.

 There's a small asymmetry in the basic rules of the game. Having 11 as an immediate winner is balanced by having 3 as an immediate loser. The fact that 2 and 12 are also losers is the basis of the house's edge of 5.5 percent (*1/18* = *5.5*) in this game. The idea is to determine which of the additional betting opportunities will dilute this edge.

A great deal of clever Monte Carlo simulation can be built with a few simple, functional programming design techniques. The monad, in particular, can help structure these kinds of calculations when there are complex orders or internal states.

Additional PyMonad features

One of the other features of PyMonad is the confusingly named **monoid**. This comes directly from mathematics and it refers to a group of data elements that have an operator, an identity element, and the group is closed with respect to that operator. When we think of natural numbers, the add operator, and an identity element 0, this is a proper monoid. For positive integers, with an operator *, and an identity value of 1, we also have a monoid; strings using | as an operator and an empty string as an identity element also qualifies.

PyMonad includes a number of predefined monoid classes. We can extend this to add our own monoid class. The intent is to limit a compiler to certain kinds of optimizations. We can also use the monoid class to create data structures which accumulate a complex value, perhaps including a history of previous operations.

Much of this provides insight into functional programming. To paraphrase the documentation, this is an easy way to learn about functional programming in, perhaps, a slightly more forgiving environment. Rather than learning an entire language and toolset to compile and run functional programs, we can just experiment with interactive Python.

Pragmatically, we don't need too many of these features because Python is already stateful and offers strict evaluation of expressions. There's no practical reason to introduce stateful objects in Python, or strictly-ordered evaluation. We can write useful programs in Python by mixing functional concepts with Python's imperative implementation. For that reason, we won't delve any more deeply into PyMonad.

Summary

In this chapter, we looked at how we can use the PyMonad library to express some functional programming concepts directly in Python. The module shows many important functional programming techniques.

We looked at the idea of currying, a function that allows combinations of arguments to be applied to create new functions. Currying a function also allows us to use functional composition to create more complex functions from simpler pieces. We looked at functors that wrap simple data objects to make them into functions which can also be used with functional composition.

Monads are a way to impose a strict evaluation order when working with an optimizing compiler and lazy evaluation rules. In Python, we don't have a good use case for monads, because Python is an imperative programming language under the hood. In some cases, imperative Python may be more expressive and succinct than a monad construction.

In the next chapter, we'll look at how we can apply functional programming techniques to build web services applications. The idea of HTTP could be summarized as `response = httpd(request)`. Ideally, HTTP is stateless, making it a perfect match for functional design. However, most web sites will maintain state, using cookies to track session state.

15
A Functional Approach to Web Services

We'll step away from Exploratory Data Analysis and look closely at web servers and web services. These are, to an extent, a cascade of functions. We can apply a number of functional design patterns to the problem of presenting web content. Our goal is to look at ways in which we can approach **Representational State Transfer (REST)**. We want to build RESTful web services using functional design patterns.

We don't need to invent yet another Python web framework; there are plenty of frameworks to choose from. We'll avoid creating a large, general-purpose solution.

We don't want to select among the available frameworks, either. There are many, each with a distinct set of features and advantages.

We'll present some principles that can be applied to most of the available frameworks. We should be able to leverage functional design patterns for presenting web content. This will allow us to build web-based applications that have the advantages of a functional design.

For example, when we look at extremely large datasets, or extremely complex datasets, we might want a web service which supports subsetting or searching. We might want a web site which can download subsets in a variety of formats. In this case, we might need to use functional designs to create RESTful web services to support these more sophisticated requirements.

The most complex web applications often have stateful sessions that make the site easier to use. The session information is updated with data provided via HTML forms or fetched from databases, or recalled from caches of previous interactions. While the overall interaction involves state changes, the application programming can be largely functional. Some of the application functions can be non-strict in their use of request data, cache data, and database objects.

In order to avoid details of a specific web framework, we'll focus on the **Web Server Gateway Interface (WSGI)** design pattern. This will allow us to implement a simple web server. A great deal of information is present at the following link:

```
http://wsgi.readthedocs.org/en/latest/
```

Some important background of WSGI can be found at

```
https://www.python.org/dev/peps/pep-0333/
```

We'll start by looking at the HTTP protocol. From there, we can consider servers such as Apache httpd to implement this protocol and see how mod_wsgi becomes a sensible extension to a base server. With this background, we can look at the functional nature of WSGI and how we can leverage functional design to implement sophisticated web search and retrieval tools.

The HTTP request-response model

The essential HTTP protocol is, ideally, stateless. A user agent or client can take a functional view of the protocol. We can build a client using the http.client or urllib library. An HTTP user agent essentially executes something similar to the following:

```
import urllib.request
with urllib.request.urlopen(""http://slott-softwarearchitect.
blogspot.com"") as response:
    print(response.read())
```

A program like **wget** or **curl** does this at the command line; the URL is taken from the arguments. A browser does this in response to the user pointing and clicking; the URL is taken from the user's actions, in particular, the action of clicking on linked text or images.

The practical considerations of the internetworking protocols, however, lead to some implementation details which are stateful. Some of the HTTP status codes indicate that an additional action on the part of the user agent is required.

Many status codes in the 3xx range indicate that the requested resource has been moved. The user agent is then required to request a new location based on information sent in the Location header. The 401 status code indicates that authentication is required; the user agent can respond with an authorization header that contains credentials for access to the server. The urllib library implementation handles this stateful overhead. The http.client library doesn't automatically follow 3xx redirect status codes.

The techniques for a user agent to handle 3xx and 401 codes aren't deeply stateful. A simple recursion can be used. If the status doesn't indicate a redirection, it is the base case, and the function has a result. If redirection is required, the function can be called recursively with the redirected address.

Looking at the other end of the protocol, a static content server should also be stateless. There are two layers to the HTTP protocol: the TCP/IP socket machinery and a higher layer HTTP structure that depends on the lower level sockets. The lower level details are handled by the scoketserver library. The Python http. server library is one of the libraries that provide a higher level implementation.

We can use the http.server library as follows:

```
from http.server import HTTPServer, SimpleHTTPRequestHandler
running = True
httpd = HTTPServer(('localhost',8080), SimpleHTTPRequestHandler)
while running:
    httpd.handle_request()
httpd.shutdown()
```

We created a server object, and assigned it to the httpd variable. We provided the address and port number to which we'll listen for connection requests. The TCP/IP protocol will spawn a connection on a separate port. The HTTP protocol will read the request from this other port and create an instance of the handler.

In this example, we provided SimpleHTTPRequestHandler as the class to instantiate with each request. This class must implement a minimal interface, which will send headers and then send the body of the response to the client. This particular class will serve files from the local directory. If we wish to customize this, we can create a subclass, which implements methods such as do_GET() and do_POST() to alter the behavior.

Often, we use the serve_forever() method instead of writing our own loop. We've shown the loop here to clarify that the server must, generally, be crashed. If we want to close the server down politely, we'll require some way in which we can change the value of the shutdown variable. The *Ctrl + C* signal, for example, is commonly used for this.

Injecting a state via cookies

The addition of cookies changes the overall relationship between a client and server to become stateful. Interestingly, it involves no change to the HTTP protocol itself. The state information is communicated via headers on the request and the reply. The user agent will send cookies in request headers that match the host and path. The server will send cookies to the user agent in response headers.

The user agent or browser must, therefore, retain a cache of cookie values and include appropriate cookies in each request. The web server must accept cookies in the request header and send cookies in the response header. The web server doesn't need to cache cookies. A server merely uses cookies as additional arguments in a request and additional details in a response.

While a cookie can, in principle, contain almost anything, the use of cookies has rapidly evolved to contain just an identifier for a session state object. The server can then use the cookie information to locate session state in some kind of persistent storage. This means the server can also update the session state based on user agent requests. It also means the server can discard sessions which are old.

The concept of a "session" exists outside the HTTP protocol. It is commonly defined as a series of requests with the same session cookie. When an initial request is made, no cookie is available, and a new session is created. Every subsequent request would include the cookie. The cookie would identify the session state object on the server; this object would have the information required by the server to provide consistent web content gracefully.

The REST approach to web services, however, does not rely on cookies. Each REST request is distinct and does not fit into an overall session framework. This makes it less "user-friendly" than an interactive site that uses cookies to simplify a user's interactions.

This also means that each individual REST request is, in principle, separately authenticated. In many cases, a simple token is generated by the server to avoid the client sending more complex credentials with every request. This leads to having the REST traffic secured using **Secured Socket Layer (SSL)** protocols; the `https` scheme is then used instead of `http`. We'll call both schemes HTTP throughout this chapter.

Considering a server with a functional design

One core idea behind HTTP is that the daemon's response is a function of the request. Conceptually, a web service should have a top-level implementation that can be summarized as follows:

```
response = httpd(request)
```

However, this is impractical. It turns out that an HTTP request isn't a simple, monolithic data structure. It actually has some required parts and some optional parts. A request may have headers, there's a method and a path, and there may be attachments. The attachments may include forms or uploaded files or both.

To make things more complex, a browser's form data can be sent as a query string in the path of a GET request. Alternatively, it can be sent as an attachment to a POST request. While there's a possibility for confusion, most web application frameworks will create HTML form tags that provide their data via a "method=POST" statement in the <form> tag; the form data will then be an attachment.

Looking more deeply into the functional view

Both HTTP response and request have headers and a body. The request can have some attached form data. Therefore, we can think of a web server like this:

```
headers, content = httpd(headers, request, [uploads])
```

The request headers may include cookie values, which can be seen as adding yet more arguments. Additionally, a web server is often dependent on the OS environment in which it's running. This OS environment data can be considered as yet more arguments being provided as part of the request.

There's a large but reasonably well defined spectrum of content. The **Multipurpose Internet Mail Extension (MIME)** types define the kinds of content that a web service might return. This can include plain text, HTML, JSON, XML, or any of the wide variety of non-text media that a website might serve.

As we look more closely at the processing required to build a response to an HTTP request, we'll see some common features that we'd like to reuse. This idea of reusable elements is what leads to the creation of web service frameworks that fill a spectrum from simple to sophisticated. The ways that functional designs allow us to reuse functions indicate that the functional approach seems very appropriate to build web services.

We'll look at functional design of web services by examining how we can create a pipeline of the various elements of a service response. We'll do this by nesting the functions for request processing so that inner elements are free from the generic overheads, which are provided by outer elements. This also allows the outer elements to act as filters: invalid requests can yield error responses, allowing the inner function to focus narrowly on the application processing.

Nesting the services

We can look at web request handling as a number of nested contexts. An outer context, for example, might cover session management: examining the request to determine if this is another request in an existing session or a new session. An inner context might provide tokens used for form processing that can detect **Cross-Site Request Forgeries (CSRF)**. Another context might handle user authentication within a session.

A conceptual view of the functions explained previously is something like this:

```
response= content(authentication(csrf(session(headers, request,
[forms])))))
```

The idea here is that each function can build on the results of the previous function. Each function either enriches the request or rejects it because it's invalid. The `session` function, for example, can use headers to determine if this is an existing session or a new session. The `csrf` function will examine form input to ensure that proper tokens were used. The CSRF handling requires a valid session. The `authentication` function can return an error response for a session that lacks valid credentials; it can enrich the request with user information when valid credentials are present.

The `content` function is free from worrying about sessions, forgeries, and non-authenticated users. It can focus on parsing the path to determine what kind of content should be provided. In a more complex application, the `content` function may include a rather complex mapping from path elements to functions that determine the appropriate content.

The nested function view, however, still isn't quite right. The problem is that each nested context may also need to tweak the response instead of or in addition to tweaking the request.

We really want something more like this:

```
def session(headers, request, forms):
    pre-process: determine session
    content= csrf(headers, request, forms)
    post-processes the content
    return the content
def csrf(headers, request, forms):
    pre-process: validate csrf tokens
    content=  authenticate(headers, request, forms)
    post-processes the content
    return the content
```

This concept points toward a functional design for creating web content via a nested collection of functions that provide enriched input or enriched output or both. With a little bit of cleverness, we should be able to define a simple, standard interface that various functions can use. Once we've standardized an interface, we can combine functions in different ways and add features. We should be able to meet our functional programming objectives of having succinct and expressive programs that provide web content.

The WSGI standard

The **Web Server Gateway Interface (WSGI)** defines a relatively simple, standardized design pattern for creating a response to a web request. The Python library's `wsgiref` package includes a reference implementation of WSGI.

Each WSGI "application" has the same interface:

```
def some_app(environ, start_response):
    return content
```

The `environ` is a dictionary that contains all of the arguments of the request in a single, uniform structure. The headers, the request method, the path, any attachments for forms or file uploads will all be in the environment. In addition to this, the OS-level context is also provided along with a few items that are part of WSGI request handling.

The `start_response` is a function that must be used to send the status and headers of a response. The portion of a WSGI server that has final responsibility for building the response will use a `start_response` function to send the headers and the status as well as to build the response text. For some applications, this function might need to be wrapped with a higher-order function so that additional headers can be added to the response.

The return value is a sequence of strings or string-like file wrappers that will be returned to the user agent. If an HTML template tool is used, then the sequence may have a single item. In some cases, like the **Jinja2** templates, the template can be rendered lazily as a sequence of text chunks, interleaving template filling with downloading to the user agent.

Due to the way they nest, WSGI applications can also be viewed as a chain. Each application will either return an error or will hand the request to another application that will determine the result.

Here's a very simple routing application:

```
SCRIPT_MAP = {
    ""demo"": demo_app,
    ""static"": static_app,
    """": welcome_app,
}
def routing(environ, start_response):
    top_level= wsgiref.util.shift_path_info(environ)
    app= SCRIPT_MAP.get(top_level, SCRIPT_MAP[''])
    content= app(environ, start_response)
    return content
```

This app will use the `wsgiref.util.shift_path_info()` function to tweak the environment. This does a "head/tail split" on the items in the request path, available in the `environ['PATH_INFO']` dictionary. The head of the path—up to the first "split" — will be moved into the `SCRIPT_NAME` item in the environment; the `PATH_INFO` item will be updated to have the tail of the path. The returned value will also be the head of the path. In the case where there's no path to parse, the return value is None and no environment updates are made.

The `routing()` function uses the first item on the path to locate an application in the `SCRIPT_MAP` dictionary. We use the `SCRIPT_MAP['']` dictionary as a default in case the requested path doesn't fit the mapping. This seems a little better than an HTTP `404 NOT FOUND` error.

This WSGI application is a function that chooses between a number of other functions. It's a higher-order function, since it evaluates functions defined in a data structure.

It's easy to see how a framework could generalize the path-matching process using regular expressions. We can imagine configuring the `routing()` function with a sequence of Regular Expression's (REs) and WSGI applications instead of a mapping from a string to the WSGI application. The enhanced `routing()` function application would evaluate each RE looking for a match. In the case of a match, any `match.groups()` function could be used to update the environment before calling the requested application.

Throwing exceptions during WSGI processing

One central feature of WSGI applications is that each stage along the chain is responsible for filtering the requests. The idea is to reject faulty requests as early in the processing as possible. Python's exception handling makes this particularly simple.

We can define a WSGI application that provides static content as follows:

```
def static_app(environ, start_response):
    try:
        with open(CONTENT_HOME+environ['PATH_INFO']) as static:
            content= static.read().encode(""utf-8"")
            headers= [
                (""Content-Type"",'text/plain; charset=""utf-8""'),
                (""Content-Length"",str(len(content))),
            ]
        start_response('200 OK', headers)
        return [content]
    except IsADirectoryError as e:
        return index_app(environ, start_response)
    except FileNotFoundError as e:
        start_response('404 NOT FOUND', [])
        return([repr(e).encode(""utf-8"")])
```

In this case, we simply tried to open the requested path as a text file. There are two common reasons why we can't open a given file, both of which are handled as exceptions:

- If the file is a directory, we'll use a different application to present directory contents
- If the file is simply not found, we'll return an HTTP 404 NOT FOUND response

Any other exceptions raised by this WSGI application will not be caught. The application that invoked this should be designed with some generic error response capability. If it doesn't handle the exceptions, a generic WSGI failure response will be used.

 Our processing involves a strict ordering of operations. We must read the entire file so that we can create a proper HTTP Content-Length header.

Further, we must provide the content as bytes. This means that the Python strings must be properly encoded and we must provide the encoding information to the user agent. Even the error message, repr(e), is properly encoded before being downloaded.

Pragmatic WSGI applications

The intent of the WSGI standard is not to define a complete web framework; the intent is to define a minimum set of standards that allow flexible interoperability of web-related processing. A framework can take a wildly different approach than an internal architecture to provide web services. However, its outermost interface should be compatible with WSGI so that it can be used in a variety of contexts.

Web servers such as **Apache httpd** and **Nginx** have adapters, which provide a WSGI-compatible interface from the web server to Python applications. For more information on WSGI implementations, visit

`https://wiki.python.org/moin/WSGIImplementations`.

Embedding our applications in a larger server allows us to have a tidy separation of concerns. We can use Apache httpd to serve completely static content, such as `.css`, `.js`, and image files. For HTML pages, though, we can use Apache's `mod_wsgi` interface to hand off requests to a separate Python process, which handles only the interesting HTML portions of the web content.

This means that we must either create a separate media server, or define our website to have two sets of paths. If we take the second approach, some paths will have the completely static content and can be handled by Apache httpd. Other paths will have dynamic content, which will be handled by Python.

When working with WSGI functions, it's important to note that we can't modify or extend the WSGI interface in any way. For example, it seems like a good idea to provide an additional parameter with a sequence of functions that define the chain of processing. Each stage would pop the first item from the list as the next step in the processing. An additional parameter like this might be typical for functional design, but the change in the interface defeats the purpose of WSGI.

A consequence of the WSGI definition is that configuration is either done with global variables, the request environment, or with a function, which fetches some global configuration objects from a cache. Using module-level globals works for small examples. For more complex applications, a configuration cache might be required. It might also be sensible to have a WSGI app, which merely updates the `environ` dictionary with configuration parameters and passes control to another WSGI application.

Defining web services as functions

We'll look at a RESTful web service, which can "slice and dice" a source of data and provide downloads as JSON, XML, or CSV files. We'll provide an overall WSGI-compatible wrapper but the functions which do the "real work" of the application won't be narrowly constrained to fit the WSGI.

We'll use a simple dataset with four subcollections: the Anscombe Quartet. We looked at ways to read and parse this data in Chapter 3, *Functions, Iterators, and Generators*". It's a small set of data but it can be used to show the principles of a RESTful web service.

We'll split our application into two tiers: a web tier, which will be a simple WSGI application, and the rest of the processing, which will be more typical functional programming. We'll look at the web tier first so that we can focus on a functional approach to provide meaningful results.

We need to provide two pieces of information to the web service:

- The quartet that we want—this is a "slice and dice" operation. For this example, it's mostly just a "slice".
- The output format we want.

The data selection is commonly done via the request path. We can request "/anscombe/I/" or "/anscombe/II/" to pick specific datasets from the quartet. The idea is that a URL defines a resource, and there's no good reason for the URL to ever change. In this case, the dataset selectors aren't dependent on dates, or some organizational approval status or other external factors. The URL is timeless and absolute.

The output format is not a first class part of the URL. It's just a serialization format—not the data itself. In some cases, the format is requested via the HTTP `Accept` header. This is hard to use from a browser but easy to use from an application using a RESTful API. When extracting data from the browser, a query string is commonly used to specify the output format. We'll use the "`?form=json`" method at the end of the path to specify the JSON output format.

A URL we can use will look like this:

```
http://localhost:8080/anscombe/III/?form=csv
```

This would request a CSV download of the third dataset.

Creating the WSGI application

First, we'll use a simple URL pattern-matching expression to define the one and only routing in our application. In a larger or more complex application, we might have more than one such patterns:

```
import re
path_pat= re.compile(r""^/anscombe/(?P<dataset>.*?)/?$"")
```

This pattern allows us to define an overall "script" in the WSGI sense at the top level of the path. In this case, the script is "anscombe". We'll take the next level of the path as a dataset to select from the Anscombe Quartet. The dataset value should be one of I, II, III, or IV.

We used a named parameter for the selection criteria. In many cases, RESTful APIs are described using a syntax, as follows:

```
/anscombe/{dataset}/
```

We translated this idealized pattern into a proper, regular expression, and preserved the name of the dataset selector in the path.

Here's the kind of unit test that demonstrates how this pattern works:

```
test_pattern= """"""
>>> m1= path_pat.match(""/anscombe/I"")
>>> m1.groupdict()
{'dataset': 'I'}
>>> m2= path_pat.match(""/anscombe/II/"")
>>> m2.groupdict()
{'dataset': 'II'}
>>> m3= path_pat.match(""/anscombe/"")
>>> m3.groupdict()
{'dataset': ''}
"""""""
```

We can include the three previously mentioned examples as part of the overall doctest using the following command:

```
__test__ = {
    ""test_pattern"": test_pattern,
}
```

This will ensure that our routing works as expected. It's important to be able to test this separately from the rest of the WSGI application. Testing a complete web server means starting the server process and then trying to connect with a browser or a test tool, such as Postman or Selenium. Visit http://www.getpostman.com or http://www.seleniumhq.org to get more information on the usage of Postman and Selenium. We prefer to test each feature in isolation.

Here's the overall WSGI application, with two lines of command highlighted:

```
import traceback
import urllib
def anscombe_app(environ, start_response):
    log= environ['wsgi.errors']
    try:
        match= path_pat.match(environ['PATH_INFO'])
        set_id= match.group('dataset').upper()
        query= urllib.parse.parse_qs(environ['QUERY_STRING'])
        print(environ['PATH_INFO'], environ['QUERY_STRING'],
        match.groupdict(), file=log)
        log.flush()
        dataset= anscombe_filter(set_id, raw_data())
        content, mime= serialize(query['form'][0], set_id, dataset)
        headers= [
            ('Content-Type', mime),
            ('Content-Length', str(len(content))),         ]
        start_response(""200 OK"", headers)
        return [content]
    except Exception as e:
        traceback.print_exc(file=log)
        tb= traceback.format_exc()
        page= error_page.substitute(title=""Error"",
        message=repr(e), traceback=tb)
        content= page.encode(""utf-8"")
        headers = [
            ('Content-Type', ""text/html""),
            ('Content-Length', str(len(content))),
        ]
        start_response(""404 NOT FOUND"", headers)
        return [content]
```

This application will extract two pieces of information from the request: the PATH_INFO and the QUERY_STRING methods. The PATH_INFO request will define which set to extract. The QUERY_STRING request will specify an output format.

The application processing is broken into three functions. A raw_data() function reads the raw data from a file. The result is a dictionary with lists of Pair objects. The anscombe_filter() function accepts a selection string and the dictionary of raw data and returns a single list of Pair objects. The list of pairs is then serialized into bytes by the serialize() function. The serializer is expected to produce bytes, which can then be packaged with an appropriate header and returned.

We elected to produce an HTTP Content-Length header. This isn't required, but it's polite for large downloads Because we decided to emit this header, we are forced to materialize the results of the serialization so that we can count the bytes.

If we elected to omit the Content-Length header, we could change the structure of this application dramatically. Each serializer could be changed to a generator function, which would yield bytes as they are produced. For large datasets, this can be a helpful optimization. For the user watching a download, however, it might not be so pleasant because the browser can't display how much of the download is complete.

All errors are treated as a 404 NOT FOUND error. This could be misleading, since a number of individual things might go wrong. A more sophisticated error handling would provide more try:/except: blocks to provide more informative feedback.

For debugging purposes, we've provided a Python stack trace in the resulting web page. Outside the context of debugging, this is a very bad idea. Feedback from an API should be just enough to fix the request and nothing more. A stack trace provides too much information to potentially malicious users.

Getting raw data

The raw_data() function is largely copied from *Chapter 3, Functions, Iterators, and Generators*. We included some important changes. Here's what we're using for this application:

```
from Chapter_3.ch03_ex5 import series, head_map_filter, row_iter,
Pair

def raw_data():
    """"""
    >>> raw_data()['I'] #doctest: +ELLIPSIS
    (Pair(x=10.0, y=8.04), Pair(x=8.0, y=6.95), ...
    """"""
```

```
with open(""Anscombe.txt"") as source:
    data = tuple(head_map_filter(row_iter(source)))
    mapping = dict((id_str, tuple(series(id_num,data)))
        for id_num, id_str in enumerate(['I', 'II', 'III', 'IV'])
)

return mapping
```

We opened the local data file, and applied a simple `row_iter()` function to return each line of the file parsed into a row of separate files. We applied the `head_map_filter()` function to remove the heading from the file. The result created a tuple-of-tuple structure with all of the data.

We transformed the tuple-of-tuple into a more useful `dict()` function by selecting particular series from the source data. Each series will be a pair of columns. For series "I," it's columns 0 and 1. For series "II," it's columns 2 and 3.

We used the `dict()` function with a generator expression for consistency with the `list()` and `tuple()` functions. While it's not essential, it's sometimes helpful to see the similarities with these three data structures and their use of generator expressions.

The `series()` function creates the individual `Pair` objects for each *x,y* pair in the dataset. In retrospect, we can see the the output value after modifying this function so that the resulting `namedtuple` class is an argument to this function, not an implicit feature of the function. We'd prefer to see the `series(id_num,Pair,data)` method to see where the `Pair` objects are created. This extension requires rewriting some of the examples in *Chapter 3, Functions, Iterators, and Generators*. We'll leave that as an exercise for the reader.

The important change here is that we're showing the formal `doctest` test case. As we noted earlier, web applications—as a whole—are difficult to test. The web server must be started and then a web client must be used to run the test cases. Problems then have to be resolved by reading the web log, which can be difficult unless complete tracebacks are displayed. It's much better to debug as much of the web application as possible using ordinary `doctest` and `unittest` testing techniques.

Applying a filter

In this application, we're using a very simple filter. The entire filter process is embodied in the following function:

```
def anscombe_filter(set_id, raw_data):
    """"""
    >>> anscombe_filter(""II"", raw_data()) #doctest: +ELLIPSIS
```

```
(Pair(x=10.0, y=9.14), Pair(x=8.0, y=8.14), Pair(x=13.0, y=8.74),
...
""""""
return raw_data[set_id]
```

We made this trivial expression into a function for three reasons:

- The functional notation is slightly more consistent and a bit more flexible than the subscript expression
- We can easily expand the filtering to do more
- We can include separate unit tests in the docstring for this function

While a simple lambda would work, it wouldn't be quite as convenient to test.

For error handling, we've done exactly nothing. We've focused on what's sometimes called the "happy path:" an ideal sequence of events. Any problems that arise in this function will raise an exception. The WSGI wrapper function should catch all exceptions and return an appropriate status message and error response content.

For example, it's possible that the set_id method will be wrong in some way. Rather than obsess over all the ways it could be wrong, we'll simply allow Python to throw an exception. Indeed, this function follows the Python I advice that, "it's better to seek forgiveness than to ask permission." This advice is materialized in code by avoiding "permission-seeking": there are no preparatory if statements that seek to qualify the arguments as valid. There is only "forgiveness" handling: an exception will be raised and handled in the WSGI wrapper. This essential advice applies to the preceding raw data and the serialization that we will see now.

Serializing the results

Serialization is the conversion of Python data into a stream of bytes, suitable for transmission. Each format is best described by a simple function that serializes just that one format. A top-level generic serializer can then pick from a list of specific serializers. The picking of serializers leads to the following collection of functions:

```
serializers = {
    'xml': ('application/xml', serialize_xml),
    'html': ('text/html', serialize_html),
    'json': ('application/json', serialize_json),
    'csv': ('text/csv', serialize_csv),
}
def serialize(format, title, data):
```

```
"""""json/xml/csv/html serialization.
>>> data = [Pair(2,3), Pair(5,7)]
>>> serialize(""json"", ""test"", data)
(b'[{""x"": 2, ""y"": 3}, {""x"": 5, ""y"": 7}]', 'application/json')
""""""

    mime, function = serializers.get(format.lower(), ('text/html',
serialize_html))

    return function(title, data), mime
```

The overall `serialize()` function locates a specific serializer and a specific MIME type that must be used in the response to characterize the results. It then calls one of the specific serializers. We've also shown a `doctest` test case here. We didn't patiently test each serializer, since showing that one works seems adequate.

We'll look at the serializers separately. What we'll see is that the serializers fall into two groups: those that produce strings and those that produce bytes. A serializer that produces a string will need to have the string encoded as bytes. A serializer that produces bytes doesn't need any further work.

For the serializers, which produce strings, we need to do some function composition with a standard convert-to-bytes. We can do functional composition using a decorator. Here's how we can standardize the conversion to bytes:

```
from functools import wraps
def to_bytes(function):
    @wraps(function)
    def decorated(*args, **kw):
        text= function(*args, **kw)
        return text.encode(""utf-8"")
    return decorated
```

We've created a small decorator named `@to_bytes`. This will evaluate the given function and then encode the results using UTF-8 to get bytes. We'll show how this is used with JSON, CSV, and HTML serializers. The XML serializer produces bytes directly and doesn't need to be composed with this additional function.

We could also do the functional composition in the initialization of the `serializers` mapping. Instead of decorating the function definition, we could decorate the reference to the function object:

```
serializers = {
    'xml': ('application/xml', serialize_xml),
    'html': ('text/html', to_bytes(serialize_html)),
```

```
    'json': ('application/json', to_bytes(serialize_json)),
    'csv': ('text/csv', to_bytes(serialize_csv)),
}
```

Though this is possible, this doesn't seem to be helpful. The distinction between serializers that produce strings and those that produce bytes isn't an important part of the configuration.

Serializing data into the JSON or CSV format

The JSON and CSV serializers are similar functions because both rely on Python's libraries to serialize. The libraries are inherently imperative, so the function bodies are strict sequences of statements.

Here's the JSON serializer:

```
import json
@to_bytes
def serialize_json(series, data):
    """
    >>> data = [Pair(2,3), Pair(5,7)]
    >>> serialize_json(""test"", data)
    b'[{""x"": 2, ""y"": 3}, {""x"": 5, ""y"": 7}]'
    """
    obj= [dict(x=r.x, y=r.y) for r in data]
    text= json.dumps(obj, sort_keys=True)
    return text
```

We created a list of dictionaries structure and used the json.dumps() function to create a string representation. The JSON module requires a materialized list object; we can't provide a lazy generator function. The sort_keys=True argument value is essential for unit testing. However, it's not required for the application and represents a bit of overhead.

Here's the CSV serializer:

```
import csv, io
@to_bytes
def serialize_csv(series, data):
    """
```

```
>>> data = [Pair(2,3), Pair(5,7)]
>>> serialize_csv(""test"", data)
b'x,y\\r\\n2,3\\r\\n5,7\\r\\n'
""""""
buffer= io.StringIO()
wtr= csv.DictWriter(buffer, Pair._fields)
wtr.writeheader()
wtr.writerows(r._asdict() for r in data)
return buffer.getvalue()
```

The CSV module's readers and writers are a mixture of imperative and functional elements. We must create the writer, and properly create headings in a strict sequence. We've used the `_fields` attribute of the `Pair` namedtuple to determine the column headings for the writer.

The `writerows()` method of the writer will accept a lazy generator function. In this case, we used the `_asdict()` method of each `Pair` object to return a dictionary suitable for use with the CSV writer.

Serializing data into XML

We'll look at one approach to XML serialization using the built-in libraries. This will build a document from individual tags. A common alternative approach is to use Python introspection to examine and map Python objects and class names to XML tags and attributes.

Here's our XML serialization:

```
import xml.etree.ElementTree as XML
def serialize_xml(series, data):
    """"""
    >>> data = [Pair(2,3), Pair(5,7)]
    >>> serialize_xml(""test"", data)
    b'<series name=""test""><row><x>2</x><y>3</y></row><row><x>5</x>
    <y>7</y></row></series>'
    """"""
    doc= XML.Element(""series"", name=series)
    for row in data:
        row_xml= XML.SubElement(doc, ""row"")
        x= XML.SubElement(row_xml, ""x"")
```

```
        x.text= str(row.x)
        y= XML.SubElement(row_xml, ""y"")
        y.text= str(row.y)
    return XML.tostring(doc, encoding='utf-8')
```

We created a top-level element, `<series>`, and placed `<row>` subelements underneath that top element. Within each `<row>` subelement, we've created `<x>` and `<y>` tags and assigned text content to each tag.

The interface for building an XML document using the ElementTree library tends to be heavily imperative. This makes it a poor fit for an otherwise functional design. In addition to the imperative style, note that we haven't created a DTD or XSD. We have not properly assigned a namespace to our tags. We also omitted the `<?xml version=""1.0""?>` processing instruction that is generally the first item in an XML document.

A more sophisticated serialization library would be helpful. There are many to choose from. Visit `https://wiki.python.org/moin/PythonXml` for a list of alternatives.

Serializing data into HTML

In our final example of serialization, we'll look at the complexity of creating an HTML document. The complexity arises because in HTML, we're expected to provide an entire web page with some context information. Here's one way to tackle this HTML problem:

```python
import string

data_page = string.Template("""""<html>
<head><title>Series ${title}</title></head>
<body><h1>Series ${title}</h1>
<table><thead><tr><td>x</td><td>y</td></tr></thead>
<tbody>
${rows}
</tbody></table></body></html>""""")

@to_bytes
def serialize_html(series, data):
    """"""
    >>> data = [Pair(2,3), Pair(5,7)]
    >>> serialize_html(""test"", data) #doctest: +ELLIPSIS
    b'<html>...<tr><td>2</td><td>3</td></tr>\\n<tr><td>5</td>
    <td>7</td></tr>...
    """"""
```

```
text= data_page.substitute(title=series,
    rows=""\n"".join(
        ""<tr><td>{0.x}</td><td>{0.y}</td></tr>"".format(row)
        for row in data)
    )
return text
```

Our serialization function has two parts. The first part is a `string.Template()` function that contains the essential HTML page. It has two placeholders where data can be inserted into the template. The `${title}` method shows where title information can be inserted and the `${rows}` method shows where the data rows can be inserted.

The function creates individual data rows using a simple format string. These are joined into a longer string, which is then substituted into the template.

While workable for simple cases like the preceding example, this isn't ideal for more complex result sets. There are a number of more sophisticated template tools to create HTML pages. A number of these include the ability to embed the looping in the template, separate from the function that initializes serialization. Visit `https://wiki.python.org/moin/Templating` for a list of alternatives.

Tracking usage

Many publicly available APIs require the use of an "API Key". The supplier of the API requests you to sign up and provide an email address or other contact information. In exchange for this, they provide an API Key which activates the API.

The API Key is used to authenticate access. It may also be used to authorize specific features. Finally, it's also used to track usage. This may include throttling requests if an API Key is used too often in a given time period.

The variations in the business models are numerous. For example, use of the API Key is a billable event and charges are incurred. For other businesses, traffic must reach some threshold before payments are required.

What's important is non-repudiation of the use of the API. This, in turn, means creating API Keys that can act as a user's authentication credentials. The key must be difficult to forge and relatively easy to verify.

One easy way to create API Keys is to use a cryptographic random number to generate a difficult-to-predict key string. A small function, like the following, should be good enough:

```
import random
rng= random.SystemRandom()
import base64
def make_key_1(rng=rng, size=1):
    key_bytes= bytes(rng.randrange(0,256) for i in range(18*size))
    key_string= base64.urlsafe_b64encode(key_bytes)
    return key_string
```

We've used the `random.SystemRandom` class as the class for our secure random number generator. This will seed the generator with the `os.urandom()` bytes, which assures a reliably unpredictable seed value. We've created this object separately so that it can be reused each time a key is requested. Best practice is to get a number of keys from a generator using a single random seed.

Given some random bytes, we used a base 64 encoding to create a sequence of characters. Using a multiple of three in the initial sequence of random bytes, we'll avoid any trailing "=" signs in the base 64 encoding. We've used the URL safe base 64 encoding, which won't include the "/" or "+" characters in the resulting string, characters that might be confusing if used as part of a URL or query string.

> The more elaborate methods won't lead to more random data. The use of `random.SystemRandom` assures that no one can counterfeit a key assigned to another user. We're using *18×8* random bits, giving us a large number of random keys.

How many random keys? Take a look at the following command and its output:

```
>>> 2**(18*8)
22300745198530623141535718272648361505980416
```

The odds of someone successfully forging a duplicate of someone else's key are small.

Another choice is to use `uuid.uuid4()` to create a random **Universally Unique Identifier (UUID)**. This will be a 36-character string that has 32 hex digits and four "-" punctuation marks. A random UUID is also difficult to forge. A UUID that includes data such as username or host IP address is a bad idea because this encodes information, which can be decoded and used to forge a key. The reason for using a cryptographic random number generator is to avoid encoding any information.

The RESTful web server will then need a small database with the valid keys and perhaps some client contact information. If an API request includes a key that's in the database, the associated user is responsible for the request. If the API request doesn't include a known key, the request can be rejected with a simple `401 UNAUTHORIZED` response. Since the key itself is a 24-character string, the database will be rather small and can easily be cached in memory.

Ordinary log-scraping might be sufficient to show the usage for a given key. A more sophisticated application might record API requests in a separate logfile or database to simplify analysis.

Summary

In this chapter, we looked at ways in which we can apply functional design to the problem of serving content with REST-based web services. We looked at the ways that the WSGI standard leads to somewhat functional overall applications. We also looked at how we can embed a more functional design into a WSGI context by extracting elements from the request for use by our application functions.

For simple services, the problem often decomposes down into three distinct operations: getting the data, searching or filtering, and then serializing the results. We tackled this with three functions: `raw_data()`, `anscombe_filter()`, and `serialize()`. We wrapped these functions in a simple WSGI-compatible application to divorce the web services from the "real" processing around extracting and filtering the data.

We also looked at the way that web services functions can focus on the "happy path" and assume that all of the inputs are valid. If inputs are invalid, the ordinary Python exception handling will raise exceptions. The WSGI wrapper function will catch the errors and return appropriate status codes and error content.

We avoided looking at more complex problems associated with uploading data or accepting data from forms to update a persistent data store. These are not significantly more complex than getting data and serializing the results. They are already solved in a better manner.

For simple queries and data sharing, a small web service application can be helpful. We can apply functional design patterns and assure that the website code is succinct and expressive. For more complex web applications, we should consider using a framework that handles the details properly.

In the next chapter, we'll look at a few optimization techniques that are available to us. We'll expand on the `@lru_cache` decorator from *Chapter 10, The Functools Module*. We'll also look at some other optimization techniques that were presented in *Chapter 6, Recursions and Reductions*.

16
Optimizations and Improvements

In this chapter, we'll look at a few optimizations that we can make to create high performance functional programs. We'll expand on the `@lru_cache` decorator from *Chapter 10, The Functools Module*. We have a number of ways to implement the memoization algorithm. We'll also discuss how to write our own decorators. More importantly, we'll see how we use a `Callable` object to cache memoized results.

We'll also look at some optimization techniques that were presented in *Chapter 6, Recursions and Reductions*. We'll review the general approach to tail recursion optimization. For some algorithms, we can combine memoization with a recursive implementation and achieve good performance. For other algorithms, memoization isn't really very helpful and we have to look elsewhere for performance improvements.

In most cases, small changes to a program will lead to small improvements in performance. Replacing a function with a `lambda` object will have a tiny impact on performance. If we have a program that is unacceptably slow, we often have to locate a completely new algorithm or data structure. Some algorithms have bad "big-O" complexity; nothing will make them magically run faster.

One place to start is `http://www.algorist.com`. This is a resource that may help to locate better algorithms for a given problem.

Memoization and caching

As we saw in *Chapter 10, The Functools Module*, many algorithms can benefit from memoization. We'll start with a review of some previous examples to characterize the kinds of functions that can be helped with memoization.

In *Chapter 6, Recursions and Reductions*, we looked at a few common kinds of recursions. The simplest kind of recursion is a tail recursion with arguments that can be easily matched to values in a cache. If the arguments are integers, strings, or materialized collections, then we can compare arguments quickly to determine if the cache has a previously computed result.

We can see from these examples that integer numeric calculations such as computing factorial or locating a Fibonacci number will be obviously improved. Locating prime factors and raising integers to powers are more examples of numeric algorithms that apply to integer values.

When we looked at the recursive version of a Fibonacci number calculator, we saw that it contained two tail-call recursions. Here's the definition:

$$F_n = F_{n-1} + F_{n-2}$$

This can be turned into a loop, but the design change requires some thinking. The memoized version of this can be quite fast and doesn't require quite so much thinking to design.

The Syracuse function, shown in *Chapter 6, Recursions and Reductions,* is an example of the kind of function used to compute fractal values. It contains a simple rule that's applied recursively. Exploring the Collatz conjecture ("does the Syracuse function always lead to 1?") requires memoized intermediate results.

The recursive application of the Syracuse function is an example of a function with an "attractor," where the value is attracted to 1. In some higher dimensional functions, the attractor can be a line or perhaps a fractal. When the attractor is a point, memoization can help; otherwise, memoization may actually be a hindrance, since each fractal value is unique.

When working with collections, the benefits of caching may vanish. If the collection happens to have the same number of integer values, strings, or tuples, then there's a chance that the collection is a duplicate and time can be saved. However, if a calculation on a collection will be needed more than once, manual optimization is best: do the calculation once and assign the results to a variable.

When working with iterables, generator functions, and other lazy objects, caching of an overall object is essentially impossible. In these cases, memoization is not going to help at all.

Raw data that includes measurements often use floating point values. Since an exact equality comparison between floating point values may not work out well, memoizing intermediate results may not work out well either.

Raw data that includes counts, however, may benefit from memoization. These are integers, and we can trust exact integer comparisons to (potentially) save recalculating a previous value. Some statistical functions, when applied to counts, can benefit from using the `fractions` module instead of floating point values. When we replace x/y with the `Fraction(x,y)` method, we've preserved the ability to do exact value matching. We can produce the final result using the `float(some_fraction)` method.

Specializing memoization

The essential idea of memoization is so simple that it can be captured by the `@lru_cache` decorator. This decorator can be applied to any function to implement memoization. In some cases, we might be able to improve on the generic idea with something more specialized. There are a large number of potentially optimizable multivalued functions. We'll pick one here and look at another in a more complex case study.

The binomial, $\binom{n}{m}$, shows the number of ways n different things can be arranged in groups of size m. The value is as follows:

$$\binom{n}{m} = \frac{n!}{m!(n-m)!}$$

Clearly, we should cache the factorial calculations rather than redo all those multiplications. However, we may also benefit from caching the overall binomial calculation, too.

We'll create a `Callable` object that contains multiple internal caches. Here's a helper function that we'll need:

```
from functools import reduce
from operator import mul
prod = lambda x: reduce(mul, x)
```

The `prod()` function computes the product of an iterable of numbers. It's defined as a reduction using the * operator.

Here's a `Callable` object with two caches that uses this `prod()` function:

```
from collections.abc import Callable
class Binomial(Callable):
    def __init__(self):
        self.fact_cache= {}
        self.bin_cache= {}
    def fact(self, n):
        if n not in self.fact_cache:
            self.fact_cache[n] = prod(range(1,n+1))
        return self.fact_cache[n]
    def __call__(self, n, m):
        if (n,m) not in self.bin_cache:
            self.bin_cache[n,m] = self.fact(n)//(self.fact(m)*self.
fact(n-m))
        return self.bin_cache[n,m]
```

We created two caches: one for factorial values and one for binomial coefficient values. The internal `fact()` method uses the `fact_cache` attribute. If the value isn't in the cache, it's computed and added to the cache. The external `__call__()` method uses the `bin_cache` attribute in a similar way: if a particular binomial has already been calculated, the answer is simply returned. If not, the internal `fact()` method is used to compute a new value.

We can use the preceding `Callable` class like this:

```
>>> binom= Binomial()
>>> binom(52,5)
2598960
```

This shows how we can create a `Callable` object from our class and then invoke the object on a particular set of arguments. There are a number of ways that a 52-card deck can be dealt into 5-card hands. There are 2.6 million possible hands.

Tail recursion optimizations

In *Chapter 6, Recursions and Reductions,* among many others, we looked at how a simple recursion can be optimized into a `for` loop. The general approach is this:

- Design the recursion. This means the base case and the recursive cases. For example, this is a definition of computing:

$$n! = n \times (n-1)!$$

  To design the recursion execute the following commands:

```
def fact(n):
    if n == 0: return 1
    else: return n*fact(n-1)
```

- If the recursion has a simple call at the end, replace the recursive case with a `for` loop. The command is as follows:

```
def facti(n):
    if n == 0: return 1
    f= 1
    for i in range(2,n):
        f= f*i
    return f
```

When the recursion appears at the end of a simple function, it's described as a tail–call optimization. Many compilers will optimize this into a loop. Python — lacking this optimization in its compiler — doesn't do this kind of tail-call transformation.

This pattern is very common. Performing the tail-call optimization improves performance and removes any upper bound on the number of recursions that can be done.

Prior to doing any optimization, it's absolutely essential that the function already works. For this, a simple `doctest` string is often sufficient. We might use annotation on our factorial functions like this:

```
def fact(n):
    """Recursive Factorial
    >>> fact(0)
    1
    >>> fact(1)
    1
    >>> fact(7)
    5040
```

```
"""
    if n == 0: return 1
    else: return n*fact(n-1)
```

We added two edge cases: the explicit base case and the first item beyond the base case. We also added another item that would involve multiple iterations. This allows us to tweak the code with confidence.

When we have a more complex combination of functions, we might need to execute commands like this:

```
test_example="""
>>> binom= Binomial()
>>> binom(52,5)
2598960
"""
__test__ = {
    "test_example": test_example,
}
```

The __test__ variable is used by the `doctest.testmod()` function. All of the values in the dictionary associated with the __test__ variable are examined for the `doctest` strings. This is a handy way to test features that come from compositions of functions. This is also called integration testing, since it tests the integration of multiple software components.

Having working code with a set of tests gives us the confidence to make optimizations. We can easily confirm the correctness of the optimization. Here's a popular quote that is used to describe optimization:

> *"Making a wrong program worse is no sin."*
>
> *-Jon Bentley*

This appeared in the *Bumper Sticker Computer Science* chapter of *More Programming Pearls*, published by Addison-Wesley, Inc. What's important here is that we should only optimize code that's actually correct.

Optimizing storage

There's no general rule for optimization. We often focus on optimizing performance because we have tools like the Big O measure of complexity that show us whether or not an algorithm is an effective solution to a given problem. Optimizing storage is usually tackled separately: we can look at the steps in an algorithm and estimate the size of the storage required for the various storage structures.

In many cases, the two considerations are opposed. In some cases, an algorithm that has outstandingly good performance requires a large data structure. This algorithm can't scale without dramatic increases in the amount of storage required. Our goal is to design an algorithm that is reasonably fast and also uses an acceptable amount of storage.

We may have to spend time researching algorithmic alternatives to locate a way to make the space-time trade off properly. There are some common optimization techniques. We can often follow links from Wikipedia: http://en.wikipedia.org/wiki/Space-time_tradeoff.

One memory optimization technique we have in Python is to use an iterable. This has some properties of a proper materialized collection, but doesn't necessarily occupy storage. There are few operations (such as the len() function) that can't work on an iterable. For other operations, the memory saving feature can allow a program to work with very large collections.

Optimizing accuracy

In a few cases, we need to optimize the accuracy of a calculation. This can be challenging and may require some fairly advanced math to determine the limits on the accuracy of a given approach.

An interesting thing we can do in Python is replace floating point approximations with fractions.Fraction value. For some applications, this can create more accurate answers than floating point, because more bits are used for numerator and denominator than a floating point mantissa.

It's important to use decimal.Decimal values to work with currency. It's a common error to use a float value. When using a float value, additional noise bits are introduced because of the mismatch between Decimal values provided as input and the binary approximation used by floating point values. Using Decimal values prevents the introduction of tiny inaccuracies.

In many cases, we can make small changes to a Python application to switch from `float` values to `Fraction` or `Decimal` values. When working with transcendental functions, this change isn't necessarily beneficial. Transcendental functions—by definition—involve irrational numbers.

Reducing accuracy based on audience requirements

For some calculations, a fraction value may be more intuitively meaningful than a floating point value. This is part of presenting statistical results in a way that an audience can understand and take action on.

For example, the chi-squared test generally involves computing the X^2 comparison between actual values and expected values. We can then subject this comparison value to a test against the X^2 cumulative distribution function. When the expected and actual values have no particular relationship—we can call this a null relationship—the variation will be random; X^2 the value tends to be small. When we accept the null hypothesis, then we'll look elsewhere for a relationship. When the actual values are significantly different from the expected values, we may reject the null hypothesis. By rejecting the null hypothesis, we can explore further to determine the precise nature of the relationship.

The decision is often based on the table of the X^2 **Cumulative Distribution Function (CDF)** for selected X^2 values and given degrees of freedom. While the tabulated CDF values are mostly irrational values, we don't usually use more than two or three decimal places. This is merely a decision-making tool, there's no practical difference in meaning between 0.049 and 0.05.

A widely used probability is 0.05 for rejecting the null hypothesis. This is a `Fraction` object less than 1/20. When presenting data to an audience, it sometimes helps to characterize results as fractions. A value like 0.05 is hard to visualize. Describing a relationship has having 1 chance in 20 can help to characterize the likelihood of a correlation.

Case study – making a chi-squared decision

We'll look at a common statistical decision. The decision is described in detail at `http://www.itl.nist.gov/div898/handbook/prc/section4/prc45.htm`.

This is a chi-squared decision on whether or not data is distributed randomly. In order to make this decision, we'll need to compute an expected distribution and compare the observed data to our expectations. A significant difference means there's something that needs further investigation. An insignificant difference means we can use the null hypothesis that there's nothing more to study: the differences are simply random variation.

We'll show how we can process the data with Python. We'll start with some backstory—some details that are not part of the case study, but often features an **Exploratory Data Analysis (EDA)** application. We need to gather the raw data and produce a useful summary that we can analyze.

Within the production quality assurance operations, silicon wafer defect data is collected into a database. We might use SQL queries to extract defect details for further analysis. For example, a query could look like this:

```
SELECT SHIFT, DEFECT_CODE, SERIAL_NUMBER
FROM some tables;
```

The output from this query could be a CSV file with individual defect details:

```
shift,defect_code,serial_number
1,None,12345
1,None,12346
1,A,12347
1,B,12348
and so on. for thousands of wafers
```

We need to summarize the preceding data. We might summarize at the SQL query level using the COUNT and GROUP BY statements. We might also summarize at the Python application level. While a pure database summary is often described as being more efficient, this isn't always true. In some cases, a simple extract of raw data and a Python application to summarize can be faster than a SQL summary. If performance is important, both alternatives must be measured, rather than hoping that the database is fastest.

In some cases, we may be able to get summary data from the database efficiently. This summary must have three attributes: the shift, type of defect, and a count of defects observed. The summary data looks like this:

```
shift,defect_code,count
1,A,15
2,A,26
3,A,33
and so on.
```

The output will show all of the 12 combinations of shift and defect type.

In the next section, we'll focus on reading the raw data to create summaries. This is the kind of context in which Python is particularly powerful: working with raw source data.

We need to observe and compare shift and defect counts with an overall expectation. If the difference between observed counts and expected counts can be attributed to random fluctuation, we have to accept the null hypothesis that nothing interesting is going wrong. If, on the other hand, the numbers don't fit with random variation, then we have a problem that requires further investigation.

Filtering and reducing the raw data with a Counter object

We'll represent the essential defect counts as a `collections.Counter` parameter. We will build counts of defects by shift and defect type from the detailed raw data. Here's a function to read some raw data from a CSV file:

```python
import csv
from collections import Counter
from types import SimpleNamespace
def defect_reduce(input):
    rdr= csv.DictReader(input)
    assert sorted(rdr.fieldnames) == ["defect_type", "serial_number",
    "shift"]
    rows_ns = (SimpleNamespace(**row) for row in rdr)
    defects = ((row.shift, row.defect_type) for row in rows_ns:
        if row.defect_type)
    tally= Counter(defects)
    return tally
```

The preceding function will create a dictionary reader based on an open file provided via the `input` parameter. We've confirmed that the column names match the three expected column names. In some cases, we'll have extra columns in the file; in this case, the assertion will be something like `all((c in rdr.fieldnames) for c in [...])`. Given a tuple of column names, this will assure that all of the required columns are present in the source. We can also use sets to assure that `set(rdr.fieldnames) <= set([...])`.

We created a `types.SimpleNamespace` parameter for each row. In the preceding example, the supplied column names are valid Python variable names that allow us to easily turn a dictionary into a namespace. In some cases, we'll need to map column names to Python variable names to make this work.

A `SimpleNamespace` parameter allows us to use slightly simpler syntax to refer to items within the row. Specifically, the next generator expression uses references such as `row.shift` and `row.defect_type` instead of the bulkier `row['shift']` or `row['defect_type']` references.

We can use a more complex generator expression to do a map-filter combination. We'll filter each row to ignore rows with no defect code. For rows with a defect code, we're mapping an expression which creates a two tuple from the `row.shift` and `row.defect_type` references.

In some applications, the filter won't be a trivial expression such as `row.defect_type`. It may be necessary to write a more sophisticated condition. In this case, it may be helpful to use the `filter()` function to apply the complex condition to the generator expression that provides the data.

Given a generator that will produce a sequence of `(shift, defect)` tuples, we can summarize them by creating a `Counter` object from the generator expression. Creating this `Counter` object will process the lazy generator expressions, which will read the source file, extract fields from the rows, filter the rows, and summarize the counts.

We'll use the `defect_reduce()` function to gather and summarize the data as follows:

```
with open("qa_data.csv", newline="" ) as input:
    defects= defect_reduce(input)
print(defects)
```

We can open a file, gather the defects, and display them to be sure that we've properly summarized by shift and defect type. Since the result is a `Counter` object, we can combine it with other `Counter` objects if we have other sources of data.

The `defects` value looks like this:

```
Counter({('3', 'C'): 49, ('1', 'C'): 45, ('2', 'C'): 34,
('3', 'A'): 33, ('2', 'B'): 31, ('2', 'A'): 26, ('1', 'B'): 21,
('3', 'D'): 20, ('3', 'B'): 17, ('1', 'A'): 15, ('1', 'D'): 13,
('2', 'D'): 5})
```

We have defect counts organized by shift and defect types. We'll look at alternative input of summarized data next. This reflects a common use case where data is available at the summary level.

Once we've read the data, the next step is to develop two probabilities so that we can properly compute expected defects for each shift and each type of defect. We don't want to divide the total defect count by 12, since that doesn't reflect the actual deviations by shift or defect type. The shifts may be more or less equally productive. The defect frequencies are certainly not going to be similar. We expect some defects to be very rare and others to be more common.

Reading summarized data

As an alternative to reading all of the raw data, we can look at processing only the summary counts. We want to create a Counter object similar to the previous example; this will have defect counts as a value with a key of shift and defect code. Given summaries, we simply create a Counter object from the input dictionary.

Here's a function that will read our summary data:

```
from collections import Counter
import csv
def defect_counts(source):
    rdr= csv.DictReader(source)
    assert rdr.fieldnames == ["shift", "defect_code", "count"]
    convert = map(
        lambda d: ((d['shift'], d['defect_code']),
        int(d['count'])),
        rdr)
    return Counter(dict(convert))
```

We require an open file as the input. We'll create a csv.DictReader() function that helps parse the raw CSV data that we got from the database. We included an assert statement to confirm that the file really has the expected data.

We defined a lambda object that creates a two tuple with the key and the integer conversion of the count. The key is itself a two tuple with the shift and defect information. The result will be a sequence such as ((shift,defect), count), ((shift,defect), count), …). When we map the lambda to the DictReader parameter, we'll have a generator function that can emit the sequence of two tuples.

We will create a dictionary from the collection of two tuples and use this dictionary to build a Counter object. The Counter object can easily be combined with other Counter objects. This allows us to combine details acquired from several sources. In this case, we only have a single source.

We can assign this single source to the variable defects. The value looks like this:

```
Counter({('3', 'C'): 49, ('1', 'C'): 45, ('2', 'C'): 34,
('3', 'A'): 33, ('2', 'B'): 31, ('2', 'A'): 26,('1', 'B'): 21,
('3', 'D'): 20, ('3', 'B'): 17, ('1', 'A'): 15, ('1', 'D'): 13,
('2', 'D'): 5})
```

This matches the detail summary shown previously. The source data, however, was already summarized. This is often the case when data is extracted from a database and SQL is used to do group-by operations.

Computing probabilities from a Counter object

We need to compute the probabilities of defects by shift and defects by type. In order to compute the expected probabilities, we need to start with some simple sums. The first is the overall sum of all defects, which can be calculated by executing the following command:

```
total= sum(defects.values())
```

This is done directly from the values in the Counter object assigned to the defects variable. This will show that there are 309 total defects in the sample set.

We need to get defects by shift as well as defects by type. This means that we'll extract two kinds of subsets from the raw defect data. The "by-shift" extract will use just one part of the (shift,defect type) key in the Counter object. The "by-type" will use the other half of the key pair.

We can summarize by creating additional Counter objects extracted from the initial set of the Counter objects assigned to the defects variable. Here's the by-shift summary:

```
shift_totals= sum((Counter({s:defects[s,d]}) for s,d in defects),
Counter())
```

We've created a collection of individual Counter objects that have a shift, s, as the key and the count of defects associated with that shift defects[s,d]. The generator expression will create 12 such Counter objects to extract data for all combinations of four defect types and three shifts. We'll combine the Counter objects with a sum() function to get three summaries organized by shift.

We can't use the default initial value of 0 for the `sum()` function. We must provide an empty `Counter()` function as an initial value.

The type totals are created with an expression similar to the one used to create shift totals:

```
type_totals= sum((Counter({d:defects[s,d]}) for s,d in defects),
Counter())
```

We created a dozen `Counter` objects using the defect type, `d`, as the key instead of shift type; otherwise, the processing is identical.

The shift totals look like this:

```
Counter({'3': 119, '2': 96, '1': 94})
```

The defect type totals look like this:

```
Counter({'C': 128, 'A': 74, 'B': 69, 'D': 38})
```

We've kept the summaries as `Counter` objects, rather than creating simple `dict` objects or possibly even `list` instances. We'll generally use them as simple dicts from this point forward. However, there are some situations where we will want proper `Counter` objects instead of reductions.

Alternative summary approaches

We've read the data and computed summaries in two separate steps. In some cases, we may want to create the summaries while reading the initial data. This is an optimization that might save a little bit of processing time. We could write a more complex input reduction that emitted the grand total, the shift totals, and the defect type totals. These `Counter` objects would be built one item at a time.

We've focused on using the `Counter` instances, because they seem to allow us flexibility. Any changes to the data acquisition will still create `Counter` instances and won't change the subsequent analysis.

Here's how we can compute the probabilities of defect by shift and by defect type:

```
from fractions import Fraction
P_shift = dict( (shift, Fraction(shift_totals[shift],total))
for shift in sorted(shift_totals))
P_type = dict((type, Fraction(type_totals[type],total)) for type in
sorted(type_totals))
```

We've created two dictionaries: `P_shift` and `P_type`. The `P_shift` dictionary maps a shift to a `Fraction` object that shows the shift's contribution to the overall number of defects. Similarly, the `P_type` dictionary maps a defect type to a `Fraction` object that shows the type's contribution to the overall number of defects.

We've elected to use `Fraction` objects to preserve all of the precision of the input values. When working with counts like this, we may get probability values that make more intuitive sense to people reviewing the data.

We've elected to use `dict` objects because we've switched modes. At this point in the analysis, we're no longer accumulating details; we're using reductions to compare actual and observed data.

The `P_shift` data looks like this:

```
{'2': Fraction(32, 103), '3': Fraction(119, 309), '1':
Fraction(94, 309)}
```

The `P_type` data looks like this:

```
{'B': Fraction(23, 103), 'C': Fraction(128, 309),
'A': Fraction(74, 309), 'D': Fraction(38, 309)}
```

A value such as 32/103 or 96/309 might be more meaningful to some people than 0.3106. We can easily get `float` values from `Fraction` objects, as we'll see later.

The shifts all seem to be approximately at the same level of defect production. The defect types vary, which is typical. It appears that the defect C is a relatively common problem, whereas the defect B is much less common. Perhaps the second defect requires a more complex situation to arise.

Computing expected values and displaying a contingency table

The expected defect production is a combined probability. We'll compute the shift defect probability multiplied by the probability based on defect type. This will allow us to compute all 12 probabilities from all combinations of shift and defect type. We can weight these with the observed numbers and compute the detailed expectation for defects.

Here's the calculation of expected values:

```
expected = dict(
    ((s,t), P_shift[s]*P_type[t]*total) for t in P_type:
        for s in P_shift
    )
```

We'll create a dictionary that parallels the initial `defects` `Counter` object. This dictionary will have a sequence of two tuples with keys and values. The keys will be two tuples of shift and defect type. Our dictionary is built from a generator expression that explicitly enumerates all combinations of keys from the `P_shift` and `P_type` dictionaries.

The value of the `expected` dictionary looks like this:

```
{('2', 'B'): Fraction(2208, 103), ('2', 'D'): Fraction(1216, 103),
('3', 'D'): Fraction(4522, 309), ('2', 'A'): Fraction(2368, 103),
('1', 'A'): Fraction(6956, 309), ('1', 'B'): Fraction(2162, 103),
('3', 'B'): Fraction(2737, 103), ('1', 'C'): Fraction(12032, 309),
('3', 'C'): Fraction(15232, 309), ('2', 'C'): Fraction(4096, 103),
('3', 'A'): Fraction(8806, 309), ('1', 'D'): Fraction(3572, 309)}
```

Each item of the mapping has a key with shift and defect type. This is associated with a `Fraction` value based on the probability of defect based on shift times, the probability of a defect based on defect type times the overall number of defects. Some of the fractions are reduced, for example, a value of 6624/309 can be simplified to 2208/103.

Large numbers are awkward as proper fractions. Displaying large values as `float` values is often easier. Small values (such as probabilities) are sometimes easier to understand as fractions.

We'll print the observed and expected times in pairs. This will help us visualize the data. We'll create something that looks like the following to help summarize what we've observed and what we expect:

```
obs exp     obs exp     obs exp     obs exp
15 22.51     21 20.99     45 38.94     13 11.56     94
26 22.99     31 21.44     34 39.77      5 11.81     96
33 28.50     17 26.57     49 49.29     20 14.63     119
74          69          128          38          309
```

This shows 12 cells. Each cell has values with the observed number of defects and an expected number of defects. Each row ends with the shift totals, and each column has a footer with the defect totals.

In some cases, we might export this data in CSV notation and build a spreadsheet. In other cases, we'll build an HTML version of the contingency table and leave the layout details to a browser. We've shown a pure text version here.

Here's a sequence of statements to create the contingency table shown previously:

```
print("obs exp"*len(type_totals))
for s in sorted(shift_totals):
    pairs= ["{0:3d} {1:5.2f}".format(defects[s,t],
    float(expected[s,t])) for t in sorted(type_totals)]
    print("{0} {1:3d}".format( "".join(pairs), shift_totals[s]))
footers= ["{0:3d}".format(type_totals[t]) for t in
sorted(type_totals)]
print("{0} {1:3d}".format("".join(footers), total))
```

This spreads the defect types across each line. We've written enough `obs exp` column titles to cover all defect types. For each shift, we'll emit a line of observed and actual pairs, followed by a shift total. At the bottom, we'll emit a line of footers with just the defect type totals and the grand total.

A contingency table like this one helps us to visualize the comparison between observed and expected values. We can compute a chi-squared value for these two sets of values. This will help us decide if the data is random or if there's something that deserves further investigation.

Computing the chi-squared value

The X^2 value is based on $\sum_i \frac{(e_i - o_i)^2}{e_i}$, where the e values are the expected values and the o values are the observed values.

We can compute the specified formula's value as follows:

```
diff= lambda e,o: (e-o)**2/e
chi2= sum(diff(expected[s,t], defects[s,t]) for s in shift_totals:
    for t in type_totals
    )
```

We've defined a small `lambda` to help us optimize the calculation. This allows us to execute the `expected[s,t]` and `defects[s,t]` attributes just once, even though the expected value is used in two places. For this dataset, the final X^2 value is 19.18.

There are a total of six degrees of freedom based on three shifts and four defect types. Since we're considering them independent, we get 2×3=6. A chi-squared table shows us that anything below 12.5916 would reflect 1 chance in 20 of the data being truly random. Since our value is 19.18, the data is unlikely to be random.

The cumulative distribution function for X^2 shows that a value of 19.18 has a probability of the order of 0.00387: about 4 chances in 1000 of being random. The next step is a follow-up study to discover the details of the various defect types and shifts. We'll need to see which independent variable has the biggest correlation with defects and continue the analysis.

Instead of following up with this case study, we'll look at a different and interesting calculation.

Computing the chi-squared threshold

The essence of the X^2 test is a threshold value based on the number of degrees of freedom and the level of uncertainty we're willing to entertain in accepting or rejecting the null hypothesis. Conventionally, we're advised to use a threshold around 0.05 (1/20) to reject the null hypothesis. We'd like there to be only 1 chance in 20 that the data is simply random and it appears meaningful. In other words, we'd like there to be 19 chances in 20 that the data reflects simple random variation.

The chi-squared values are usually provided in tabular form because the calculation involves a number of transcendental functions. In some cases, libraries will provide the X^2 cumulative distribution function, allowing us to compute a value rather than look one up on tabulation of important values.

The cumulative distribution function for a X^2 value, x, and degrees of freedom, f, is defined as follows:

$$F(x;k) = \frac{\gamma\left(\dfrac{k}{2}, \dfrac{x}{2}\right)}{\Gamma\left(\dfrac{k}{2}\right)}$$

It's common to the probability of being random as $p = 1 - F(\chi^2; k)$. That is, if $p > 0.05$, the data can be understood as random; the null hypothesis is true.

This requires two calculations: the incomplete gamma function, $\gamma(s, z)$, and the complete gamma function, $\Gamma(x)$. These can involve some fairly complex math. We'll cut some corners and implement two pretty-good approximations that are narrowly focused on just this problem. Each of these functions will allow us to look at functional design issues.

Both of these functions will require a factorial calculation, $n!$. We've seen several variations on the fractions theme. We'll use the following one:

```
@lru_cache(128)
def fact(k):
    if k < 2: return 1
    return reduce(operator.mul, range(2, int(k)+1))
```

This is $k! = \prod_{2 \le i \le k} i$: a product of numbers from 2 to k (inclusive). We've omitted the unit test cases.

Computing the partial gamma value

The partial gamma function has a simple series expansion. This means that we're going to compute a sequence of values and then do a sum on those values. For more information, visit `http://dlmf.nist.gov/8`.

$$\gamma(s,z) = \sum_{0 \le k \le \infty} \frac{(-1)^k}{k!} \frac{z^{s+k}}{s+k}$$

This series will have a sequence of terms that—eventually—become too small to be relevant. The calculation $(-1)^k$ will yield alternating signs:

$$-1^0 = 1, -1^1 = -1, -1^2 = 1, -1^3 = -1$$

The sequence of terms looks like this with $s=1$ and $z=2$:

```
2/1, -2/1, 4/3, -2/3, 4/15, -4/45, ..., -2/638512875
```

At some point, each additional term won't have any significant impact on the result.

When we look back at the cumulative distribution function, $F(x;k)$, we can consider working with `fractions.Fraction` values. The degrees of freedom, k, will be an integer divided by 2. The X^2 value, x, may be either a `Fraction` or a `float` value; it will rarely be a simple integer value.

When evaluating the terms of γ, the value of $\frac{(-1)^k}{k!}$ will involve integers and can be represented as a proper `Fraction` value. The value of z^{s+k} could be a `Fraction` or `float` value; it will lead to irrational values when $s+k$ is not an `integer` value. The value of $s+k$ will be a proper `Fraction` value, sometimes it will have the integer values, and sometimes it will have values that involve $1/2$.

The use of `Fraction` value here—while possible—doesn't seem to be helpful because there will be an irrational value computed. However, when we look at the complete `gamma` function given here, we'll see that `Fraction` values are potentially helpful. In this function, they're merely incidental.

Here's an implementation of the previously explained series expansion:

```
def gamma(s, z):
    def terms(s, z):
        for k in range(100):
            t2= Fraction(z**(s+k))/(s+k)
            term= Fraction((-1)**k,fact(k))*t2
            yield term
        warnings.warn("More than 100 terms")
    def take_until(function, iterable):
        for v in iterable:
            if function(v): return
            yield v
    ε= 1E-8
    return sum(take_until(lambda t:abs(t) < ε, terms(s, z)))
```

We defined a `term()` function that will yield a series of terms. We used a `for` statement with an upper limit to generate only 100 terms. We could have used the `itertools.count()` function to generate an infinite sequence of terms. It seems slightly simpler to use a loop with an upper bound.

We computed the irrational z^{s+k} value and created a `Fraction` value from this value by itself. If the value for z is also a `Fraction` value and not a `float` value then, the value for `t2` will be a `Fraction` value. The value for `term()` function will then be a product of two `Fraction` objects.

We defined a `take_until()` function that takes values from an iterable, until a given function is true. Once the function becomes true, no more values are consumed from the iterable. We also defined a small threshold value, ε, of 10^{-8}. We'll take values from the `term()` function until the values are less than ε. The sum of these values is an approximation to the partial `gamma` function.

Here are some test cases we can use to confirm that we're computing this properly:

- $\gamma(1,2) = 1 - e^{-2} \approx 0.8646647$

- $\gamma(1,3) = 1 - e^{-3} \approx 0.9502129$

- $\gamma\left(\dfrac{1}{2}, 2\right) = \sqrt{\pi} \times \operatorname{erf}\left(\sqrt{2}\right) \approx 1.6918067$

The error function, `erf()`, is another interesting function. We won't look into it here because it's available in the Python math library.

Our interest is narrowly focused on the chi-squared distribution. We're not generally interested in the incomplete gamma function for other mathematical purposes. Because of this, we can narrow our test cases to the kinds of values we expect to be using. We can also limit the accuracy of the results. Most chi-squared tests involve three digits of precision. We've shown seven digits in the test data, which is more than we might properly need.

Computing the complete gamma value

The complete gamma function is a bit more difficult. There are a number of different approximations. For more information, visit `http://dlmf.nist.gov/5`. There's a version available in the Python math library. It represents a broadly useful approximation that is designed for many situations.

We're not actually interested in a general implementation of the complete gamma function. We're interested in just two special cases: integer values and halves. For these two special cases, we can get exact answers, and don't need to rely on an approximation.

For integer values, $\Gamma n = (n-1)!$. The gamma function for integers can rely on the factorial function we defined previously.

For halves, there's a special form:

$$\Gamma\frac{1}{2} + n = \frac{(2n)!}{4^n n!}\sqrt{\pi}$$

This includes an irrational value, so we can only represent this approximately using `float` or `Fraction` objects.

Since the chi-squared cumulative distribution function only uses the following two features of the complete gamma function, we don't need a general approach. We can cheat and use the following two values, which are reasonably precise.

If we use proper Fraction values, then we can design a function with a few simple cases: an integer value, a Fraction value with 1 in the denominator, and a Fraction value with 2 in the denominator. We can use the Fraction value as follows:

```
sqrt_pi = Fraction(677622787, 382307718)
def Gamma_Half(k):
    if isinstance(k,int):
        return fact(k-1)
    elif isinstance(k,Fraction):
        if k.denominator == 1:
            return fact(k-1)
        elif k.denominator == 2:
            n = k-Fraction(1,2)
            return fact(2*n)/(Fraction(4**n)*fact(n))*sqrt_pi
    raise ValueError("Can't compute Γ({0})".format(k))
```

We called the function Gamma_Half to emphasize that this is only appropriate for whole numbers and halves. For integer values, we'll use the fact() function that was defined previously. For Fraction objects with a denominator of 1, we'll use the same fact() definition: $\Gamma n = (n-1)!$.

For the cases where the denominator is 2, we can use the more complex "closed form" value. We used an explicit Fraction() function for the value $4^n n!$. We've also provided a Fraction approximation for the irrational value $\sqrt{\pi}$.

Here are some test cases:

- $\Gamma(2) = 1$

- $\Gamma(5) = 24$

- $\Gamma\left(\frac{1}{2}\right) = \sqrt{\pi} \approx 1.7724539$

- $\Gamma\left(\frac{3}{2}\right) = \frac{\sqrt{\pi}}{2} \approx 0.8862269$

These can also be shown as proper Fraction values. The irrational values lead to large, hard-to-read fractions. We can use something like this:

```
>>> g= Gamma_Half(Fraction(3,2))
>>> g.limit_denominator(2000000)
Fraction(291270, 328663)
```

This provides a value where the denominator has been limited to be in the range of 1 to 2 million; this provides pleasant-looking six-digit numbers that we can use for unit test purposes.

Computing the odds of a distribution being random

Now that we have the incomplete gamma function, gamma, and complete gamma function, Gamma_Half, we can compute the X^2 CDF values. The CDF value shows us the odds of a given X^2 value being random or having some possible correlation.

The function itself is quite small:

```
def cdf(x, k):
    """X² cumulative distribution function.
    :param x: X² value -- generally sum (obs[i]-exp[i])**2/exp[i]
        for parallel sequences of observed and expected values.:
        param k: degrees of freedom >= 1; generally len(data)-1
    """
    return 1-gamma(Fraction(k,2),
    Fraction(x/2))/Gamma_Half(Fraction(k,2))
```

We included some docstring comments to clarify the parameters. We created proper Fraction objects from the degrees of freedom and the chi-squared value, *x*. When converting a float value to a Fraction object, we'll create a very large fractional result with a large number of entirely irrelevant digits.

We can use Fraction(x/2).limit_denominator(1000) to limit the size of the x/2 Fraction method to a respectably small number of digits. This will compute a correct CDF value, but won't lead to gargantuan fractions with dozens of digits.

Here are some sample data called from a table of X^2. Visit http://en.wikipedia.org/wiki/Chi-squared_distribution for more information.

To compute the correct CDF values execute the following commands:

```
>>> round(float(cdf(0.004, 1)), 2)
0.95
>>> cdf(0.004, 1).limit_denominator(100)
Fraction(94, 99)
>>> round(float(cdf(10.83, 1)), 3)
0.001
>>> cdf(10.83, 1).limit_denominator(1000)
Fraction(1, 1000)
>>> round(float(cdf(3.94, 10)), 2)
0.95
>>> cdf(3.94, 10).limit_denominator(100)
Fraction(19, 20)
>>> round(float(cdf(29.59, 10)), 3)
0.001
>>> cdf(29.59, 10).limit_denominator(10000)
Fraction(8, 8005)
```

Given X^2 and a number of degrees of freedom, our CDF function produces the same results as a widely used table of values.

Here's an entire row from a X^2 table, computed with a simple generator expression:

```
>>> chi2= [0.004, 0.02, 0.06, 0.15, 0.46, 1.07, 1.64, 2.71, 3.84,
6.64, 10.83]
>>> act= [round(float(x), 3) for x in map(cdf, chi2, [1]*len(chi2))]
>>> act
[0.95, 0.888, 0.806, 0.699, 0.498, 0.301, 0.2, 0.1, 0.05, 0.01,
0.001]
```

The expected values are as follows:

```
[0.95, 0.90, 0.80, 0.70, 0.50, 0.30, 0.20, 0.10, 0.05, 0.01, 0.001]
```

We have some tiny discrepancies in the third decimal place.

What we can do with this is get a probability from a X^2 value. From our example shown previously, the 0.05 probability for six degrees of freedom has a X^2 value 12.5916

```
>>> round(float(cdf(12.5916, 6)), 2)
0.05
```

The actual value we got for X^2 in the example was 19.18. Here's the probability that this value is random:

```
>>> round(float(cdf(19.18, 6)), 5)
0.00387
```

This probability is 3/775, with the denominator limited to 1000. Those are not good odds of the data being random.

Summary

In this chapter, we looked at three optimization techniques. The first technique involves finding the right algorithm and data structure. This has more impact on performance than any other single design or programming decision. Using the right algorithm can easily reduce runtimes from minutes to fractions of a second. Changing a poorly used sequence to a properly used mapping, for example, may reduce run time by a factor of 200.

We should generally optimize all of our recursions to be loops. This will be faster in Python and it won't be stopped by the call stack limit that Python imposes. There are many examples of how recursions are flattened into loops in other chapters, primarily, *Chapter 6, Recursions and Reductions*. Additionally, we may be able to improve performance in two other ways. First, we can apply memoization to cache results. For numeric calculations, this can have a large impact; for collections, the impact may be less. Secondly, replacing large materialized data objects with iterables may also improve performance by reducing the amount of memory management required.

In the case study presented in this chapter, we looked at the advantage of using Python for exploratory data analysis—the initial data acquisition including a little bit of parsing and filtering. In some cases, a significant amount of effort is required to normalize data from various sources. This is a task at which Python excels.

The calculation of a X^2 value involved three `sum()` functions: two intermediate generator expressions, and a final generator expression to create a dictionary with expected values. A final `sum()` function created the statistic. In under a dozen expressions, we created a sophisticated analysis of data that will help us accept or reject the null hypothesis.

We also evaluated some complex statistical functions: the incomplete and the complete `gamma` function. The incomplete `gamma` function involves a potentially infinite series; we truncated this and summed the values. The complete `gamma` function has some potential complexity, but it doesn't happen to apply in our case.

Using a functional approach, we can write succinct and expressive programs that accomplish a great deal of processing. Python isn't a properly functional programming language. For example, we're required to use some imperative programming techniques. This limitation forces away from purely functional recursions. We gain some performance advantage, since we're forced to optimize tail recursions into explicit loops.

We also saw numerous advantages of adopting Python's hybrid style of functional programming. In particular, the use of Python's higher order functions and generator expressions give us a number of ways to write high performance programs that are often quite clear and simple.

Index

Symbols

@lru_cache decorator 197
@then_convert(converter) style
    decorator 225
@total_ordering decorator 197
@wraps decorator 216

A

access_detail_iter() function 235
AccessDetails objects 241
access_iter() function 235
accumulate() function
  about 165, 167
  totals, running with 167, 168
accuracy
  optimizing 311, 312
  reducing, based on audience
    requirements 312
alt_range() function 269
anscombe_filter() function 294
Anscombe's Quartet 48
Apache httpd 290
API Key
  about 301
  usage, tracking 301-303

B

base case states 13
bind() function 274, 275
binning 127
bisect module
  used, for creating mapping 55, 56

body mass index (BMI) 265
by_dist() function 91

C

Callable class
  higher-order functions, building
    with 111, 112
Cartesian product
  enumerating 182
CDF values
  computing 327-329
chain() function
  about 165, 169
  iterators, combining with 169
chi-squared decision
  alternative summary approaches 318, 319
  making 312-314
  probabilities, computing from Counter
    object 317, 318
  raw data, filtering with Counter
    object 314-316
  raw data, reducing with Counter
    object 314-316
  summarized data, reading 316, 317
  threshold, computing 322, 323
  value, computing 321, 322
chunking 107
classes
  defining, with total ordering 201-203
  number classes 203, 204
Clojure 53
collections.Counter method 127
combinations() function 181

F

faster() function 40
file parsers, reductions
  CSV files, parsing 137, 138
  plain text files, parsing with
      headers 138-140
  writing 135-137
fillvalue parameter 258
filterfalse() function
  about 165, 175
  filtering with 175
filter() function
  about 96
  filtering with 175
  used, for identifying outliers 98, 99
  used, for passing data 96-98
  used, for rejecting data 96-98
  using 256
finite iterators
  accumulate() 165
  accumulate(), used for running
      totals 167, 168
  chain() 165
  chain(), used for combining iterators 169
  compress() 165
  compress(), filtering with 171, 172
  dropwhile() 165
  dropwhile(), stateful filtering with 173, 174
  enumerate() 165
  enumerate(), used for assigning
      numbers 166, 167
  filterfalse() 165
  filterfalse(), filtering with 175
  filter(), filtering with 175
  groupby() 165
  groupby(), used for partitioning
      iterator 170, 171
  islice() 165
  islice(), subsets picking with 172, 173
  starmap() 165
  starmap(), used for applying function to
      data 176, 177
  takewhile() 165

  takewhile(), stateful filtering with 173, 174
  tee(), iterators cloning with 177
  using 165
  zip_longest() 165
  zip_longest(), used for merging
      iterables 171
first-class functions 24
first-class objects 39, 40
First Normal Form 136
flatten function 179
float_lat_lon() function 136
Fortran code 18
functional composition
  about 264
  example 265
  PyMonad multiplication operator,
      using 268, 269
functional features
  about 23
  advanced concepts 34
  familiar territory 34
  first-class functions 24
  functional type systems 33
  higher-order functions 25, 26
  immutable data 26, 27
  non-strict evaluation 27-29
  pure functions 24, 25
  recursion 29-33
  strict evaluation 27-29
functional hybrid
  using 14, 15
functional paradigm
  using 12-14
functional programming
  about 9
  classic example 17-20
functional type systems 33
functions, as first-class objects 39-41
function tools 198
functools.reduce() function 260, 266
functools.wraps() function 215
functor
  about 270
  applicative functors 270, 271

G

generator expressions
  combining 47, 48
  limitations 46, 47
  using 43-46
generator functions
  used, for cleaning raw data 48, 49
  writing 108-111
Global Interpreter Lock (GIL)
  about 229
  URL 229
groupby() function
  about 165, 170
  iterator, partitioning with 170, 171
group-by reductions
  from many to fewer 126, 127
  writing 132, 133
grouper function 179
group() function 129

H

Haskell 16, 33
higher-order functions
  about 25, 26, 87
  building, with Callables 111, 112
  filter() function 96
  good functional design, assuring 112-114
  iter() function 99
  lambda forms 91
  map() function 93
  max() function 88-91
  min() function 88-91
  sorted() function 100
  writing 101
higher-order mappings and filters
  additional data, wrapping while
    mapping 104, 105
  data, flattening while mapping 106, 107
  data, structuring while filtering 107, 108
  data, unwrapping while mapping 103, 104
  writing 101-103
higher-order reductions
  writing 133-135

HTTP request-response model
  about 282, 283
  functional view 285
  server, considering with functional
    design 284, 285
  services, nesting 286, 287
  state, injecting via cookies 284

I

imap(function, iterable) method 246
**imap_unordered(function, iterable)
  method 246**
immutable namedtuple
  rewrapping 150, 151
  Spearman rank-order correlation,
    computing 152, 153
  statistical ranks, assigning 148, 149
  using 145-147
  using, as record 142-144
  wrapping 149, 150
immutable objects
  about 26
  Higher-order Functions, using 26
  Wrap-Process-Unwrap pattern, using 26
infinite iterators
  count() 160
  count(), counting with 160-162
  cycle() 160
  cycle(), used for reiterating cycle 162-164
  repeat() 160
  repeat(), used for repeating single
    value 164
  working with 160
islice() function
  about 165-173
  subsets, picking with 172, 173
itemgetter() function 257
iterables
  all() function, using 73-75
  any() function, using 73-75
  counts, using for statistics 76-78
  file, parsing at higher level 63-65

complex multiprocessing architectures 248
concurrent.futures module, using 248, 249
concurrent.futures thread pools, using 249
concurrent processing, designing 250-252
map_async(), using 247
queue module, using 250
starmap_async(), using 247
threading module, using 250
using 244-246
**Multipurpose Internet Mail Extension
    (MIME) 285**
multy() function 40
myreduce() function 267

N

named attributes
obtaining, when using higher-order
    functions 257, 258
namedtuples
building, with functional constructors 145
using 42, 43
ncycles function 178
nested generator expressions 14
Nginx 290
non-strict dictionary rules
exploiting 255
non-strict evaluation 27-29
nth function 178
null_wrapper() function 215
num variable 259

O

**Object-Oriented Programming (OOP)
    language 26**
OCaml 16
operator module
named attributes, obtaining when using
    higher-order functions 257, 258
using 256, 257
operators
reducing with 260, 261
starmapping with 258-260

operators.truediv() function 259
optimization techniques
accuracy, optimizing 311, 312
caching 306, 307
memoization 305
storage, optimizing 311

P

padnone function 178
pairwise function 179
parallelism 149
parameterized decorator
about 221
abstract decorator 222
decorating wrapper 222
overall decorator 222
partial() function
about 197, 205
used, for applying partial arguments 205
partial gamma value
computing 323-325
partition function 179
path_filter() function 241
PATH_INFO request 294
Peano axioms 118
permutations() function 181
point_roll() function 277
polymorphism pattern matching 153-158
powerset function 194
previous results
caching, lru_cache decorator used 198-200
procedural paradigm
functional hybrid, using 14, 15
functional paradigm, using 12-14
object creation 15, 16
stacks of abstractions 16, 17
subdividing 11, 12
product() function 181
product, reducing
about 182, 183
all pixels and all colors,
    enumerating 185, 186
collection of values, permuting 190, 191

WSGI
about 287, 288
application, creating 292-294
exceptions, throwing 288, 289
pragmatic WSGI applications 290

X

XML serialization 299

Z

z() function 98

zip() function
about 78, 96
alternate approach, for structuring flat
sequences 83, 84
flat sequences, structuring 81-83
used, for flattening sequences 80, 81
using 78-80
zipped sequence, unzipping 80
zip_longest() function
about 165, 171
iterables, merging with 171

Thank you for buying
Functional Python Programming

About Packt Publishing

Packt, pronounced 'packed', published its first book, *Mastering phpMyAdmin for Effective MySQL Management*, in April 2004, and subsequently continued to specialize in publishing highly focused books on specific technologies and solutions.

Our books and publications share the experiences of your fellow IT professionals in adapting and customizing today's systems, applications, and frameworks. Our solution-based books give you the knowledge and power to customize the software and technologies you're using to get the job done. Packt books are more specific and less general than the IT books you have seen in the past. Our unique business model allows us to bring you more focused information, giving you more of what you need to know, and less of what you don't.

Packt is a modern yet unique publishing company that focuses on producing quality, cutting-edge books for communities of developers, administrators, and newbies alike. For more information, please visit our website at www.packtpub.com.

About Packt Open Source

In 2010, Packt launched two new brands, Packt Open Source and Packt Enterprise, in order to continue its focus on specialization. This book is part of the Packt Open Source brand, home to books published on software built around open source licenses, and offering information to anybody from advanced developers to budding web designers. The Open Source brand also runs Packt's Open Source Royalty Scheme, by which Packt gives a royalty to each open source project about whose software a book is sold.

Writing for Packt

We welcome all inquiries from people who are interested in authoring. Book proposals should be sent to author@packtpub.com. If your book idea is still at an early stage and you would like to discuss it first before writing a formal book proposal, then please contact us; one of our commissioning editors will get in touch with you.

We're not just looking for published authors; if you have strong technical skills but no writing experience, our experienced editors can help you develop a writing career, or simply get some additional reward for your expertise.

Mastering Object-oriented
Python

Grasp the intricacies of object-oriented programming in Python in order to efficiently build powerful real-world applications

Steven F. Lott   [PACKT] open source

Mastering Object-oriented Python

ISBN: 978-1-78328-097-1   Paperback: 634 pages

Grasp the intricacies of object-oriented programming in Python in order to efficiently build powerful real-world applications

1. Create applications with flexible logging, powerful configuration and command-line options, automated unit tests, and good documentation.

2. Use the Python special methods to integrate seamlessly with built-in features and the standard library.

3. Design classes to support object persistence in JSON, YAML, Pickle, CSV, XML, Shelve, and SQL.

Learning Python
Data Visualization

Master how to build dynamic HTML5-ready SVG charts using Python and the pygal library

Chad Adams   [PACKT] open source

Learning Python Data Visualization

ISBN: 978-1-78355-333-4   Paperback: 212 pages

Master how to build dynamic HTML5-ready SVG charts using Python and the pygal library

1. A practical guide that helps you break into the world of data visualization with Python.

2. Understand the fundamentals of building charts in Python.

3. Packed with easy-to-understand tutorials for developers who are new to Python or charting in Python.

Please check **www.PacktPub.com** for information on our titles